Long Way Round

Long Way Round

CHASING SHADOWS ACROSS THE WORLD

EWAN MCGREGOR *and*
CHARLEY BOORMAN

with ROBERT UHLIG

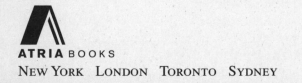

ATRIA BOOKS

NEW YORK   LONDON   TORONTO   SYDNEY

For my sister Telsche, whose presence I felt throughout my journey, and whose memory still lives on.

Charley Boorman

This is for my Eve and our children Clara and Esther.

Ewan McGregor

ATRIA BOOKS
1230 Avenue of the Americas
New York, NY 10020

Copyright © 2004 by Long Way Round Limited

ISBN-13: 978-0-7434-9933-0
ISBN-10:   0-7434-9933-6
ISBN-13: 978-0-7434-9934-7 (Pbk)
ISBN-10:   0-7434-9934-4 (Pbk)

First Atria Books trade paperback edition November 2005

10 9 8 7 6 5 4

ATRIA BOOKS is a trademark of Simon & Schuster, Inc.

Manufactured in the United States of America

For information regarding special discounts for bulk purchases, please contact Simon & Schuster Special Sales at 1-800-456-6798 or business@simonandschuster.com

Contents

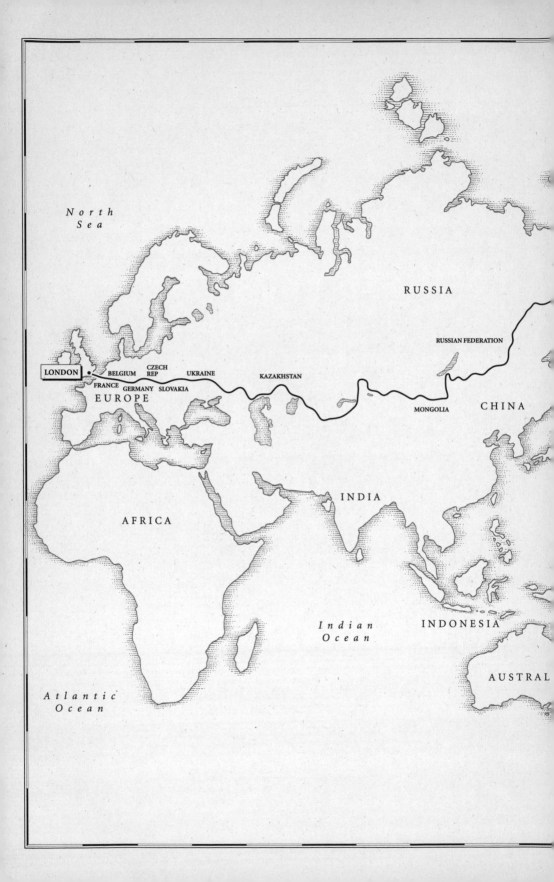

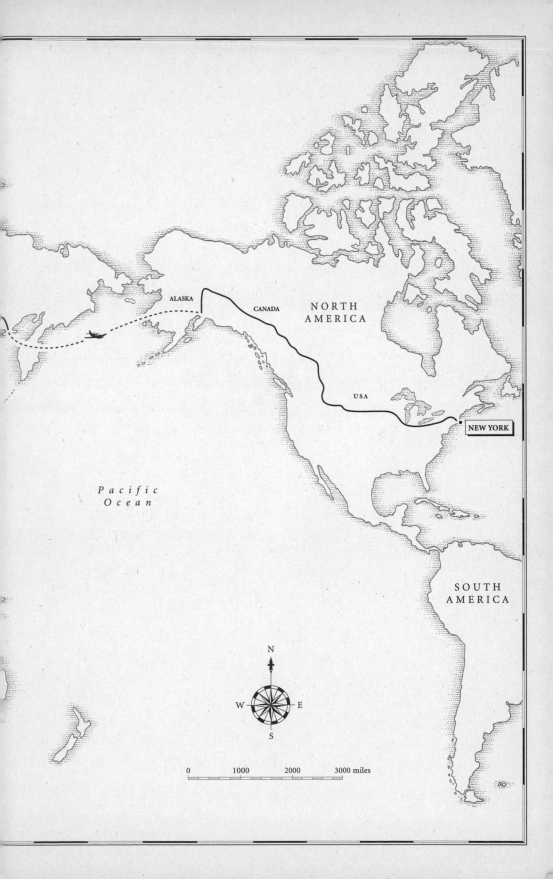

ALASKA

CANADA

NORTH
AMERICA

USA

NEW YORK

Pacific
Ocean

SOUTH
AMERICA

N

W   E

S

0   1000   2000   3000 miles

1
The long way home

MAGADAN

EWAN: On the last day, I walked down to the harbour. Having slept late, I had breakfast on my own and went for a wander. I wanted to get to the ocean; I needed to see the Pacific. Not knowing the right way, I stumbled down the hill, through rows and rows of tenements, nodding, smiling and waving at the people I passed, eventually arriving at the waterfront. I turned around, lifted my camera to my eye and took a photograph. There it was: Magadan, Siberia. The place that had been in my dreams and thoughts for two years, like a mythical city forever beyond my reach. I wanted to capture it, somehow hold on to it and take a part of it with me when we began the long journey home.

I walked on. The path led to the beach. Although it was the last day of June, it was the first day the sun had shone in Magadan that year. Three weeks earlier, it had snowed. But that day, the air was warm and soft, the sky a cloudless blue. Women wore bikinis and small children were running naked across the sands. Families were eating picnics or cooking on barbecues. I walked past them all, along the entire length of the beach, until I came to the harbour. I climbed up on to a quayside and sat on a mushroom-shaped bollard. An Alsatian came over and sat next to me. I scratched its head for a while, gazed out at the ocean and thought back to the day when Charley and I had sat in a little workshop in west London, surrounded by motorbikes, with dreams of the open road in our heads. All we knew then was that we wanted to get from London to Magadan. With the maps laid out in front of us, we drew a route, arbitrarily assigning mileage to each day, not knowing anything about the state of the roads. We guessed our way from west to east, across two continents, from the Atlantic to the Pacific, as far as it was possible to ride a motorbike in a straightish line. Time and again we were told by experienced travellers that our plans were wildly optimistic and that we didn't know what we were letting ourselves in for. I'd never ridden off-road and Charley had never properly camped. The chances of failure were high, they said. Yet here we were in Magadan, as far around the globe from home as it was possible to go, and we'd arrived one day ahead of our schedule.

I thought back to the day a month or so earlier when we had been in Mongolia. It was mid-afternoon and we were riding through a beautiful valley. I pulled over and got off my bike. Charley, ahead of me, stopped too. He swung his bike around and rode back towards me. Before he even arrived, I could feel it coming off him: why are we stopping? We're not getting petrol, we're not stopping to eat: why are we stopping?

I walked away from Charley. I didn't want to tell him that I had stopped because we'd passed the place. The place that had been in my dreams. The place we'd fantasised about months before we'd even set off from London. A place with a river of cool, white water and a field nearby to pitch our tents. The place we were going to stop at in the middle of an afternoon so that we could cool our sweaty feet in the river while catching fish that we'd cook that evening on an open fire under a star-speckled sky.

I'd seen that river half an hour earlier. There was no question at all that it was the place. A beautiful big white river and nobody for hundreds of miles. And we had ridden straight past it.

I sat down for five minutes, just needing to look at the countryside around us. The countryside that we often didn't have time to take in because we were always so intent on keeping to our schedule.

Then we got back on our bikes and moved on. A few weeks later, we arrived at the first big river in Siberia. It was too wide, too fast and too deep to cross on a motorbike. There was a bridge, but it had collapsed. I thought Charley would be itching to get ahead, impatient with the hold-up. But he was in his element. He knew that someone or something would be along to help. The delays *were* the journey. We'd get across it when we got across it.

I understood now that it didn't really matter that we hadn't stopped beside that cool, fast-flowing Mongolian river. The imperfections in our journey were what made it perfect. And maybe we wouldn't be in Magadan now if we'd not had that burning desire to keep going. After all, the river would always be there. Now that I knew what was out there, I could always return.

2
On yer bike

EWAN: Every journey begins with a single step. In our case it was eight years ago, when Charley walked up to me in Casey's, a pub that was more like someone's living room than a bar, at Sixmilebridge in County Clare. Except for an eager and winning smile, there was nothing in the way of an introduction.

'You ride bikes,' he said.

'Yeah,' I replied hesitantly, taken aback by the gregarious, long-haired stranger in front of me.

With our wives and daughters we had moved into cottages on location in Ireland to shoot *Serpent's Kiss*, a movie I will always remember fondly for the many long nights of drinking, partying and discussing bikes. It was the kick-off party on the eve of the first day's shooting and although Charley and I didn't know it yet, we had a lot in common. We were both married with daughters only a few months old, we'd both been successful actors for some time and we were facing weeks of working closely together. There was a lot we could have talked about, but Charley has an instinct for cutting through social niceties straight to the subject closest to a person's heart. This time was no exception. Charley's in-your-face affability had got the better of my reserve.

'Yeah . . . yeah, I ride a '78 Motoguzzi,' I said, referring to my first big bike, a heavy Italian machine built like a tractor. And with that, we were away. The evening dissolved into a long night of biker anecdotes and bonding over tales of fatherhood.

Over the next few days and weeks, I came to realise our first meeting was typical for Charley, who always seemed to come into a conversation from the opposite end to anyone else, an enviable trait that swiftly broke the ice. The shoot was very slow and there was even more hanging about than usual on a film set, so we just headed down to Casey's Bar, where we joined Pete Postlethwaite and other cast members, playing poker, sinking pints of Guinness and Harp and spinning yarns. It was a great time, and an opportunity to relax and have some fun in an otherwise quiet, small town in the middle of rural Ireland, and the more we got to know each other, the more we found we had in common. We shared the same attitude to parenting – one of total integration of our children into our lives. As a child, Charley had been through many of the experiences with his father – travelling the world from film set to film set, changing schools every few months – that I suspected my children would face. We got on so well that by the time of the wrap party I had asked Charley to be godfather to my daughter, Clara.

Many location friendships burn bright but short, doused soon after shooting finishes. Others turn into lasting friendships, but of the type in which you meet and speak infrequently. With Charley it was different: we kept in touch and our families met up regularly. And events soon turned our relationship into something deeper than a shared passion for bikes and a good party.

I had flown to Chicago and Los Angeles to make an episode of *ER*, coincidentally called *Long Way Round*. While I was on set in America, lying in a hospital bed with tubes up my nose, by some weird and horrible irony my Clara was being rushed into hospital in London. At first I thought it was just a bad cold or flu, but it turned out to be a severe case of meningitis.

I flew straight home to spend the next fortnight in hospital, sitting at my wee girl's bedside with my wife, Eve. It was a terrible time and I turned to Charley, who, just before we had met in Ireland, had himself gone through a difficult period when his eldest daughter, Doone, had been severely ill with a white blood cell deficiency. Charley and his wife, Olly, were a great support. One afternoon after Charley had visited us at the Chelsea and Westminster Hospital I saw him out. It was so serious, what was happening to Clara upstairs. Charley could see how it was grinding me down and he knew how awful it was to be in hospital like that with your kid. He turned to me and simply said: 'It's okay. It can get better.' He reminded me that all children get ill, and at some stage many children become very ill. Out of everyone I knew, Charley understood just how frightening and isolating it can be if you are dealing with your child's illness all by yourself. He knew just what to say. He gave me a big hug, then swung his leg over his Honda XR600R, pulled out into the traffic, lifted the front wheel and hoicked a huge wheelie all the way down the Fulham Road. Something about that really got through to me. That wheelie was so brilliantly inappropriate and spontaneous that it cut through my anxiety and worries, lifting my spirits more than any words could have done. And it was very much in keeping with Charley's true spirit of optimism. It was a strange period but I'll never forget Charley roaring away on his back wheel. Just when I needed it, he really cheered me up and in that moment our friendship was sealed for good.

CHARLEY: When I met Ewan in Casey's in 1997, I immediately recognised a kindred spirit. Someone with big passions in his life, and with biking at the centre of them. I've been obsessed with bikes for as long as I can remember. Growing up on a farm in County Wicklow, in Ireland, there was a guy just up the road who had a motorbike and I always saw him bombing past. I was about six years old then and I just thought 'Wow'. Around that time my father, John Boorman, was filming *Zardoz* in Ireland with Sean Connery, who was staying at our house during the shoot. One weekend, Sean's son Jason came to visit. Jason was quite a bit older than me and spent most of his stay forcing me to push him up and down the drive on a little monkey bike. Eventually, long after I had got the bike started and Jason had spent a long time riding it around the farm, he let me have a go. I promptly fell off, but that one moment, that twist of the grip, the roar of the engine, the smell of the exhaust and the petrol and the thrill of the speed was enough. I was hooked. I pestered my parents to indulge my nascent passion. Before long I'd persuaded them to let me buy a motorbike, a Yamaha 100 miniature trials bike that I've kept to this day and which I bought with my earnings as a featured extra in *The Great Train Robbery*. It was fabulous.

Most days I would see a neighbour shoot past the farm on a Maico 500, an Italian bike that was the best thing around in those days. Tommy Rochford, the man on that bike, soon became my idol. His father, Danny, was a master gardener who looked after my parents' gardens. Like his father, Tommy was kind and generous, but, most importantly, he let me ride up to his house on my bicycle and tinker with his Maico. Tommy would lift me on to the bike, start it up and hold it upright until I moved off. I was small at the time and my feet did not reach the ground, so I would go flying around the field until I'd had enough, at which point I would race towards Tommy, slam on the brakes and, as the bike dropped to the deck, leap off.

By the time I was twelve, I had a 125cc and, like Tommy, I was into motocross whenever I wasn't making films. At about that time I got to know Kaz Balinski, a fellow motorbike fanatic in the making who lived across the river from our farm. Kaz, who had a Yamaha YZ-80, had built a motocross track that soon became Tommy's and my primary destination. We would race our bikes down to the bottom of my parents' fields, through the river into the Balinski's field and up the hill to Kaz's motocross track, where we would bounce around the circuit, racing, tumbling and falling until it got dark.

A couple of years later, I wanted a bigger bike, a 250cc. My dad said it was too big and I was too young, but I persisted and eventually I became the proud owner of a Yamaha YZ-250. The day I first climbed on to that 250 my father was out playing tennis with a neighbour. The bike was all I had ever wanted and I was determined not to be intimidated by its size and power. I shot along a dirt track and raced past the tennis court, hoicking a huge wheelie in defiance of my father as I passed by. Glaring at my dad as if to say 'look, I *can* ride this thing, you see', I felt blissfully pleased with myself until I looked ahead to see a stone wall topped by barbed wire looming up only a few feet away. I slammed the bike down and hauled on the brakes, but I was on lush, green grass, almost knee-high, and there was nothing doing. I was going to slide. I felt the bike slip away beneath me as I skimmed across the grass, hit the wall, bounced over it and wrapped myself in barbed wire. My father came running up to me as I lay helpless on the ground but the look in his eyes told me that there was no way he was going to help me. Standing above me, he shouted in my face: 'You fucking idiot. I told you that you were too small for that thing.' With the bike beside me, its engine still thundering away, there was little I could do but plead forlornly: 'Yeah, okay, but can you just get this thing off me?'

Shortly after that, I sold the Yamaha and got another 125cc. My father was right: the YZ-250 really was just too big, but before I waved it goodbye I went out for a spin on the roads with Tommy's brother, Kevin, who had a fully equipped road bike, whereas my YZ-250 was an untaxed motocross machine with no lights – so I strapped a torch on the front. Having spent a few hours riding through the Wicklow countryside, we came to a junction, the turning for the road home. There, standing in the middle of the road, was Sergeant Cronen, the local policeman. His arms were folded on his chest and he had a stern look on his face. I was baffled. How had he spotted us? Simple, he said. He had stopped to examine an abandoned car and noticed, going up the hill, a white light, a red light, a white light and no red light. He thought it was a simple case of pulling the rider over to tell him that his rear light was not working, but then I came shooting around the corner: bang. Done.

Sergeant Cronen looked at me with one eyebrow raised and just murmured quietly in his soft Irish brogue: 'Charley, Charley, Charley. Tsk, tsk, tsk. What the feck are yer doin'?'

I didn't even have my helmet off. How could he have known who I was? I never found out. He went through the whole process. Fourteen offences. No tax, no insurance, no licence, riding with illegal tyres, illegal bike, not a proper helmet, insufficient due care and attention, and so on, not to mention the torch strapped to the bike as a front light. Sergeant Cronen ordered Wicklow's most wanted to head back immediately, but I was in the middle of nowhere, about seven miles from home, so I started pushing the bike. He was having none of it. 'Get on yer bike and drive it straight home,' he said. 'Yer in serious trouble.'

By the time I got home, Sergeant Cronen had already rung my dad, who was really pissed off. Striding into the living room, he threw the phone book at me. 'You'll need a lawyer,' he snapped. 'Look it up yourself.'

'But Dad, I'm dyslexic,' I whimpered, the tears rolling down my cheeks. 'I don't even know how to spell it.'

It took a long time for my father to stop ribbing me about it but even after two run-ins with him my passion for motorbikes remained undimmed. Soon after that encounter with Sergeant Cronen I was heading up to Tommy Rochford's house in my usual manner. I would come out of our driveway and jump on my motorbike, sitting side saddle as I rode up the hill so that if someone spotted me I could jump off and pretend I was walking.

This time, I came screaming up the hill, doing about 30mph, when Garda Jackson, Sergeant Cronen's superior, stepped out of the village shop. There was no time to brake. I jumped off the bike. Garda Jackson looked round to see me running flat out – uphill – trying to keep up with my bike. I knew it was a fair cop but to my amazement he just stood there and shook his head. He was speechless. It was only a few days after I'd been let off by Sergeant Cronen and here I was taking on the law yet again.

'Charley! What the hell are yer doin'?' he bellowed when he'd come to his senses. I expected the book to be thrown at me but Garda Jackson turned a blind eye and for many years my motorcycle escapades continued in the same vein, evading the law until I passed my test when I was about twenty-one and living in London. Then I got my Kawasaki Zephyr 750, my first big bike.

EWAN: My biking baptism can be summed up in two words: teenage love. My first girlfriend was petite with short mousy blonde hair, a smile that was as wicked as her character, and I was mad about her. Whereas I was a day pupil, she was a boarder at Morrison's Academy, our school in Crieff, a small Perthshire town. She and I went out for a while when I was about thirteen or fourteen. Her personality was a beguiling mix of contradictions and maybe that was why I couldn't stop thinking about her. She was very sweet-natured but at times she could be really hard core, quite a tough cookie. Her right breast was the first girl's breast that I ever touched. In a bush off Drummond Terrace.

Then she went off me. We were on, we were off; we were on, we were off. So whenever we were off I went out with lots of other girls. That's what you did at my school but I always came back to her. Our on-off romance came to an abrupt end, however, when she started going out with another guy from Ardvreck, the other school in Crieff. He rode a 50cc road bike first and then a 125. And whereas I had always walked my girlfriend back to Ogilvy House, where she boarded, and snogged her at the gate, suddenly she was going back with this guy. He would meet her at the back gate, snog her and then he would go screeching around Ogilvy House on his motorbike all night long. It drove everyone to distraction. He was doing it for her. And I knew what he felt like. And I knew what it made her feel like.

I was nearly sixteen by then and already heartbroken. Then one day, on the way back from a shopping trip to Perth with my mum, we passed Buchan's, the local bike shop. I urged my mother to stop the car. I got out, walked up the short hill to the shop and pressed my nose to the window. There was a light blue 50cc bike on display right at the front of the shop. I didn't know what make it was, or if it was any good. Such trivialities were irrelevant to me. All I knew was that I could get it in three or four months' time. I could ride it at sixteen and maybe even get my girlfriend back.

I'd ridden my first bike when I was about six. My father, Jim, was chairman of the Crieff Round Table and had organised an event for disadvantaged children. It was a kind of *Jim'll Fix It* and one small boy's fix it was to ride a motorbike. My father organised a wee red Honda 50cc and we headed off to a field that belonged to a family friend. After the kid had a go, they asked me if I wanted a ride. Of course I did. I clambered on and shot off. It was just a twist and go, and I went all over the field. I thought it was just the best thing. I loved the smell of it, the sound of it, the look of it, the rush of it, the high-pitched screaming of the engine. Best of all, there was a Land-Rover parked next to two large loads of straw bales with about a metre and a half between them. I knew that from where the adults were standing it looked as if there was no distance between them. Just one large heap of straw.

I thought I would have a go. I came racing towards the adults, shot right through the gap in the straw bales, thrilled to hear the adults scream and elated that it had frightened them witless. It was my first time on a motorbike and I wanted more. A few months later, my Uncle Kenny turned up at the house with a motorbike and rode me up and down the drive on it. That just made me hanker for one all the more: motorbikes had become my object of desire.

So when I looked through Buchan's window in Perth that day,

it suddenly all made sense to me. It was what had to happen. I needed the bike to be able to ride around. I can't remember whether it was to win back my ex-girlfriend's heart or not, but more than anything it meant that, instead of having to walk everywhere, I could ride my motorbike to school and the games fields at the bottom of Crieff and when I went out at weekends. I knew what had to happen: somehow I had to have that bike. I started to fantasise about it. I spent all my waking hours thinking about getting on and starting up the bike, donning the helmet and riding around Crieff. I couldn't sleep. Driven to desperation by my desire for a bike, I made a series of promises to my mum: I won't leave town. I'll be very safe. I won't take any risks. I won't do anything stupid. But, in truth, I was making it up as I was going along.

Crieff is built on a hill. It's a small town and I used to walk everywhere. It takes less than half an hour to walk from one end of the town to the other. My whole childhood was spent walking around the town, from my parents' house to school to friends' houses. It was great, but I was getting to that age when children become aware of the possibilities of venturing further afield. Crieff is smack in the middle of Scotland, only fifty miles north of both Edinburgh and Glasgow, and no more than a day's drive from anywhere in the country. Unless, like us, you went everywhere by bicycle. With so many beautiful places within easy striking distance, the idea of getting a motorbike was too much to resist.

I asked my mother, promising and bargaining the world just for the chance of having a bike. 'I'll only go thirty miles an hour, just please let me have the bike,' I begged.

'I'll speak to your dad,' Mum replied. I thought there was a vague possibility, a glimmer of hope, but my parents never gave in. I just wasn't allowed. 'If something happened to you, I couldn't possibly forgive myself,' my mother told me.

She was probably right, too. When Charley and I visited her during a four-day trip to Scotland that served as the dress rehearsal for our round-the-world journey, I showed Charley the Buchan's shop window where I'd spent many hours gazing longingly at that little 50cc bike. Charley teased my mother: 'Dreadful parents. All that denial. Denying his need as a man to straddle that motorbike.'

But my mother didn't rise to Charley's bait. 'You see, when he was sixteen, he was a bit . . . he would probably have fallen off and then he might not be going round the world now,' she said.

'I might not be here at all,' I chipped in.

'So you know – maybe we did the right thing,' Mum said.

'You definitely did the right thing,' I told her. And she had. At the time that I was begging for a bike I'd already had a close scrape with a 100cc four-stroke belonging to George Carson, the school laboratory technician. I was playing Sganarelle in a school production of the eponymous Molière play. During a break in rehearsals I casually popped the question to Mr Carson.

'Can I have a go on your motorbike, sir?'

'Yeah, of course,' he replied, not knowing I didn't have a clue how to ride it.

The bike was in a wee alleyway up the side of the refectory building that doubled up as the school hall and theatre. I managed to kick-start it, but, unable to control the clutch, stalled it three times. On the fourth attempt, I took off on the bike, zooming down the alleyway until I crashed smack into a wall, bending the wheel and snapping the handlebars. Mr Carson came out to find me looking very red-faced. The bill for the damage came to more than £80, a fortune to a fifteen-year-old in those days and one that took me months of working as a dishwasher and waiter at the Murray Park Hotel to pay back.

So when my mother refused my pleas for a bike part of me understood her concerns but the rest of me knew there was something missing. Spiritually I was already a biker but I just didn't have a bike.

A year or so later I left home for drama school. First to Fife for a year and then down to the Guildhall in London, where I soon became friends with Jeremy Spriggs, another aspiring actor. When I was nineteen, Jeremy took me to a country pile that belonged to someone he knew in Cambridgeshire. There, in a delapidated shed, I found an old off-road bike. It was broken, with its engine in a plastic bag and the rest of the bike in bits. But it was a bike. That was all that mattered. Determined to buy it and get it working, I paid Jeremy's friend £150. When we got it back to London, Jeremy took it away to get it fixed. A few days later he told me it couldn't be repaired. I was gutted. Jeremy had probably spoken to my mum. He didn't want me to have it, knowing that if I killed myself on it he would feel responsible. Another bike had slipped through my fingers.

As soon as I graduated from the Guildhall and started working, I headed for a bike shop in Kentish Town in north London. For years I had frequented bike shops just to look at bikes and gear and all the stuff that goes with biking. To this day, I will quite happily read motorcycle catalogues about gloves and foot pegs – biker porn. Sitting in that shop was a Honda 100cc bike that I could ride on a car licence. I bought it straightaway and loved it. I rode it everywhere. I would go to parties on it, to auditions, absolutely anywhere. For the first time, I felt totally independent. I didn't need to go on the tube. And I wore all the gear.

One day I was sitting in traffic having come down the hill from Hampstead Heath. I was dressed like the archetypal greasy biker: denim jacket, leather jacket, an open-faced helmet with goggles. I really looked the part. And approaching me, on the other side of the column of traffic, was a very cool rider, dressed almost the same. As he drew level, Zen biker nodded over to me, across the top of a car bonnet, to say 'How you doing?' I nodded back. The lights turned green and we moved away. As the traffic cleared, Zen biker could see that, while he was sitting on a big Harley-Davidson, I was straddling a wee Honda 100cc. His withering look could have shrivelled a pomegranate. I was mortified.

That embarrassing episode only strengthened my resolve to get my biker's licence and to buy a large bike. The day I passed my test, I hot-footed it to a bike shop in north London and bought a very old 1970s Motoguzzi, sold to me as a Motoguzzi Le Mans. I loved the look of it, but it turned out to be a far cry from the salesman's claims. It had clip-on bars and it was in the racing position, but it was like riding a tractor. It was a dog. Someone had obviously traded it in and I bought it because I liked the way it looked and because I really didn't know anything about bikes at the time. But I had just passed my test, I was desperate to ride a big bike and it was perfect for me – noisy, oily, good-looking and messy. My only regret about the Guzzi, which I restored and customised until it was a beauty, is that I eventually sold it.

The only problem was what to do with the Guzzi when my parents visited. I was living the life of Riley in a bachelor pad in Primrose Hill. I partied every weekend, from Friday night, when I would meet my friends in town, to Sunday evening, when all the parties would invariably wind up at my flat. At about this time, a beautiful Australian girl, Elska Sandor, moved in upstairs. She was studying textiles, but all she wanted to do was design skateboards. She introduced herself – I had been too embarrassed to speak to her because I was always at the tail end of a weekend's partying whenever I bumped into her – and we became good friends. Every time my parents came to visit, I would rush upstairs to Elska's flat with all my biking gear – helmet, gloves, clothing, magazines – and hide it with her. For several years my parents blithely walked past my bike, chained to a lamppost outside my flat, never realising it was mine.

At about this time, while filming an episode of *Kavanagh QC*, I met a beautiful French production designer. I fell head over heels in love with Eve Mavrakis and we married soon afterwards. From the very early days of our romance, Eve made it clear that she didn't care for bikes at all. She thought they were dangerous. And if Eve seriously asked me to stop riding, I would hang up my leathers, but she knows that bikes are my passion and, because of that, my wife has always tolerated my bike riding. Even when

Clara was born, Eve didn't place demands on me. While Clara was still a little baby I met Charley and, thanks to his friendship, became an even more fanatical biker.

Not long after Charley and I met I began work on *The Phantom Menace*, the first of the *Star Wars* prequels, and met up with Charley and some of his biker mates. They were all on sports bikes and Charley had one too. I could see how much fun they were, but it wasn't until Sasha Gustav, a Russian photographer friend, lent me his sports bike that I found out for myself. It was the first brand new bike I had ridden – I was used to riding my old Guzzi – and I was in for quite a shock. Going down Haverstock Hill in Hampstead I pulled away gently from the lights and looked down at the speedometer to discover I was already doing 80mph. Alarmed at the speed, I hit the brakes and stopped almost instantaneously. I was gobsmacked. Sports bikes excel at what they do in the most exhilarating way. I decided there and then to get a new bike and to make it a sports bike, and, as I had a bit of cash from making *Star Wars Episode One*, I thought I'd get a brand new Ducati 748.

When the shooting started at Leavesden Studios, north of London in Hertfordshire, I embarked on an all-out campaign to get the Ducati, importing it from Italy through James Wilson, a friend of Charley's who ran Set Up Engineering, a racing suspension specialist in south London. Importing the Ducati from Europe made it slightly cheaper but I had to pay cash. Every few weeks I would bowl into the *Star Wars* accounts department at Leavesden to ask for an advance, taking out many thousands of pounds each time. It was a lot of cash to ask for against my wages and it all had to be authorised. They were making *Star Wars* and all I was thinking about was this wonderful Ducati.

One afternoon I got a phone call from Rick McCallum, the producer and George Lucas's right-hand man. He wanted to speak to me about the bike. My first thought was: 'Oh fuck, I'm in trouble.' I guessed I had taken out too much money – as if the *Star Wars* producers didn't have that much cash. But guilt is always the first response and I thought I had done something wrong. I went up to the producers' office, knocked on the door and walked in. Rick was waiting.

'George and I want to know how much this bike is costing you?' he said. I told him how much, thinking I was about to be castigated for bothering the production accountants.

'George and I would like to buy it for you,' Rick said. I was stunned. For the next few years, I rode around on what was in effect George Lucas's bike, until I passed it on to Charley, who rides it to this day.

It was quite ironic that George Lucas bought me the Ducati. My contract usually forbids me from riding a bike while shooting a movie. The only location where I was allowed to ride to work was Australia; I spent almost two years there on and off, shooting *Moulin Rouge* and the second and third *Star Wars* episodes. Working in America, where I had to take the company limousine, or drive by car to the studio, had driven me nuts, so when I first met Baz Luhrman, the director of *Moulin Rouge*, I told him that if he wanted me to sign up for eight months to rehearse and shoot his film – a much longer period than the usual three months a film takes – I had to be allowed to ride a bike.

'I act. I am with my wife and kids. And I ride motorbikes. That's it, that's all I do,' I said. 'If you don't let me ride a motorbike for eight months, it's like forbidding me from listening to music. It's that big a deal to me. I cannot stay off bikes for eight months.' I made it clear to Baz that in my eyes it was unreasonable and unacceptable, and somehow in Australia they got their insurers to okay it.

Midway through the eight-month shoot, I rode off into the outback. It was the first time I had done a solo bike tour to get away from a movie set. I was having a great time making *Moulin Rouge* with Nicole Kidman, but I was surrounded by people every day and I needed a break. Before I left, everyone in the cast and crew, including Baz and all the producers, showed me maps and suggested routes. It was unheard of for a leading actor to take off on a bike in the middle of a movie and they were scared stiff. But there was nothing they could do about it. I needed to make decisions for myself and I wasn't going to let anyone stop me.

I rode for several hours, camped and, after pitching my tent, I just stayed there. I didn't do anything, just sat in a field beside a tent for a day, keeping the fire going. I fell asleep and woke up at four in the morning, staring at the stars, lying in the grass next to the burnt-out fire. It was just what I needed. I did nothing, but that was my decision. No one to pick me up at dawn and tell me what I could have for lunch. No one telling me to stand over there, to say this line, or to do that. Film-making is a fantastic experience but the technicalities are deadly dull. It's boredom, peppered with moments of passion.

When I leave work on a motorbike, pull on my helmet and move off, it doesn't matter if I've had a good day or not. With no phone, no stereo and no traffic to sit in for forty minutes, contemplating what's happened during the day, I am concentrating so hard on what I'm doing and where I'm going, and making sure that no one is pulling out to kill me, that by the time I get home my mind has been cleared of any troubles. Motorcycling gives me anonymity and I don't have much of that in my life. It's an escape from being stared at. When I'm flashing around on my bike with my helmet on I'm just another geezer on the road and that's nice. But, above all, there's something about riding a bike – the concentration and the single-mindedness of it, and the desire to get it right, taking a corner fast without losing control, doing it beautifully, getting into a groove and winning the battle between your head telling you to do one thing, the bike wanting to do another and your body in between – that I miss like hell if I don't get to ride it every day. I walk into the house and I'm chilled.

CHARLEY: For most bikers, commuting around town is never enough. The urge to go faster and further takes over, and the open road beckons. For years, I would get up early on Sunday mornings to meet hundreds of other bikers at a petrol station near Box Hill, south of London, shortly after 6.30 a.m. By midday we would have burned down to the south coast, downed a fry-up breakfast and raced back to London for lunch with the family. Whenever I had a couple of spare hours, I would head for the roundabouts south of the river at Wandsworth Bridge or beneath the A40 at White City to practise my cornering, circling again and again to see how low I could get my knee down, clocking up thirty miles or more each session, orbiting for hours until I'd achieved a perfect lap. When you're leaning over and it's really hot, worn rubber builds up on the edges of the tyre. It means everything to a biker and I would get to a point where I would be going around for so long that when I pulled up to go straight, it all felt really wrong. The whole bike felt lopsided because I had become used to hanging down just one side.

On trips across London with Olly and our daughters, Doone and Kinvara, I would shoot ahead on my bike. As Olly negotiated roundabouts, she would pass me and see me in her mirror, going round and round. Then my headlight would appear in her mirror as I approached, pulling a wheelie and grinning wildly at the kids as I drew level, before racing past.

But my obsession with bikes and speed was accompanied by increasingly close scrapes with injuries and a series of almost fatal accidents. Days after returning home from shooting *Serpent's Kiss* in Ireland, I set off with about fifteen other bikers, one a scaffolder in his early twenties, another the retired chairman of ICI in his sixties, for the twenty-four-hour Superbike race at the Paul Ricard racetrack in southern France. After a long and tiring first day eating up the miles through northern France, we spent the night at a cheap hotel and departed early the next morning, hoping to make the racetrack at Le Castellet, a tiny village in Provence, by midday. The afternoon before I had been right on the pace, but shortly after we set off, I hit a little wet patch and just felt the front end tuck and lose its grip. It made me nervous. I had a hangover from a few too many drinks the previous night and I was struggling to regain my feeling for the roads. The road was narrow and twisty, with a succession of switchbacks, but continued round for almost three-quarters of a full circle. Concentrating intensely on the road in front of me, I looked up to find I was on the wrong side of the road with a car coming straight towards me. Clouds of blue smoke and the stench of burning rubber filled the air as we both slammed on our brakes. Gritting my teeth, I tightened my grip on the brake lever and prepared for the worst. Seconds before impact, we both came to a standstill. My front tyre was just inches from the car's front bumper. I looked through the windscreen to see a middle-aged father, with his wife and three kids, staring back at me, the look on his face a mixture of obvious relief, blind fear and outright indignation. I knew just what he was thinking: 'What the fuck are you doing?'

In the enjoyment and excitement of a fortnight devoted to the adulation of motorbikes at the Paul Ricard racetrack I soon forgot the close encounter, but my next scrape, a year or so later, was much more serious. Racing along twisty country roads with a mate, I entered a corner far too fast. We were travelling at 100mph and I knew there was no way I was going to come out of that hairpin in one piece. Looking around for an exit route, I spotted a clear run-off directly ahead. Good news: maybe I would survive the inevitable crash after all. Then I noticed a tiny little lip at the edge of the tarmac. At a safe speed, I would have passed over it without incident, but at more than 100mph it was going to cause serious trouble. Moments later, my front tyre hit the lip, denting the rim. Then the back wheel went over it and the rear swing arm snapped. The bike went down and it completely disintegrated, leaving me lying in the long grass with the remnants of the bike still beneath me.

'Charley, Charley, where are you?' It was David Healey, one of the many riders I used to meet for those Sunday morning burn-ups to the coast. Dazed, bewildered, but still alive, I popped up from the grass like a startled meerkat. Bits of bike were scattered in a wide circle around me. My back and one of my shoulders hurt like hell. I had damaged some ligaments and broken a four-inch-thick fence post, but it was the bike, not me, that was written off. And for me that was much more galling.

'Charley,' David said again. 'You need a track day. You can do all this, much faster, but in an environment where there's less chance of you killing yourself.'

My first day at Snetterton, a simple, fast two-mile racetrack built on a Second World War airbase in Norfolk, was a revelation. It was the only time in my life that I ended a day thinking that if I had known about this when I was younger I would have made a career of it. I'd had a fabulous time, but it was also a terrible moment. I realised then what I really wanted to do with my life, but I was too old to do it.

EWAN: I soon followed Charley on to the racetrack. I'd had fewer close calls than he had, although exaggerated accounts of my falling off a Honda Blackbird had made the newspapers, which reported that I had narrowly escaped a fatal 180mph collision on a tour of the Scottish Highlands with my father in March 1999 when I should have been at the Oscar's ceremony in Hollywood. In fact, in that instance my rear wheel had slipped sideways on a diesel spill, tipping me off the bike at about 30mph as I was exiting a roundabout more than a week after the Academy Awards. I was never very good at being fast on the roads. I'd had near misses where I had strayed over to the other side of the road as I was going around a corner, inwardly screaming 'Oh, my God' as a car was coming towards me, and I had thought it was just stupid. I remember looking in the windscreen of an oncoming car, seeing the bewildered face of the driver, and my only thought was: 'What for?' I was just trying to keep up with the rider ahead of me. Riding fast on a racetrack makes sense: you're never going to meet someone coming the other way.

My first track day was an event organised by Ducati at the Brands Hatch Indy circuit. Carl Fogarty, the legendary four-time World Superbike champion, was to be there and Ducati, knowing I rode a 748, had asked me to join them. Arriving at Brands Hatch on my bike, I found the flies had broken on my particularly garish two-piece leather suit, given to me by *Bike* magazine. I'd acquired the leathers after doing a photo shoot on my Motoguzzi for them. Asked what colour I wanted I said: 'Well, my bike's yellow. So maybe something yellow and black.' I was actually thinking of something predominantly black with a little bit of yellow piping. Then the suit arrived. It was like a diagonal chequered flag, all yellow and black squares, like a rotten banana. The boots looked as if someone had splashed luminous paint all over them. Pink, purple and green – absolutely awful. The gloves were no better. And here I was, turning up for a track day – my first ever – with a bunch of bike journalists, many of whom are complete nutters on bikes because they are paid to thrash the living daylights out of them, and my flies were gaping wide open. Someone gave me some silver gaffer tape. I taped it over the crotch of my yellow, fluorescent nightmare leather suit. It wasn't the greatest look.

The journalists pestered me with questions about how I was feeling. I was so sick with fear and anticipation that I just wanted them to leave me alone and ask me questions afterwards. Ducati paired me off with the oldest participant. As we walked down to the track, he asked me how fast I was. 'Oh, pretty quick,' I replied. The old guy told me he was worried about the pace. 'We'll just take it steady at first,' he suggested. We eased out on to the track, I tucked in behind him, and then he and all the other biking journalists disappeared, just evaporated into thin air. Taking it easy, apparently. It left me thinking that if that was taking it easy, then I didn't stand a chance. And so it was for the first session of eight or ten laps. I hadn't been riding bikes for long enough to know the essentials: what gear to be in, how to keep the racing line and how to make a bike really move. But the learning curve is very steep on a track day and it didn't take long to learn the ropes. Hanging off your bike, your backside nearly scraping the tarmac, is a very strange thing to do, but it's the most exhilarating experience I've ever had, one that becomes more technical and less frightening as it goes on. Even now, after many track days, my nerves will be shredded before the first session of the day because racing is all about telling your brain to ignore its natural instincts, particularly on corners. Resisting until the very last moment, braking as late as you can, the whole back end of the bike lifting, trying to overtake itself as you struggle to do everything as smoothly and gently as possible, while your brain screams at you to slow down. It's a fabulous feeling when you get it right.

However, riding a bike is not just about going flat-out fast. It's also about taking your time, steadily eating up the miles, cruising the highways, letting the road take you wherever it's going and not worrying about the destination, just enjoying the journey. Whenever I can grab the chance I get on my bike and take off for a few days. A few years ago, I rode from London to my parents-in-law's home in north-east France. I didn't want to be recognised so I shaved my head into a Mohawk in the hope it would be enough to ensure that I was left alone. After a day riding through central France, I stopped at a campsite at the Tarn Gorge and put my tent up. Dressed in shorts and a vest, with my six-inch Mohican and a large, freshly tattooed heart incorporating my wife and daughters' names on one bared shoulder, I entered the local bar. Sipping a drink at the bar and planning on staying another few days to do some sightseeing and relax, I was just about to ask the barman if I could book a table that evening when a customer at the bar gave me a look that made me want to leave immediately. He looked at me as if I was a piece of dirt, with real hatred in his eyes. With a Gauloise wedged between his thin lips, this Frenchman, quietly smoking at the bar, clearly thought I was despicable, worthy only of his contempt because of my appearance. It shocked me that one person could look at another with such hatred. And all because I had spiky hair.

I crossed the road to a restaurant with dozens of empty tables inside and outside. I walked in and asked for a table for later that evening. The waitress looked at the barman. They both looked at me, silent for a few seconds. And then she said simply: *'Non.'*

I couldn't believe it. What was she thinking? 'It's just for me – *pour moi.'*

'Non.'

'How about out of sight?'

'Non.'

I crawled back into my tent and went to sleep hungry and thirsty, surrounded by hundreds of happy British holidaymakers. Because of their presence on campsites across France, I'd shaved my hair into a Mohican to avoid detection. My disguise had succeeded so comprehensively that now I couldn't even buy a meal in a local bar. In a week of travelling around the country, I don't think I was recognised once, but, shunned by restaurateurs and barkeepers across France, I soon became very lonely and hungry, and rolled up at my parents-in-law's home several days earlier than intended.

A few years later, shortly after I finished shooting *Big Fish* in Alabama, I encountered a similar experience. Wanting to ride to Los Angeles before flying home to London, I bought myself a big Harley-Davidson Roadglide and headed for Oklahoma to cruise along one of the few remaining stretches of the original Route 66. Three days into the journey, I arrived at Elk City, a mythical Route 66 destination, far off the beaten track, stuck in a 1930s time warp and immortalised in Woody Guthrie's *Dust Bowl Ballads*. I stumbled into an old pool hall, wishing I had someone to play with at one of the dozen or so empty tables. Oozing authenticity and history, it had the Stars and Stripes in one corner and it made you want to stand there with your hand clutched to your chest, humming 'The Star-Spangled Banner'. A young guy was playing pool with a girl, and a trio of good old boys were sitting at a table at the far end, playing cards. Next door was a gun store with two signs in the window – 'We Don't Ring 911' and

'We Keep Indian Time' – and further down the road was the Elk City Holiday Inn Express. Having taken in the pool hall, I pulled up outside its front doors. A force five wind had been blowing all day and I'd been riding at a tilt of about 45 degrees since getting on the road. I was exhausted, in need of food and a bed. 'Can we help?' the manager asked.

'Yeah, I'm just looking for a room,' I said, asking for a double to get a larger room.

'No. We're full.'

Outside, the parking lot was empty. It was late afternoon and there wasn't a single car to be seen.

'Really? Haven't you got anything?'

'We're full.'

I crossed the road and took a room in a motel. A few months later, on *The Jay Leno Show*, I mentioned being turned away from what appeared to be a totally empty Holiday Inn Express. Jay invited me back on his show to publicise *Long Way Round* in December 2003 and made a great thing of presenting me with a voucher for a free night's stay, breakfast included, sent in by the Elk City Holiday Inn Express. Not that I was going to take them up on it.

These short breaks from the routine of home and movie-making made me hanker for more. I'd never really travelled on my own because by the time I was sixteen I was totally focused on becoming a professional actor. Holidays were spent stitching sacks in a potato shed, cleaning cars at a garage and, dressed in waders and clutching a barrel, scooping rancid fish, stiff with rigor mortis, out of festering pools at a trout farm, all to pay for the next term's tuition and living expenses at drama school. But I had loved camping, travelling with my parents to Brittany and to Camusdarach, where my uncle and mentor, Denis Lawson, shot *Local Hero* with Burt Lancaster in the early eighties. I loved that beach and the little camping ground nearby; it put camping in my blood and made me appreciate the liberating virtues of self-sufficiency.

Gradually a trip started to take shape in my head. I'd mentioned to Charley the idea of riding down to Spain with our wives, but it was something that we were going to do when the kids were older. I couldn't wait that long. I wanted to do something sooner. Much sooner. One Saturday afternoon, therefore, I headed off to a map shop in Primrose Hill with Clara, my eldest daughter. I bought a very basic world map, spread it out on a pool table in my basement and indulged in a bit of daydreaming. My wife had grown up in China, so I thought of riding there. Then I noticed that if I headed from Mongolia north into Siberia, instead of south to China, it wasn't that much further east to the edge of Asia. Once there, it was only a relatively short leap across the Bering Strait to Alaska, and from Alaska, I reckoned, surely it would be hardtop all the way across North America. London to New York – the long way round: it had an appealing, exciting ring to it. I was looking at it when Charley phoned. 'I think you ought to come over for dinner,' I said.

By the time Charley and Olly arrived, I had made up my mind. Charley needed little persuading. Knowing that I become obsessive about things as soon as they enter my head, my wife thought it might be just another madly ambitious scheme and, because it seemed so far away, immediately said 'Of course you should go'. Olly, although supportive, was taken aback. She knew how determined I am to see things through and she realised probably more than any of us what we were letting ourselves in for. I had three more films to shoot – *Big Fish*, the third episode of *Star Wars* and *Stay* – then I would be free. I'd take three or four months off, I figured, and we'd do the trip in the spring of 2004.

The first thing we did was to buy *The Adventure Motorcycling Handbook*. The first word of chapter one leapt from the page. 'Prepare,' it warned. 'As a rule a first time, multinational, trans-continental journey such as crossing Africa, the Americas or Asia needs at the very least one year of preparation,' it said, emphasising 'one year' in bold type. 'If you're heading right around the world, double that time.' Two years! My Los Angeles agent was nervous enough about me taking a few months off as it was. I couldn't afford to take two years off for career reasons and the need to earn a living meant Charley couldn't afford not to work for two years. It was out of the question for both of us, yet the book regarded as the bible for motorcycle circumnavigations said it would take that long to plan the journey and map out the route, organise visas, permits and other documentation, select and prepare the right motorbike, learn basic medical and mechanics' skills, get the vaccinations, source the camping equipment and motorcycle spares, learn languages, get fit and generally prepare ourselves. It looked like the trip would remain for ever a pipedream.

Then we hit on a way of making it work: we would film the trip and sell it as a television series. Surely there would be interest in two well-known actors circumnavigating the globe and that would finance a production company to help us with the preparation. We would concentrate on the bikes, the physical preparation and choosing the equipment. The production staff would help us with the paperwork, source the equipment and deal with logistics. If we produced it ourselves, we would retain control of the filming and ensure the spirit of the trip – two friends alone on the road, surviving on their wits, a friendship united in adversity – would not be forgotten. As I had those three films slated for 2003, we decided that Charley would take on the responsibility of finding the producers.

CHARLEY: It was April 2003 and I was in London when the call came. It was Ewan. 'I'm taking January to August off next year,' he boomed down the line, his voice filled with excitement. 'Let's do it then. I've spoken to my agents in London and LA, and I've blocked eight months out of the calendar. What have you done about the producers?'

Caught on the hop, I bluffed. 'Oh . . . yeah . . . loads. I've got a few people to meet, I've got a few meetings lined up,' I said. Then I put down the phone, stared out of the window and just thought 'fuck'.

Fortunately, in my wallet I had the business card of a very energetic and ambitious producer I'd met at a party about two weeks earlier. Russ Malkin was brash and cocky – essential qualities in a good producer – and ran a production company, called Image Wizard, that specialised in taking on television challenges that no one else would have considered possible. He'd earned a place in *The Guinness Book of Records* for making the fastest ever feature film: thirteen days from start to finish, including writing the script, shooting, editing and projection at a charity premiere in London. He obviously knew how to get things done against very tight deadlines. He'd produced programmes about powerboat racing and other adrenalin sports, and he was a biker, so he understood the passion for speed and the draw of the open road. Russ seemed to be just the man we needed.

I met Russ and told him our plans. Ewan was coming to town, so I arranged another meeting. Then Ewan cancelled and I could tell that Russ was becoming increasingly suspicious, unsure that there really was a Ewan involved, and, if he was involved, that he would ever appear. Fortunately Ewan turned up at the next appointment. He hit it off with Russ and we went on a tour of big league independent television production companies. At every single one we heard the same spiel: 'Yeah, yeah, we can do that. Not a problem. We'll get the BBC involved. They'll put up the money. Leave it to us. We'll take care of it all.' It all sounded very impressive, but it was the last thing we wanted to hear. Our dream of two mates on the road was in danger of being taken over by corporate executives with ponytails, dressed in the Soho uniform of baggy jeans, T-shirts over long-sleeved tops and baseball caps. Ewan had learned the hard way that it was important to retain control several years earlier, when he made a film about polar bears near Churchill, on the Hudson Bay in northern Canada. The production company re-edited and sold it to broadcasters around the world, making a mint out of it, but Ewan, who would have given his share to the polar bear conservationists, wasn't entitled to a penny. It taught Ewan that spending a few weeks seeing something entirely new was a much more fulfilling holiday than lying on a beach and that he had a taste for adventure. And it taught us that if we were going to make a television series, then we wanted to dictate the terms. But how?

Russ's answer was to enlist David Alexanian, an old friend from Los Angeles, who made low-budget independent feature films. With his sister Alexis, who had a long track record producing major studio and independent films, David specialised in projects that other producers shied away from, the kind of ventures that don't fall into some easily defined category and which rely on passion, integrity and imagination instead of big budgets and formulaic production values. Russ said he needed David, the consummate negotiator who had made his money on Wall Street, to broker an American deal. We met David and immediately liked him. He was clearly a player, a typical LA dealmaker, somebody who made things happen come what may, but who was not ashamed of showing his passion for something and who was generous in every way. Most importantly, David was also a biker and, Russ assured us, would understand and protect the spirit of our adventure.

In September, Russ, David and I flew to Sydney, where Ewan was finishing shooting on episode three of the *Star Wars* prequels. We hired two Yamaha Super Ténéré trail bikes and took off into the outback, where David and Russ shot a video of us that we could use to pitch our idea to broadcasters.

After *Star Wars*, Ewan flew to New York to shoot *Stay*, working his arse off on his third back-to-back film to justify taking most of the next year off. Ewan had taken only eight days off in the previous twelve months and, with only a short while to go before his planned career break, Ewan's family and agents, who had originally thought our scheme was no more than the idle fantasy of a man yearning for some relief from a highly pressured career, were starting to take the trip seriously. Meanwhile, my friends and most of my family just humoured me every time I mentioned it. Ewan had lined the inside of his trailer on the *Stay* set in New York with maps of the countries we hoped to pass through and was meticulously planning the journey. In London, however, nothing was going right. We had no bikes or offices, no money, no staff, no camping equipment, no bike gear. Nothing but a dream and Ewan badgering us to get a television deal double-quick.

EWAN: In December, Russ and David flew to the US to meet with my Los Angeles agents. They knew I was doing a trip – I had been very open with them and they knew I had blocked the time off. Unfortunately, the meeting didn't go as well as we'd hoped. My agents weren't sure that people would be interested in our television series. Without TV support we would really struggle to finance the trip.

I phoned up Charley from my car. 'Charley, my agents aren't sure we'll get a deal,' I said. I could tell he was devastated. Having given up his work from the new year, I could hear in Charley's voice that his world had fallen away. He had pinned his hopes on the trip, and on the television series to finance it, but now he had to face going home to Olly and telling her: 'Maybe no one will buy it.'

For the first time since I'd hatched my plan and got Charley on board, our dream trip was in jeopardy. As the implications sank in, I began to think of it as a small disaster. But to Charley, who had no work booked after Christmas, who was about to go away for the holiday break and for whom money was tight, it was a nightmare and he panicked about it. 'Hang on a minute guys,' he said, 'we are in the process of selling the foreign rights to the television series. Someone clearly thinks it's interesting enough to want to watch it and there's got to be money there to make it work.'

But my agents' concerns made us wonder. Perhaps no one would buy our programme or find it interesting. After all, we hadn't been able to convince a big Hollywood agency; my agency. My immediate response was that we would have to find some way to fund the trip ourselves. I was about to broach the subject with my wife when she said: 'You should start looking into a way of doing the trip without David and Russ, without any television deal or any other way of funding it. Without anything. Just look into how you are going to do the trip, funding it yourself.'

Eve's unprompted endorsement was just what we needed to hear. It made us realise she was absolutely behind us. Her support restored our confidence. We knew a film of our journey was a good idea. Everyone we had spoken to seemed interested in it. So we phoned David and Russ. Wondering what they might have said at the meeting, we told them to stay in L.A. But they were one step ahead. They had already met with William Morris, another large TV and film agency, who seemed excited about the project. They had lined up a series of meetings with broadcasters in January. The trip might be back on.

Meanwhile, in London we were searching for offices. We needed somewhere like a garage to prepare our bikes, but also with office space for the production staff and an editing suite. For weeks we trudged around premises all over the city. Most were ludicrously expensive, others were too small or too far out of town. Depressed by the troubles we'd had in LA and bored by visiting empty, unsuitable buildings, Charley rolled up outside an unprepossessing block in a residential street in Shepherd's Bush in west London a few days before Christmas. Dejected and tired, he was on the point of not bothering to view the property, but when he went inside it was a revelation. It had a workshop which opened straight on to the street with a roll-up metal shutter to let the bikes in. There was a kitchen and office downstairs and more rooms upstairs. It was perfect. With only days left to Christmas, our adventure was suddenly taking shape. All we needed now was to test and get hold of some bikes, kit them out with touring equipment, order spares, source some camping gear, work out the route, organise visas and documentation, do some off-road training, and secure a television deal to pay for it all. So not much pressure then.

3
From chaos to bliss

DEPARTURE DAY

EWAN: On Wednesday 14 April, shortly after 9 a.m., we set off. Ahead of us, three continents stretched eastwards. All of them would have to be crossed before we reached New York. With 20,000 miles, 108 days and 19 time zones to go, we roared away from the workshop and offices in Bulwer Street, our friends, family and the team cheering behind us. Turning the corner, we drove out of their sight, advancing little more than a few tens of yards east before we came to our first stop: a BP petrol station. We needed to fill up. Then Charley dropped his bike. For the second time that morning.

We looked at each other. It was unusual for Charley ever to lose control of his bike but we both knew exactly what was running through each other's minds. Had we chosen the wrong bikes? Were they too heavy? Had we overloaded them? And how the hell would we cope with them on the rough roads, swamps, marshes, and deserts of Asia when we couldn't balance them on the flat tarmac of Shepherd's Bush in west London? There was no getting away from it: the bikes were overloaded and heavy. But the explanation for Charley's sudden weakness was rather less prosaic.

CHARLEY: After months of anticipation, at last the day of departure arrived and I was on the way to Bulwer Street with my wife, Olly, and my daughters, Kinvara and Doone. I felt excited and nervous, the children were more clingy than usual, but otherwise it was just like any other morning. With the four of us in the car, the girls giggling in the back, Olly and me chatting in the front, it was as if we were driving away from home for a run-of-the-mill day out. Then, turning the corner into Bulwer Street, we were confronted by a scene of total chaos. People everywhere. And those who weren't busy strapping things to cars were ticking items off checklists or carting heavy boxes out of the offices into the support vehicles, or milling around, waiting for us. I was consumed by nerves.

With much of the equipment, including the two Mitsubishi support vehicles, finalised only hours before we were due to leave, the crew had been working flat out for a week and had not slept for forty-eight hours. Ewan, of course, was ready and packed days earlier. There's nothing he likes more than a chance to tidy up and put things away neatly, preferably clearly labelled for future reference. The night before departure, Ewan later told me with a degree of pleasure, he had gone to bed with his clothes for the morning carefully stacked – underpants and socks on the top of the pile – beside his meticulously packed bags. I, on the other hand, had left everything to the last moment. With Ewan looking on, I hastily bundled clothes, equipment and bike spares into my bags with such little regard for order and process that I could see Ewan was alarmed. So it was with some delight that I managed to pack all my things into a considerably smaller space and strap my bags to my bike with greater ease than he did. Nevertheless, our bikes topped the scales at almost a third of a ton fully laden with two side panniers, a top box containing communications and filming equipment specially designed for us by Sonic, a tank bag and a large holdall and tent strapped to the rear seat.

Pushing the bikes gingerly out into the street, we were petrified they would topple over when we propped them on their side stands. Olly and the children were watching, and my friend Roy, who runs the Bullet motorcycle shop and who had been a great help in the last few days of preparation, was there. My twin sister Daisy turned up with her boyfriend, Peter, waving a huge banner made from an old bedspread painted with the words 'Charley and Ewan. Good Luck. Float Like Butterflies'. A wonderful, warm gesture. They also gave us crosses to accompany the St Christopher medals, trinkets and good-luck charms we were wearing around our necks. Peter, meanwhile, cruised through the crowd and workshop, his arms wide apart, booming: 'The Time Has Come! The Time Has Come!'

Milling around in the street were some of Ewan's friends and family, including his Uncle Denis. Olly made me a cup of coffee, but generally kept out of the way. The kids were dancing around me, coming up to hug me and asking questions, but I was too stressed to answer. It was the first time I'd felt any real nerves. Certainly, I'd had dark moments, waking up in the middle of the night, especially between Christmas and New Year, when the prospect of a television deal seemed remote. Worrying about whether I was doing the right thing going off for three months, leaving everybody behind, I was plagued with thoughts of what might happen if something went wrong. Any biker knows the rule of the road: one big fall and you're toast. And, knowing I couldn't really talk about such things with my wife, I felt completely alone with my demons. Ewan told me the same thoughts went through his head. He also had nights when he didn't sleep. There were mornings when we would turn up at our workshop and we could see in each other's tired, bloodshot eyes that we had both spent half the night thinking about the same thing.

Ewan described it as the longest goodbye. Day after day in the last fortnight of preparation, he would arrive at the workshop and unload tales of immense sadness at home. Particularly subdued one morning, he described how he had been dancing to the new Proclaimers album, whirling around the kitchen with Clara, his eldest daughter. 'She really loved it,' he said. 'I had her in my arms. We were reeling away when I looked around to see Eve crying. It was terrible ... there's nothing to do in those circumstances but be sad.' On other occasions, feeling his home was so brimming with unhappiness about his imminent departure, he couldn't get out of the house fast enough. Whereas Olly was bored with four months' preparation and just wanted us to get on with it, Ewan's family was having a much tougher time coming to terms with his departure. Just days before we left he told me: 'I feel so sick in my stomach, so sick I couldn't stand it at home yesterday. It's been unbelievably sad and horrible, that feeling where you just want to run away from it because it is just awful. I feel it all the time. I feel it with Eve. She is so unhappy and not herself. It's not to make me guilty or anything like that. It's just that she knows I'm leaving. I just want to run away from the pain.'

By the Monday before departure, with just two days to go, I, too, felt sick to my stomach. Pushing my fears and thoughts to the back of my mind, I told myself everything would be all right. I just got on with the job. There was no time for second thoughts.

Before we pushed the bikes outside, Russ and David arrived with Jo Melling, the project manager, carrying a sheaf of documents. Jo explained they were copies of all the visas, driving licences, passports and papers that we needed, but I saw red. 'Just come and fucking give it to us at 8.15 in the morning, when we are trying to leave and we have to unpack everything just to get these things in,' I shouted. 'Why couldn't you just fucking give us this fucking stuff yesterday or the day before yesterday instead of keeping it all upstairs for fucking hours and hours and hours?' I was livid, but my anger soon gave way to guilt. Jo had worked tirelessly on all the visas and, while I had been asleep at home, she had toiled through the night to get everything ready. It was the first time in a long while that I had lost my temper. I gave Jo a hug, apologised and told her I felt stupid. But underneath I was still angry that, because I had to repack things, the bike was now even more top-heavy than before.

So when it came to saying our last goodbyes, I was shaking with nerves. Ewan had already said goodbye to Eve, his daughters and his mother at his home, riding away from them with tears streaming down his face. Fortunately my daughters, Doone and Kinvara, were fairly cool and reserved because we'd discussed it at home. I gave them a big hug and told them to look after their mum. Then I kissed Olly and squeezed her tight, holding my emotions in check until I swung my leg over the bike, at which point I overbalanced. Unable to support all that weight, I dropped the bike in front of thirty people. I looked over at Olly and I just knew what she was feeling. I could see the tears welling up in her eyes and I lost it. With the help of a few of the onlookers, I hoisted the bike back up and, gritting my teeth, rode away from my family and friends, deeply relieved that Ewan was in the front as we pulled off. I was so wobbly I couldn't hold the bike. I couldn't steer properly. I couldn't drive the bike. I couldn't do anything. Shepherd's Bush Green dissolved in a flood of tears as I struggled to see through my visor. By the time we reached the petrol station, I had lost all my energy. The emotions involved in leaving my wife and children, and all the domestic hassles we'd had in the last few days, frantically trying to get things done before I left, welled up inside me. I dropped the bike again, smashing the indicator lamp. The bike would survive, but I had severely dented my pride.

With Roy, who had followed us to the petrol station on a waspy, backfiring little Italian bike, Ewan helped me pick up the bike. Struggling to pull myself together, I remembered the words of Jamie Lowther-Pinkerton, a former SAS officer who had taught us how to survive in hostile environments: 'If you can survive the prep, the mission will be fine.' We had indeed survived the preparation, three months of it, but I still harboured a nagging doubt that we had chosen the wrong bike. I'd always favoured the lighter KTM over the BMW. And now it seemed I might have been right.

EWAN: From the moment we decided to ride around the world, Charley was convinced we should ride customised dirt bikes built by

KTM, a small Austrian company that specialises in off-road enduro and motocross bikes. The only KTM he'd ever ridden was my KTM Duke, but Charley knew KTM's enduro and motocross bikes had dominated the Paris–Dakar rally, the toughest of all off-road races, and won the enduro world championship for the last four years. In 2004, every rider in the top five rode a KTM bike, endorsement enough for any biker. But it was more than that. Among bikers, KTM has a much tougher hard-core image than better known, more mainstream bike manufacturers. Charley's assessment was 'KTM is the Rolling Stones. Anything else is Take That.'

Even before we began our bike assessment in early January, Charley had made his mind up. 'I've always wanted the KTM,' he said. 'It's built very differently. It's much lighter and much thinner than other bikes. It answers all the requirements I would need for this trip. Plus it has that GF, that grin factor, about it. It's more fun to ride. And I think that the people behind the scenes, the KTM guys, are much more fun and up for a bit of a laugh.'

But I needed more convincing, so early January found us outside the Abercrave Inn, near BMW's off-road training facility in the Brecon Beacons in south Wales. It was a miserable, misty day. The ground was wet, but at least it wasn't raining. A squad of BMW engineers and executives led us through the 1150 GS Adventure, their top-of-the-range endurance touring bike. Shaft-driven and stacked with servo-booster ABS brakes, a huge 1150cc Boxer engine, heated grips, a 30-litre tank for a 200-mile range, and loads of gadgets, it was a massive, heavy machine.

While David and Russ held a meeting inside the oak-beamed pub with the BMW executives, Charley and I sped off for a couple of hours, first on local roads then off-road on BMW's 2,100-acre test area. After the ride, even Charley had to concede he was surprised by the BMW. 'They were a lot better than I thought they were going to be,' he said. 'I had a preconceived idea of what a BMW would be like and I was proved wrong. I'm man enough to admit that. But it's still fucking heavy and there were times I struggled to bring the bike up when it dipped beneath me.'

I thought the BMW was a beautiful machine. Even though I dropped the bike when doing a slow U-turn on a dirt track, I was extremely impressed. But, most of all, I liked it because when we got back on the road it felt really sweet. I wanted to start back to London on it. I was surprised because BMWs come with a certain stigma about the people who ride them. But that had been blown away. It handled fantastically, I was really comfortable and I felt that this machine would go for ever. It was so solid and that slow revving engine just felt like it would get us around the world.

Two days later we were at KTM's offices on a nondescript industrial estate in Milton Keynes. The windowless workshop might not have been as plush as the Abercrave Inn, or as imposing as several thousand acres of Welsh hills, but I could see from Charley's face that for him this was oily biker heaven. From the moment we entered the whitewashed breeze-block building, Charley's face bore a grin that reached from ear to ear. 'Ooh, look at that,' he exclaimed as soon as we walked in. Right in front of us stood two gleaming KTM bikes, a 640cc and the 950 Adventurer. From that moment on, as far as Charley was concerned BMW didn't stand a chance.

We tested the 640 and 950 on KTM's test ground, a scrappy area of concrete beside a disused airfield. With a few traffic cones dotted across the broken surface and some lengths of wood thrown on the ground, it couldn't hold a candle to BMW's facilities in Wales. No matter: the KTMs performed brilliantly, inspiring us with more confidence in our abilities than the BMWs had done. The choice was between the KTM 640, which was lighter and better suited to off-road biking, and the KTM 950 Adventurer, which would be hard work off-road but which would cruise happily at 90 or 100mph on the thousands of miles of hardtop across North America. The KTM mechanics warned us that the 950 Adventurer would not be as simple to service on the road as the 640 and pointed out that just about every Paris–Dakar rider used a 640, but our hearts were set on the bigger machine. The fuel tank on the 950 was a bit small, but we didn't want to let that bother us. We were convinced we could find a way around its limited range.

By lunchtime, Charley was so enthused by the bikes he didn't want to leave the test track. He wanted to have his lunch in the saddle. 'It's just fantastic, it's everything that I thought it would be,' he said. 'And maybe a bit more.' Eating with the KTM mechanics, we discussed the relative merits of the bikes and were set on KTM until Russ asked which bike we would choose if we had to set off immediately on a long journey.

'When you ask that,' I said, 'and there's the KTM sitting next to the BMW GS Adventure and I have to ride to Scotland right now and I've got both sets of keys, my immediate thought is that I'd go on the GS.'

Charley immediately cut in: 'But it's so . . . so . . . there's no excitement in it. There's no . . . it's just *nothing* sitting on it. BMW, you know . . . it's like their cars. I mean, they're lovely cars but they're boring to drive. You sit there and everything's functional.'

'Not the 325i I drove at Christmas. It wasn't boring,' I said.

'Sure – but I don't know . . . I just find it very clinical.'

'You're right. The BMW is practical, because they absolutely fucking do what they're meant to do. Which is keep going for a very long time.'

David interjected: 'You guys . . .'

But I couldn't let it lie: 'All right, here's one other thing. A lot of the KTM guys we just met were slightly nervous about taking the bike around the world. Whereas the fucking BMW has been round the world for the last fifty years. That bike is proven.'

'So what?' said Charley. 'We're only doing twenty thousand miles. And any bike or car or any vehicle, you know it's going to do it. You would do it on any vehicle you could buy these days. I mean, the guy was saying couriers are using these. He said couriers use these and they fucking love them.'

I was just exploring all the options, keeping an open mind.

Charley might well be right, I thought, but it was too early to make a final decision.

David cut in again: 'You know what it looks like? The KTM sits there in the drive and it looks like a supermodel. It's, like, do you want to go out with Claudia Schiffer tonight? I mean, it's the sexiest fucking bike on the planet.'

'Or do you want to go out with the BMW,' Charley added, warming to David's theme, 'which is one of the kitchen girls from the cooking programme.'

'Absolutely. You know you're going to get laid,' David added, 'so it's . . .'

'Two fat ladies or two supermodels,' Charley chipped in.

'Don't get so worked up about it,' I said. 'I'm not going to prevent you going on the fucking KTM. It's just that there are so many good points about the BMW too, that's all. The KTM 950 is a sweet bike, but I still don't get the feeling that it's as robust as the BMW. I think BMW make a bike that goes round the world and I think they're probably the only ones that do. If you think about it, it's the only bike that is really designed and built to do what we want to do, but that's not to say that we can't make the KTM work for us. I think we can; I'm sure we can.'

'I was just . . .,' Charley started.

'Listen, this is a fucking nice problem to have,' I said. 'This is a high-class dilemma. Okay? Which fantastic motorcycle will we choose? This is a top-league problem, baby. So let's not lose sight of that.'

The next week we visited Honda. From the moment we stepped into their enormous factory hall, lined with just about everything Honda produces, from trucks and cars to bikes and lawnmowers, we knew Honda wasn't right for us. Honda makes some great bikes. Its Africa Twin is an endurance classic and its Varadero had been recommended to us, but we felt neither could match KTM for sex appeal or the BMW for ruggedness. After a test ride through the streets of Swindon and along the M4, we left Honda for a pub lunch, where we discussed the events of the morning. At last we agreed on something: Honda was too corporate and its bike was not what we were looking for.

'I think there's only one bike that's built for this,' I said.

'And that's the KTM,' Charley cut in.

'Now listen, listen, listen. In terms of a bike that's built for this trip, there's only the one that we've ridden so far . . .'

'And which one's that?' Charley demanded.

'The Beamer.'

'I don't think so.'

'It's built for this kind of trip. It doesn't mean it's the only one we have to use but . . .'

'I think the BMW will give us the same thing as the Varadero did,' Charley insisted. 'After a period of time we'll be bored of it. And when it's loaded up, the BMW . . .'

'After a time we'll be bored with any bike. We're going to get bored with it because we're going to be riding it six days a week for fifteen weeks. So listen, let's not worry about being bored after ten minutes. I think you've . . .'

But Charley cut straight across me: 'The KTM is a better choice. It's easier to ride. It's better balanced.'

'. . . I think you've got to think in terms of reliability,' I finished.

Somehow, by the end of January, Charley had got his way. The grin factor won out over rugged reliability and we decided the KTM was for us. By the time we went to meet Erlan Idrissov, the Kazakh ambassador, at his embassy in London, even I was enthusing about the maverick Austrian bike. All we had to do now was persuade KTM to back us. Knowing they didn't have the resources of a company such as BMW, we had downgraded our expectations of sponsorship. All we wanted was a small financial contribution to the cost of the trip and four 950 Adventurers plus necessary spare parts. It was a big climb-down from our ambition of full sponsorship, one that David found hard to deal with – 'All this exposure for their bikes has a value,' he insisted. 'If they're advertising *Long Way Round* in the TV guide, starting at eight o'clock, and there's your two faces and their two motorcycles, that's bullshit that we're not getting any dough.' But we had to accept there was a price to pay for our decision.

Once again, we were being confronted with the dilemma that plagued our entire adventure. Time, not money, was the primary controlling factor. Because of my work commitments, we didn't have one or two years to prepare for the trip. We had three and a half months. We had to employ people to help us. And that meant we had to pay them. To finance their salaries, we were making a television series, but that required even more staff, who also had to be paid. So we entered the murky world of corporate sponsorship. David, in his unique style, summed up what corporate sponsorship meant the night before KTM arrived at our offices: 'You can go out and buy a bike retail, cut a film in your own time and do it off your own back. But if you want everything for free, you're going to have to – how do I say it? – bend over and grab your ankles.'

KTM told us they would bring Thomas Junkers, a German film-maker who had ridden the 950 Adventurer to Siberia, to a meeting at our offices at which we hoped to finalise the deal. That worried us. The night before the meeting, Charley said we had to be really careful. 'KTM are bringing this guy who's done it, who's gone through Siberia, and they want him to have a look at our schedule. But he could just poo-poo it.'

I was sceptical for other reasons. 'I want to ride across Siberia, but I don't know that I want to speak to someone who's already done it. Why? Because he tells you all the stuff he did and you copy him. What's the point in that?'

The next day Georg Opitz, KTM's marketing representative, arrived in London with Junkers. Standing in front of us in the workshop was the man we needed to impress if we were to get KTM's backing, a huge, fleshy beast who we knew would not be easily persuaded that we were up to the job. He had very few words of encouragement, particularly when he saw our proposed route. Large tracts of north-west Kazakhstan were to be avoided, he said, because the Soviets used it as a biological weapons test ground. 'There is a lot of throat disease around here because of whatever the Soviets were doing,' he said loftily. 'If you stay here, never drink water. No open food. No open vegetables.'

North-east Kazakhstan was also to be avoided: 'No, no, no. These roads are not good,' Junkers insisted. Sweeping his thick fingers across the map, he berated us: 'Up here is only coal mines' . . . 'Until 1989, this was the area for the nuclear bombs' . . . 'This is the only way you can go, whatever they tell you' . . . 'You will find here a lot of cemeteries. This is a no-go area' . . . 'You can go there, but it is an area totally destroyed and with a high radiation. Very high.'

We had arranged with the Kazakh ambassador in London – who had assured us his young country was safe, beautiful and well worth visiting – to pass into Russia through a border usually restricted to freight traffic.

Thomas raised his eyebrows: 'You are sure? This area is normally a no-go area,' he said categorically. 'Here you will find military. And then you have to show them something. It is a major problem.'

Thomas's persistent negativity was grinding us down. Charley attempted to humour him: 'We can only try and, if it's not possible, then we just have to go round until we find the next available crossing point.'

'There is only one entrance and the problem is, you are not allowed to go through it on your own bike,' Thomas snapped, then stood back triumphantly. Crossing his arms, he looked at us as if we were naïve idiots even to consider any route other than his.

And so it went on. The borders we wanted to use would be closed, according to Thomas. The routes we wanted to take would be impassable, he said. The petrol stations we were counting on for fuel would be empty. The permits, visas and border documents that our back-up team were organising would be worthless in the face of local bureaucracy, he insisted. The contacts we had made with ambassadors, local police and the governments of Kazakhstan, Mongolia and Russia would not help us at all. Again and again he pointed at the map and said: 'If you are stuck here, that's the end of your journey. There is no way out.' And as for our maps, in Thomas's opinion they were useless compared with Russian military 1:500,000 maps. 'All I can say is go and buy them,' he declared.

His harshest criticisms were targeted at our plans for eastern Siberia, where we knew we would face our toughest test on the Road of Bones from Yakutsk to Magadan on the Pacific coast. 'What do you know about this road?' he demanded.

'We've spoken to people and we've got some details from people who did a motorcycle journey around the world called the Millennium Ride,' I said.

'You want to take fourteen days for this?'

'I think so. We reckoned on fourteen days for it,' Charley said.

'Actually, I think we've allowed eighteen days for it,' I chipped in.

'What do you think if I tell you now you need six weeks for this one?' Thomas barked.

'We know that two years ago, one guy did it in . . . I can't remember in how many days he did it, but it wasn't eighteen days. It was less,' Charley said. 'There was another group of people who did it last year, this particular bit of the road. And they did it, I think, in sixteen days.'

Thomas was having none of it. He said we were going at the wrong time of the year. In June, he said, Siberia would not yet have fully recovered from its severe winter. Parts of Mongolia and Kazakhstan would also be impassable. It was a fair point, but in complete contrast to the advice given to us by locals. Again and again, Thomas shook his head and tutted, turning down the corners of his mouth in disagreement. We knew we had lost the battle to convince the man with KTM's ear. Our only hope was that KTM had the balls to back us.

Two days later, on Friday 13th, the call came from KTM. Russ walked into the workshop after speaking on the phone to Georg. 'Bad news,' he said. 'Georg said he had a long meeting yesterday and that it had been a very hard decision. We love the project, Georg said, but Thomas Junkers came back from the meeting in London on Wednesday and said there were bits about Siberia that he was worried . . .'

'So they're withdrawing their offer, they're not going to give us the bikes or anything?' I said.

'Correct,' said Russ. KTM, for all its Paris–Dakar experience and hard-core image, was concerned that its bikes were not up to carrying two actors on a holiday trip around the world.

The news hit Charley like a ton of bricks: 'I told you it was a mistake to let him come here. What did Thomas say? That we couldn't do it? I mean, that it was not possible to do this?'

Charley was pacing the room, running his hands through his hair and swearing. 'I feel like my whole world has just been . . . just been taken from under me,' he wailed. I phoned Georg Opitz.

'Hello, it's Ewan McGregor here. Charley and I are a bit shell-shocked about why you've withdrawn your offer and I'm very interested to find out why. What Mr Junkers has said seems to have influenced you and I feel that's slightly unfair.'

'You were presented with a lot of opportunities for failure . . .' Georg said enigmatically and went on to list KTM's concerns.

I came off the phone. 'They think there's a huge potential for us to fail. Thomas Junkers said we were better prepared than he thought we would be, but that there were things that could happen that we could not prepare for. He said there are areas that will be unknown to you – and I said yes, that's what our journey is all about, that's why we're doing it. Don't they get it? It's an adventure, not a package holiday. And adventures are not adventures if there isn't a degree of danger and uncertainty about them.'

I turned to Charley: 'You know we now have to look at whether we go on the BMWs. Or do we get two new Honda Africa Twins and kit them out? What do we do? We have to look at our options now.'

Charley's response was immediate: 'We'll do it with BMW and show them what a fucking great big mistake they made.' But I could see that Charley was really disappointed.

CHARLEY: KTM saying no was a complete and utter bombshell. I didn't know what to say or do. I was really impressed that Russ went immediately to BMW and that they came back straight away. They were straightforward and they offered us so much, expressing great happiness and joy and pride at being part of the project. There were no questions about whether we could or couldn't do it. They really felt it was a great thing and that it was exactly what their bike had been made for. We said, what about eastern Siberia? They said, part of the adventure is to try. If you fail, then that's fine. As long as you've given it a good chance. But I couldn't get over my disappointment with KTM. I so desperately wanted to go with them, but having spoken to BMW I was really happy now to go on a BMW. It wasn't the purest kind of bike, but it was probably best suited to the job.

But, most of all, I was really impressed with Ewan. Deep down in his heart, I think he had wanted to go on a BMW right from the off, but he stuck by me and believed in my passion for the KTM, even though I'd become quite blinkered. I really appreciated what Ewan did. He was going with the KTM for me and I felt really honoured about that. It was a big thing. And I really loved him for it.

Exactly two months later we were on the forecourt of the BP garage in Shepherd's Bush, the glass from my indicator light lying in shards on the tarmac. It was an inauspicious start to the journey. Two months of getting used to the bikes, and a two-day off-road course with BMW, had taught us that the Beamers needed to be treated with respect. These were not two lightweight dirt bikes but a pair of the heaviest bikes on the road. Knowing we would face much more demanding terrain and conditions, we rode out of the petrol station and down Hammersmith Road with our hearts in our mouths. Approaching Hammersmith roundabout, one of the busiest intersections in London, we stopped beside a white van full of builders. 'Hey, we saw you on TV yesterday,' one of them shouted out of the window. 'When are you off?'

'Now. Right now. We're on our way to Folkestone. To the Channel tunnel,' we shouted.

'I don't believe it. You're going right now?' he shouted back, now leaning right out of the side window. 'Good luck!' he yelled, waving his arm. From inside the van came the sound of cheering and his mates roaring: 'We'll follow you in *Motorcycle News*. Have a great time! It's brilliant what you guys are doing! Have a good one!'

For the first time, it dawned on us that we were really on the road. The day we thought would never come had arrived. The preparation was over and we were taking off, riding towards the sunrise, two mates on the road together for the next three and a half months. It was a great feeling. We whooped and shouted to one another over the intercom radio, giddy with the feeling of escape. It was a beautiful spring day, the kind you dream about, the sky a brilliant cloudless blue, the air warm and soft. The sixty miles to the coast passed in a blur, as all the way to Folkestone people cheered, waved, tooted their car horns and shouted good luck. The big BMWs were purring beneath us, the first miles were under the wheels and it felt great to be alive.

4

No surprises

LONDON TO THE UKRAINIAN BORDER

EWAN: Before we knew it we were boarding the train under the English Channel, leaving behind Britain, our friends and families for three and a half months. When we next glimpsed daylight, we would be in the first of many foreign lands, as Charley pointed out when we swung off our bikes once inside the train.

'You know after this is France and tonight we'll be sleeping in a foreign bed. Suddenly I've got a sinking feeling. I don't want to leave England,' he said, laughing at the farcical nature of his feelings. 'Now that we're on the way, I don't want to go to all these foreign countries. I'm not having a good bike day, I'm really not, and more than anything I just need to go home, have a nice meal and go to bed at nine o'clock and then maybe cry a little. Because I actually feel a bit tearful. I'm really quite excited about the whole trip, but I just don't want to leave England.'

After weeks of feverish preparations, it was the first time we'd had time to consider our feelings. We were missing our families, the support staff, and, in no small measure, the workshop in Shepherd's Bush. It was all either of us had ever wanted: a garage with roller-shutter double doors opening directly on to the street so that we could ride our bikes straight into the building. It had space for our tool chests and a counter for laying out bike accessories and clothing. It even had a sofa, although Charley rejected the first one because it was too small to get horizontal on.

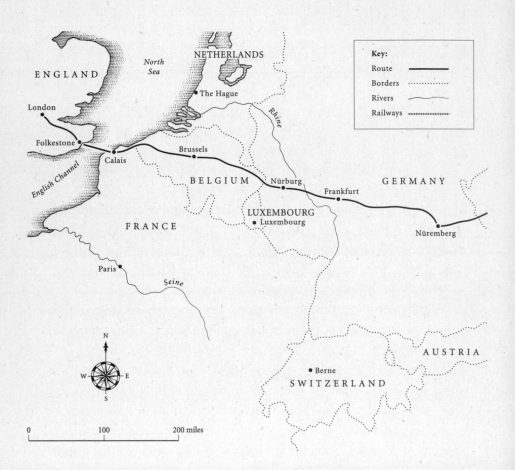

He wanted somewhere he could have his afternoon naps and gaze at the maps and bike posters on the wall.

Now, after months of dreaming about the trip, we had to get out into the cuds, as Jamie Lowther-Pinkerton and his SAS colleagues called unknown territory. We were so nervous we found it hard to come to terms with our feelings. Everything we said seemed a cliché. I was sounding like John Wayne in a bad Western: 'Ain't nothing stopping us now but leaving' and 'Ain't got nothing else to do now but leave this town', I kept saying.

We met a few other holidaymakers on the train, I signed some autographs and read some text messages from friends wishing us good luck, and then we were out of the tunnel and riding the autoroute through the flat plains of northern France. It was sweet riding and we were in a happy state of mind, the miles passing effortlessly beneath our tyres. Before we knew it we had crossed the border to Belgium and arrived in Brussels, even if our baffling GPS navigation systems, both programmed with exactly the same succession of cities, waypoints and destinations, were insisting we take completely different routes. By early evening, we were ensconced in a room in a hotel that Charley had pulled up outside at random. Relieved the first day's riding was behind us and astonished it had been so easy, we showered, dressed and hit the town. This is what we had dreamed of eighteen months earlier, when we first hatched our plan. A few hours of smooth roads, a light lunch, some more easy riding in the afternoon, an early stop and then time to explore our destination. We could only hope that it would always be this easy.

Brussels was a surprise. Not the city of Euro bureaucrats and dusty bourgeois burghers it is often said to be, it was far trendier than we expected, like the more laid-back quarters of Paris fifteen or twenty years ago, with lots of bars and crowds of young people eating outside. We wandered along narrow streets, tree-lined avenues and across pretty squares, soaking up the atmosphere, listening to buskers and street performers, enjoying the sunshine and looking forward to dinner. When a policeman pulled up and beckoned us over, we thought the spell would be broken. 'Hey, you! Come here,' he shouted out of the side window of a police van. 'Yeah, you! Here! You.'

Thinking we had inadvertently done something wrong, we both immediately felt guilty. Day one of a world trip and we were already in trouble with the police. Silently rehearsing our excuses – 'We haven't done anything. We've only just arrived' – we made our way cautiously over to the van.

'Hey! I like your films,' the policeman said in a very strong accent. '*Trainshpotting!*' he added. 'Is good, yeah?'

Wandering on for a couple of hours, we stopped in a church, where Charley lit a candle for Telsche, his sister who died of ovarian cancer eight years ago, and I lit a candle for the journey and for my family. Gazing at the sites and feeling as if we were on holiday, we stumbled on a square where two middle-aged men were playing jazz, a saxophonist in a beret and his tanned grey-haired accomplice tapping a tambourine. With tables and chairs dotted randomly around the square and people drinking beer, the ambience was great. Just the right place to stop for dinner in a bar. But as soon as we sat down, I wanted a cigarette. Having given up smoking more than a year ago, this was the moment I had dreaded. We both associated smoking with bike trips and Max, a friend who had helped me kick the habit using hypnotherapy, had warned I had begun making excuses for taking up smoking again even before I had left.

'I'm really hungry, but all I can think about is a cigarette. Day one, nothing stressful has happened, it's been an easy day and all I want is a smoke,' I told Charley.

'Would you be able to do it just in the evening? A couple of cigarettes with dinner and then never . . .?' said Charley, who could confine his own smoking to a few sociable cigarettes when he had a drink.

'Yeah, yeah, yeah,' I said unconvincingly. 'I promise. Yeah . . . probably . . . I'm going to have a Silk Cut tonight after dinner and see how it goes.'

'Shall we have dinner then?' Charley said.

'Let's pretend we've eaten already, then I can have a cigarette now . . . My God, what am I saying? Cigarette today, heroin tomorrow. Reasons? Who needs reasons when you've cigarettes.'

'No, that's not true, you know that's not true,' Charley said.

'Let's see. I'll play it by ear. After dinner I'll have a Silk Cut. And then we'll see how it goes. Take it from there.'

'Play it by ear?' Charley said. 'I think that sounds more like a decision than anything else.'

It was the first time in months we'd had time just to chat. No lists to make, no routes to consider, no equipment to think about or bikes to prepare. Reminiscing about when we first met, we talked about *Serpent's Kiss* and the people we'd known then. Then, dog-tired after so little sleep during the previous three or four nights, we headed back to our hotel with a warm sense of satisfaction and a good meal in our bellies, longing for a sound night's sleep.

The next day we headed for the Nürburgring in Germany, a mecca for petrolheads forever associated with Niki Lauda's horrific crash. In 1976, Lauda slammed his Ferrari into an embankment during the German Grand Prix, almost losing his life and bringing to an end the Ring's golden days but cementing its reputation as the longest, most beautiful and most challenging Grand Prix racetrack ever built. With music from our iPods blaring into our helmets, the GPS navigation system relieving us of map-reading tasks and the fabulous weather still holding, we swept through the flat landscape of eastern Belgium, dotted with windmills – old ones converted into homes and modern turbines generating electricity – and crisscrossed by canals. A few hours later, we left Belgium, entered Germany and soon exited the autobahn on to a beautifully built road leading to the racetrack. It was the kind of road about which bikers dream. Long, sweeping bends and smooth tarmac winding through lightly wooded hills and valleys. Blissful riding at a reasonable speed and easy, low-risk thrills when riding fast. We weren't surprised to see regular signs urging motorcyclists to keep their speed in check. It was the kind of road that asked to be taken full pelt and, with the ultimate racetrack in their sights, it was inevitable that many bikers would be tempted to race most of its length. Dozens of bikers on R1s and other racing bikes came the other way, and with several petrol stations selling high-octane fuel for the racetrack, we were tempted to have a quick burn around the Ring, but couldn't risk having an accident on only the third day of our journey. As we drew up at the Ring's parking lot, I wondered how long it would take Charley to suggest we go out for a burn. Before I even had my helmet off, Charley was bounding over.

'Shall we take these panniers off, buy some tickets and rip around the Ring?' he asked.

'Why don't we get some lunch first?' I replied.

CHARLEY: We checked into the Lindenhof, a hotel better known to Nürburgring aficionados as Renate's place because of its warm and welcoming landlady. As much a fixture of the Nürburgring as the Nordschleife (the name given to the historic thirteen-mile former Grand Prix circuit at Nürburgring), the Lindenhof's restaurant and bar were steeped in Ring history. Lined with pictures of racing cars on the Ring, motorbike club flags, metal signs from racing car manufacturers, petrol and motor oil stickers, manufacturers' marques, traffic cones, accessory makers' stickers, trophies and racetrack maps, it was a temple to motorbike and car racing.

'Last time I was here I met this English guy on a GSXR-750 like mine,' I told Ewan over lunch in Renate's restaurant. 'I was struggling to learn the track. The English guy said: "I'll slow down and you come with me. I'll take you round." We rode two or three laps together, faster and faster each lap. It was great. I learned a lot. Then when we stopped and he took his helmet off he must've been sixty-five years old. He rents a flat near the track and leaves his GSXR there. He'd done four or five hundred miles on the road. The rest of the mileage was on the Nürburgring and he had something like nine thousand miles on the clock. There are tons of people like that here, keeping their motorbikes or a sports car here, maybe renting a flat in the summer and coming here every weekend. Ringheads, I suppose you'd call them.'

After lunch, we explored the track, walking the perimeter, chatting to other bikers and waiting for five o'clock, when the track would be opened to the public.

'Where you going?' several German bikers asked us. 'You going to Italy?'

'No, not Italy. Actually we're going to New York,' we said.

'Huh?' ... 'What?' ... 'How?' they chorused. It was really quite funny to watch their baffled faces until we explained our route.

EWAN: Just hanging out with nothing to do was a delight. Getting into my own clothes, having lunch, sitting in the bar in the afternoon, maybe writing a few things, having the whole day just to relax was quite new to me. No demands on my time, no phones ringing. Nothing else to do all day. Just take it easy. It was unreal.

We found a good vantage point on a fast double right-hand bend, but it was purgatory watching other bikers scream past, knowing they had the full run of the Ring's fourteen-plus miles, with its eighty-four right-handers, eighty-eight left-handers, long straights, steep hills and winding track through four villages. Charley felt sick he wanted so much to get on his bike and take to the track. 'It's almost like you with cigarettes. I am just desperately trying not to get on my fucking bike,' he said. 'I'm gonna go and buy a ticket . . . No, I'm not . . . I'm gonna go and buy a ticket . . . No I'm not.'

'Look!' I shouted over the roar of the track. 'There's someone going around in their people carrier, a dad taking it flat out with his wife in the front and their two children strapped in the back.' The people carrier was being chased by a young lad in a cardigan driving a tiny clapped-out hatchback, careening around the circuit at breakneck speed but driving quite nonchalantly, his elbow poking out of his side window as he steered with just his left hand, chatting to his mate in the passenger seat. And then a bike passed by relatively slowly, the rider taking it easy with his girlfriend riding pillion on the back.

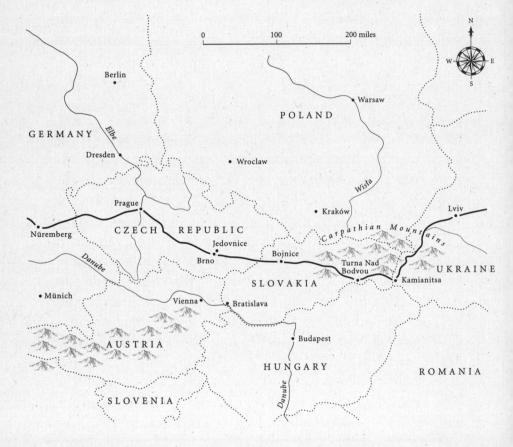

'Aaah,' we both shouted. There was something very touching about that biker cautiously circuiting the Ring and it made us both think of our wives and children at home. 'That's really affected

On our hostile training course with Jamie Lowther-Pinkerton. We were to see a lot more guns before our trip was over, and not always in such a safe pair of hands.

We spent a couple of days in Wales practising our off-road skills. It was meant to reassure us, but it left Ewan, in particular, with even more concerns.

Wednesday 14 April 2004. After months of preparation, at last it was time to leave our workshop on Bulwer Street.

On the starting line. Leaving was both exhilarating and heartbreaking, as we knew we wouldn't be seeing our friends and families for months.

Ewan looks out at the rooftops of Prague.

The cemetery in Prague's Jewish quarter. Our visit proved to be a moving experience.

Charley takes a break in Slovakia.

Ewan with a Slovakian woman. They managed to have a long conversation despite the language barrier.

What do you do when you don't have secure parking? In Lviv our hotel manager pulled up the carpets and let us park our bikes in the lobby.

In Kiev, at the Unicef centre set up to help children affected by the Chernobyl disaster. Our trips to Unicef projects here and in Kazakhstan and Mongolia had a profound impact on both of us.

At Igor's house in Antratsyt. Igor is on Charley's right, and Vladimir is seated at the front. Large selection of guns not pictured.

Preparing to go down the mine in Antratsyt. With no ventilation, we were left completely drained after forty minutes, yet the miners endured six-hour shifts in the same conditions.

A Russian newspaper heralds our arrival. Once we arrived in Kazakhstan the media's interest often caused problems on the road.

Ewan riding on blissful tarmac . . .

. . . and an example of a
main road in Kazakhstan.

Over the page: Despite all
the obstacles we faced in
Kazakhstan, it was worth it
both for the people and the
stunning scenery.

me for some reason,' I said. 'I've got a bit choked up about that, a bit teary, a guy taking his girlfriend round on his bike. It's put a lump in my throat.'

But Charley was still fixated on having a go on the track. 'I can feel that track-day sick feeling inside me now,' he said. 'It feels like my gut is dragging me to the bike going "Come on! Climb on, so we can get on to the track" while I am forcing myself back.'

'If you want to do it, just go and get your ticket,' I said, despairing of Charley's impetuosity. 'Stick some gaffer tape on the sides of your jeans and go and do it. I'll continue on my own if you fall off . . .'

Placated by a promise that we would return to the Ring for a race day in the autumn, after our circumnavigation, Charley was persuaded not to succumb to temptation. As the sun was setting, we climbed up to Schloss Nürburg, a twelfth-century castle overlooking the circuit. It had, we agreed, been a perfect day. I was just starting to realise that part of the point of this whole thing was just to get out and knock about, like I used to do with my mates on street corners when I was a kid. I still couldn't get my head around the fact that this was the way it would be for the next three and a half months. It might be different and it would probably change and it would definitely get harder, but I had to recognise that I was extremely fortunate. 'God, it's beautiful here, isn't it,' I said to no one in particular.

CHARLEY: The next morning, we decided to ride the 470 miles to Prague in one hit. Having eaten too much rich German food and drunk several cups of strong coffee the night before, we had slept fitfully and the idea of an extra day in Prague recuperating, instead of breaking the journey in Bamberg, our next scheduled stop, appealed to us both. We set off early in the morning to give ourselves plenty of time. At midday we reached Bamberg, a beautiful medieval city with steep hills topped by spectacular castles which looked as if they had been plucked from a Brothers Grimm fairytale, but we thought it was too touristy to stop at for lunch. Pulling over outside Bamberg to discuss the journey ahead, we discovered we had both been mulling over the same anxieties all morning.

'I am really apprehensive about getting to Prague,' Ewan said. 'Right now I'm just out on my bike with my best mate on a biking holiday. When we get to Prague, we'll have to meet up with Russ and David to do the filming. That feels just like work to me: another day on the set – just the thing I was trying to get away from. And when the four of us are together it gets so confusing. Everyone's got opinions about everything.'

I felt just the same. Maybe it was that huge pork knuckle or that strong coffee, but I'd had weird anxiety dreams during the night about meeting up with the others, particularly Claudio von Planta, our cameraman. Again, we were faced with the dilemma central to our trip. The journey was meant to come first. The documentary series was meant to be secondary, the means to an end. But if you decide to film a journey, everything about that journey – the route, the itinerary, the logistics – changes because you are filming it. We'd only been on the road for two and a half days, but we were already heartily fed up with filming ourselves. It got in the way of the journey, so the only solution was to have Claudio travel with us permanently. That meant an end to our dream of two mates on the road alone. And once Claudio was with us, inevitably the humdrum logistics of shooting a documentary would intrude even more into our romantic adventure.

But there was another problem: the day before we had left London, Claudio had failed his bike test. Claudio had come on board as our cameraman at the very last minute. He had told us he was an experienced biker. He was experienced all right. Nearly twenty years in the saddle. But most of them on a moped, not a big BMW with an 1150cc engine and a quarter of a ton dead weight. A few days before departure, Claudio discovered his licence didn't allow him to ride large bikes. 'Doesn't matter,' he said. 'I'll take my test. I've been riding for so long it'll be easy.' But Claudio's hubris stung him where it hurts. He failed his test and threw our plans into disarray.

With these thoughts racing through our heads, we hardly noticed the last few miles on German soil, riding along wonderfully smooth roads past gingerbread houses, through the Bavarian Forest to the Czech frontier. It was only when we drew up beside a Czech border guard that we realised we were leaving behind the ordered security of western Europe. 'This is giving me the heebie-jeebies,' I shouted over the radio shortly after we crossed into the Czech Republic.

'Me too,' Ewan replied. 'I guess it's because the unknown starts now and it'll be like this until we reach Alaska.' Despite our best efforts to learn Russian during the preparation period, we hadn't advanced beyond a few basic phrases. And as for Czech, Ukrainian, Kazakh and Mongolian, we couldn't speak a word.

The first thing we noticed about the Czech Republic was that the road leading away from the border was teeming with prostitutes. Within a couple of miles, we spotted half a dozen streetwalkers hanging out in lay-bys or just standing on the side of the road. One of the buildings in the border town, festooned with a neon sign flashing 'Non-Stop Joy Clubhouse Spot', was obviously a brothel. It was a shock, not for prurient reasons but because it immediately brought home the contrast between wealth and poverty in the west and east.

We pressed on into the Czech Republic: our third day on the road and already our fifth country. The landscape was the same as in Germany – wide plains dotted with small copses and woods – but it felt different. The road was rougher, narrower and more potholed. The villages we passed through were shabby. There was very little advertising, a legacy from the country's days as an Eastern Bloc satellite of the Soviet Union.

The drive into Prague was long and tiring. Having ridden 470 miles since leaving the Nürburgring, we were tired and hoped we would not spend too many days riding non-stop for ten hours. Even I was pleased we'd chosen the BMWs. We'd covered almost a thousand miles in three days and we didn't feel physically tired. My bum didn't hurt, my muscles didn't ache. If we'd covered that many miles on a sports bike, I'd have been pole-axed by now. Everything would hurt. The Beamers were a good choice, but they were still scary full of petrol. *Really* scary when you got on with a full tank. Jesus.

Although the BMW made few physical demands, the riding was mentally exhausting and the trek through the suburbs of Prague dragged on like the final hours of a long-haul flight. The last minutes ticked by ever so slowly, until we found ourselves crossing an ornate road bridge into the city, a magnificent view of the spires of Prague spanning the opposite riverbank and on a hill above us a massive monument with a ticking arm. And all of it washed in the light from the blood-red sun. It was a stunning entrance.

That evening we met up with Russ, David, Claudio and Jim Simak, the second unit cameraman. It was a chance to get to know Claudio. We hadn't really spent any time with him and he turned out to be very easy-going, filling us with confidence that he would not intrude on our journey. As far as Claudio was concerned, it seemed our vision was still intact. But over a long dinner in a comfortable restaurant, the grievances and petty disputes between Russ, David and ourselves came tumbling out. Afterwards, over a drink, Russ told me that Dave was really concerned that when Ewan and I arrived, I would find something wrong and lay into him about it. He said Dave was getting pins and needles in his arms, he was so worried that I was going to blow up again. In fairness, I had flown off the handle a couple of times through sheer frustration with the stresses of making the documentary. But Russ pointed out that I didn't appreciate the difficulties of getting everything ready in time for departure. Russ said we needed to work as a team together, as buddies. I said I thought that was what we were doing, but Russ said I tended to fly off the handle and that I could be a bully.

I didn't agree at all with Russ's assessment of my failings. I certainly didn't think I was a bully. I knew I got irritated when things weren't going right and I thought I dealt with those frustrations quite well. By the time I went up to my hotel room, I was a bit miffed. I didn't think it was at all fair that Russ had given me this big old chat.

The next day we took to the streets of Prague. Neither of us had visited the city before and we were staggered by its beauty. Wandering across the bridges that spanned the winding Vltava River, climbing up towards Hradcany Castle and exploring the narrow streets and baroque buildings of the old quarter, we were like any other tourists – albeit tourists with two cameramen constantly in tow. And like many tourists before us, we paid over the odds for souvenirs, Ewan buying watches for his daughters that he spotted for half the price fifteen minutes later and realised the next day had second hands that spun anticlockwise. And like thousands of visitors to Prague, we sat on the Charles Bridge while an artist sketched us in caricature, watching the world go by, although we briefly became a tourist attraction ourselves as dozens of passers-by stopped to snap Ewan with their cameras and mobile phones. We met a bunch of British visitors who'd read about us doing the trip and who wished us good luck. It was really encouraging to feel the warm support from the people we met.

After that we headed for Prague's Jewish quarter and the Old Jewish Cemetery. Because the Prague authorities allowed Jews only a small amount of space in which to bury their dead, the cemetery has to be one of the most overcrowded burial sites anywhere. It's believed there are seven or eight layers of graves. Whenever the cemetery was full, more earth was simply piled on top of the graveyard until there were layers of bodies. Even now the graveyard was chock-a-block with old tombstones, all jumbled and rammed together.

But as the day went on it became apparent that our sightseeing route had been chosen by Russ and David to suit their planned filming opportunities. The caricatures on Charles Bridge, it turned out, had been set up. Then came a visit to Parvina, a gypsy Russ had briefed to tell our fortunes. With mounting scepticism, we went down an alleyway to a whitewashed concrete courtyard at the back of a house, where four white plastic garden chairs and a picnic table, covered in a red and black tablecloth and with a candle in a glass lantern, had been set up. A dark-haired middle-aged woman in a housecoat, Parvina dealt some tarot cards on to the table. Pointing to a card labelled The Lady, which appeared every time she dealt the tarot deck, the gypsy told Ewan he would meet a significant person on the trip. But she also said he would meet someone who would double-cross him. It could be someone you know already, she warned him. My tarot revealed little, merely that I had a long journey ahead and that I was missing my family. Parvina also predicted that a member of our team would lose some money, but these were hardly revelations from the other side.

After the tarot reading, we made it clear to Russ and David that we wanted no more set-ups. We appreciated all the hard work they'd put in but it didn't fit with our vision of the trip. We'd prefer it if from now on we let the journey dictate the filming, we said, and not the other way round.

'Yeah, yeah, absolutely. Whatever you guys want, we'll do it,' David reassured us. 'We don't want to endanger the spirit of your trip. You guys know that's the most important thing to me. And from now on that means a spirit of no surprises, no set-ups.'

'In the spirit of no surprises . . .,' David began – we were back at the hotel, discussing what to do that evening – 'we've arranged for you to eat at a medieval restaurant in the centre of Prague and we've got a few things for you to do.'

'And what might those *things* be?' Ewan asked.

'Don't worry,' Russ said, 'you'll be totally cool with it.'

Russ was half right. We had better things to worry about. A few hours earlier, we'd unloaded Claudio's bike from its trailer only to find one of the pistons wasn't firing properly. Since then, I had been sweating over the bike trying to get it to start. I'd loosened the petrol tank to fit a new battery, refitted it, checked the spark plugs and tried everything we could think of, but I still couldn't get the bike to work. It was Saturday night, so the BMW dealership in Prague was closed, and we were hoping to leave the next morning. More than anything, we wanted Claudio to ride with us so that we could enjoy the trip and he could film it. But if we couldn't get his bike to start, we would have to trailer it to the next BMW dealership in Kiev. It was shaping up to be, as I told Ewan, a 'fucking nightmare'.

Then we struck on the idea of phoning Howard Godolphin, our technical contact at BMW in England. I spoke to him, explained what had happened and immediately got a suggestion.

'Look at the pistons,' Howard said. 'Coming into the piston is the carburettor, where the air and fuel get mixed together, and on top of the carburettor is a little injector which injects the fuel into the air. There's a little cable, which is the throttle control. It sits on the injector, like a bicycle cable with a plastic sheath. If you've pulled the petrol tank off, there's a good chance the sheath was trapped, overstretching the cable and starving the engine of fuel. Just lift the sheath and pop the cable back in.'

I looked at the cable. He was right. It did look pinched. We popped it back in, as instructed, and fired the ignition. The engine started with a roar. If only everything could be that easy.

EWAN: We arrived at the medieval restaurant with little appetite for what lay ahead. With period music, a contrived menu and the waiting staff dressed in period costumes, this was the kind of theme restaurant from which we would normally run a mile. We descended into a dank dungeon, ostensibly the party room, and sat around, feeling like a bunch of gormless goons, waiting for the planned surprise. David and Russ persuaded me to try on a male chastity belt with a massive iron penis covered in spikes. Reluctantly I put it on, then we settled down, unable to relax because we were expecting something momentous to happen. After the main courses, they announced that they'd arranged with the chef for us to cook a traditional pudding, a medieval pancake. Under the chef's instruction, we made up some batter and threw it into a frying pan, but with the chef and kitchen staff gazing at us with a mixture of amusement, disbelief and contempt, we found it impossible to muster enthusiasm for the sorry charade. We were embarrassed, but David and Russ pressed on regardless, telling us to commentate as we fried the pancakes.

'This is really cool,' David said. 'We organised it in such a short time. We could do around the world in ten local dishes.'

He had really not got the plot. Christ! If this was the kind of thing they were going to organise, this trip was going to be a disaster. Unable to see a way forward, worried that our dream of getting away from it all was disappearing before our eyes and blaming ourselves for creating a monster that was now raging out of control, neither of us slept well that night.

The next morning, as we were getting our bikes ready and Russ and David were packing the support vehicles, I approached David. 'These set-up things and your surprises are just not going to work,' I said. 'The real story last night was that Claudio's bike wasn't working, but Claudio wasn't there to film it because he was off trying to light that ridiculous event in that theme-restaurant kitchen. You've got to concede that learning how to make a medieval omelette – or whatever that pancake was – was pants. The whole thing was a disaster, but you and Russ thought it went really well. I'm telling you it didn't and it just proved to Charley and me that your set-ups just aren't going to work.'

I'd made my feelings very clear in the calmest way I could, but I was seriously worried. This trip was turning into work, and hard work at that. I'd hoped to escape from the hassles and rigours of film-making, but, without fully contemplating what I was letting myself in for, I had signed up for a three-month round-the-world shoot. We could always snatch a few days away from the cameras and shooting deadlines, but if we didn't sort out things now the spirit of the journey would be lost. Charley and I knew deep down that if we could just stick to our ethos of 'journey first, documentary second' the result would be a better film as well as a more enjoyable trip.

We knew relations between the four of us wouldn't be this strained for the coming three and a half months of the trip simply because it hadn't always been like this in the past. We'd been through a lot together to get this far. Our friendships were built on strong foundations, well and truly cemented when in early January we had flown to Los Angeles to pitch the big American networks. We'd checked into the Château Marmont in LA, a hotel I used to stay in a lot. Because we were doing it on the cheap, flying coach and watching the pennies, we were all checked into one room. It was the middle of the night. We had jetlag and we were pumped up because we knew we had a backbreaking schedule of meetings in the morning. It was no surprise that we all woke up at about 3 a.m., hungry, nervy and restless. Sitting around in towels, T-shirts and boxer shorts, we ordered sandwiches and coffee from room service in the early hours of the morning, four half-naked men in a bedroom.

There was a knock at the door. In walked the room-service waiter, a man in his early sixties with a bit of a twinkle in his eye. He put the tray down. Pouring the coffee, he turned to us, raised an eyebrow, grinned, and said in a very camp voice: 'See you later, chaps.'

The penny didn't drop until he left. Then we realised what four half-naked and clearly exhausted men, ordering room service in the middle of the night, must have looked like to the waiter. We looked at each other and cracked up.

At eight the next morning we started our pitches. Seeking a $6 million budget, Russ got his laptop out, already missing a key because Charley had dropped his bag on it on the flight over, and we started a spiel that we would repeat a dozen times that day.

It was hard work. The television people put us through the mill, making us fight for their attention, something I had never had to do before. None of them gave anything away. Poker-faced, arms crossed, silent. No indication of their interest or feelings. We were watching people exercising their power over us and enjoying every minute of it.

At NBC/Bravo, one of the last studios we visited, we met an executive who someone had told us was just like the sergeant major from *Forrest Gump*. Staring straight through us for ninety minutes, completely expressionless, he made the other executives look animated in comparison. At the end of the meeting, as we were getting up to leave, Charley commented on a poster on the wall of a Farrah Fawcett lookalike in a red bathing costume with very prominent nipples.

'Jesus, look at her nipples. They look like they're fake,' Charley said.

All at once the NBC exec became animated. 'It's funny you should say that,' he grinned, 'because they are fake and we spent hours moving them around to get them in the right place. We worked at them so hard, but they were never quite right.'

We went back to the Château Marmont, not really knowing what to say to each other. With meetings all day, but no sign of a deal, we were worried it was turning into a disaster. We'd been back in our room for twenty minutes, exhausted after the day of presentations on top of waking at three in the morning, when David came storming out of the bathroom, clutching his mobile phone in front of him like a relay baton. David shouted in the direction of its mouthpiece: 'All right. We're all on speaker phone. Tell the boys.'

While we had been fretting in the bedroom, David had been speaking to a television agent at William Morris, who in turn had been negotiating with the sergeant major at NBC/Bravo. It seemed the fake nipple conversation might have done the trick.

A voice came out of the phone: 'Hey guys. Listen. They want six to eight episodes. They'll pay well in excess of half a million dollars an hour.'

Suddenly we were looking down the barrel at several million dollars for our television show. 'Are you sure? Are you really sure?' we shouted back at the phone.

David interrupted: 'I asked him several times if I could tell you guys about this. I asked him: "Are you sure it's real? I'm not going to tell them about this unless it's real." It is real, isn't it?'

'Absolutely.' The agent paused for effect and then he added: 'You guys go out, get something to eat. Celebrate. I'll see you in the morning.'

Click, brrrrrr. The sound of a phone being hung up filled the bedroom. The four of us stood, stunned into silence, looking at each other and unable to believe what we'd just heard him say.

Within seconds a tiny hotel room in Los Angeles was filled by four male voices all shouting 'holy fuck'. We were running around the room, screaming our heads off, each of us working out what it amounted to split four ways and shouting with joy. At last we had the money to make our dream of adventure come true.

Two days later, the guys dropped me off at the airport. I had to get back to London before them. Sitting in an airport lounge for four hours waiting for my delayed flight to board, listening to a continuous loop of flute musak while I wrote my diary, my cellphone rang. It was the TV agent. 'Listen, when Bravo said six to eight hours, they want six hours,' he said. 'And when they said $600,000 to $800,000 an hour, they meant maybe $100,000 to $200,000.'

In one phone call we lost millions. They had got the rates mixed up. It was still a very good deal, so we couldn't really get upset about it. After all, how many people are lucky enough to get paid to live their dream? Nevertheless, we felt as if we had lost it all in the blink of an eye. It felt like we were searching around on the floor, frantically lifting the carpets and peering through the cracks in the floorboards, going 'Whoah, where did all the money go?'

It was a disappointment, but, as with other setbacks during the preparation period, it served to pull us closer together, teaching us that the journey was the most important aspect of our adventure. Now, bickering in Prague, we desperately needed to remind ourselves of our original vision.

CHARLEY: We set off in convoy, riding for about two hours behind Russ and David in their Mitsubishi 4×4s from Prague to near the Slovak border, stopping at a Cistercian monastery in Sedlec, a suburb of Kutná Hora, to visit the All Saints chapel. Built in the fifteenth century and known as the Kostnice, the Ossuary or the Beinhaus, the latter a typically pragmatic German word meaning the bone house, this ghoulish place contained the skeletons of more than forty thousand people. In the late thirteenth century, King Otakar II of Bohemia sent Henry, the abbot of Sedlec, on a diplomatic mission to the Holy Land. Henry brought back a handful of earth from Golgotha, the skull-shaped hill upon which Jesus is believed to have been crucified. Sprinkling it over the monastery cemetery, he transformed it into the most desirable graveyard in central Europe. A succession of plagues in the fourteenth century, the Hussite wars in the early fifteenth century and an enormous demand for burial plots from the wealthy, who had made vast fortunes from a local silver mine, filled the cemetery with tens of thousands of graves and the bones began to pile up. During the plague epidemic of 1318 alone, more than thirty thousand people were buried at Sedlec.

In the early fifteenth century a church was built in the middle of the cemetery and a half-blind Cistercian monk assigned the task of stacking a chapel beneath it with bones exhumed from earlier graves. Then, in 1870, František Rint, a local woodcarver, began turning the bones into a particularly macabre work of art. The centrepiece is a chandelier comprising every bone in the human body. Huge arrangements of bones in the shapes of bells hang in each corner of the chapel. A coat of arms and various ornaments, all made entirely from bones, fill the chapel.

EWAN: Maybe it didn't help that I'd been listening to Wagner on my iPod as we rode through scrappy Czech towns, along cobbled roads and down tree-lined avenues, their branches still bare from winter, towards Sedlec, but as we walked around the chapel in our motorbike kit, staring at the eerie display, I couldn't decide whether it was very beautiful or very disturbing. Charley thought it was 'a bit of a cool idea because instead of having all these bones just going to waste, stacked up outside, this groovy abbot had this great idea to do this. It's a kind of homage to the people really. People walk in, smile and think "wow, this is incredible". It's nice that the place is filled by the spirits of all the people that are here.'

But I just thought it was weird to have what looked like Christmas decorations hanging from chandeliers, images on walls and inscriptions all made from human bones. Skulls and jawbones and teeth and fingers and hips and shoulder blades and arms and lots of femurs. It was the most gruesome and chilling thing I'd ever seen, but at the same time it was actually quite beautiful and even a little bit naff. I don't know why, but it was just a bit cheesy, even if it was made out of people's bones.

In a way, it didn't really matter what we thought. If they were happy to have their bones stacked up against the back wall, I suppose they wouldn't mind being made into some kind of decoration. But it was human decoration. And it was like a serial killer's wet dream in that chapel. It put me right off my lunch.

CHARLEY: After the Bone Church, we split from Russ and David and headed off on our own with Claudio, who was very nervous of the big BMW but turned out to be a natural motorbike rider. So much for him being worried about not having a licence: he took off like a rocket. We didn't see him for dust.

We stopped off for lunch in a beautiful medieval square that could have been a set from Disneyland it was so picture perfect. We walked around the square, gazing at the painted shop fronts, stopping to look at market stalls and a beautiful fountain in the centre, while Claudio quietly got on with the filming. Within a few minutes we had the whole thing in the bag. It was such a relief to discover that between the three of us we could get it done simply and easily and without any fuss.

From the square we rode for several hours through a valley with a river flowing beside a road lined with cliff walls and dotted with abandoned factories and industrial plants, until we started climbing to the Punkva Caves at the Pusty zleb in the Moravian Karst, a wild mountainous area north of Brno. With more than a thousand caves, the region has been designated a World Heritage site. And if there's one reason to come to the Czech Republic, it's to come and see these caves. They're really quite something.

We hopped into a boat and entered the caves with the whole place to ourselves because we had arrived late in the day. We spent about an hour exploring a maze of stalagmites and stalactites, arguing over which was the one that hung down from the ceiling and which one grew up from the floor, open-mouthed at the scale and beauty of it all. While the guide explained that the caves were three hundred million years old and that the stalagmites grew by one millimetre every thirty years, we walked deep into the mountain, along tiny alleyways between the rock formations, through a door, down a short path and then into the most incredible gorge. It was immense, with green moss and algae everywhere and even patches of snow because it had its own microclimate. On the far right, a river emerged from a cliff into a large lake. It was astonishing, like a set from *The Lord of the Rings*, or, in Ewan's words, 'like the inside of Jabba the Hutt's arsehole'. We just looked at it in silence for several minutes, bowled over by it all, our arms around each other, soaking it all in.

The gorge was more than 450 feet high, nearly 600 feet wide

and almost completely enclosed, except for a small opening at the very top, ringed by pine trees silhouetted against the sky, letting in light from above. The story went that a nasty stepmother and her two stepsons were walking along the top of the cliffs above the huge bowl. Fed up with their stepmother's nagging, the stepsons led her to the edge of the gorge and, while she was still going on at them, grabbed her and threw her over. Since then, it's been called the Stepmother's Abyss.

After a night in a traveller's hotel in a small village and riding through a landscape that Ewan said reminded him of Perthshire, we rendezvoused with the support team at the Slovakian border. David's Mitsubishi Shogun and Russ's Mitsubishi pick-up truck – now christened Warrior and Animal – were parked up near the customs offices. Even before we got off our bikes, Russ ran over to speak to us.

'Did you get your carnet stamped on the way in?' he yelled.

'No,' I said.

'You really didn't?'

'We really didn't. We just drove through.'

'This is giving me a brain ache,' Russ said. 'Do you know how important that carnet is?'

'We're only travellers,' I replied. 'Surely if we can enter the country without stamping the carnet, we can do the same when we leave it.'

'You can't, mate. The carnet's a bond kinda thing. You can't play around with the rules, do you know what I mean? Believe me, mate, you can't do that to these things.'

Russ was in a state of panic, talking ten to the dozen and not finishing any of his sentences. '. . . I've been caught out with these things before . . . they are all . . . let me find out . . . let's phone back to the office before we do anything and get some advice on that . . . otherwise I'd be tempted almost to . . .'

'Russ, what's the matter?' I said. 'Let's just keep this calm, okay? We'll make the phone call. We're not going to do anything. And once we've found out what we need to do, we'll go from there.'

Everything had been so sweet and so smooth until we met up with the crew. Suddenly we were embroiled in a massive drama at the border, a place where we needed to keep a low profile. We hadn't stamped our carnet coming into the Czech Republic, which we needed to prove we hadn't sold any of our equipment. If anyone had told us we'd need it, we'd forgotten.

David was running back and forward in a bright red jacket, a walkie-talkie clipped to his belt and a look of terror on his face, drawing an enormous amount of attention to us just when we were trying to slip out of the Czech Republic unobtrusively.

While Ewan munched on some nuts and I adjusted some of the bags on my bike, Russ berated us for not getting our carnet stamped. Eventually, I'd had enough.

'Listen, Russ,' I said. 'Just calm down. You're getting really worked up about this when we need to keep our cool. Just calm down.'

Russ lost it altogether. 'You deal with it,' he snapped and stomped off.

David was looking very stony-faced. He'd just spoken to a trucker who had told him he'd been waiting for five hours to get through the border. 'There's no fuckin' way we're waiting for five hours,' he declared, as if we had any choice. Gabbling into his cellphone, seeking advice, he spotted Russ heading towards the customs office. 'Just don't show the carnet!' he hollered after him. 'Russ . . . just so you are in the loop on this . . .'

But Russ kept walking. He was clearly furious with me. He had a point, but there was a way to deal with these things. It takes time to get through a border and you've just got to let it happen. It didn't help that Russ and David were running around like blue-arsed flies, filming everything, Dave ordering Jim to shoot him. 'Jim, come here! I've got to tell you this!' he shouted. And then at the camera: 'I'm with the boys . . . *Long Way Round* . . . and we've just arrived at the border . . .'

It just seemed like everyone was overreacting. Russ and I needed to do something about the tension between us, but I was convinced everything would settle if he just relaxed. We always knew Europe would be touristy and fairly uneventful. The real drama would come when we got further east. Why create a crisis when we were confident the road would provide enough to satisfy our hunger for adventure, as well as the documentary's desire for incident?

Eventually we got it sorted. The border guards had spotted us causing a commotion outside and knew they had to check our documents carefully. We paid a small fee for not having stamped our carnet and that was that. Fifteen minutes later, we were in Slovakia. What a faff about nothing. It reinforced the belief that the best approach is always to stay nice and cool and get the job done.

EWAN: I didn't mind hanging around for however long a border crossing would take, but I did mind wasting time unnecessarily. Riding into Slovakia for a couple of hours, I sunk into a very blue mood, getting annoyed at silly little things such as the chitchat on the radio and Charley poking fun at me. I let the banter get the better of me, probably because I needed a little bit of rest, a little bit of time on my own to phone my wife and get away from full-on male company. I'm not very good at laddish repartee at the best of times, but now it really seemed to land a punch and I was failing to roll with it. It made me miss Eve and my girls all the more. It was only the end of the first week, but I was really longing for them, feeling a bit low and a bit lonely and letting things get to me, my self-esteem falling through the floor. Every border crossing just made me pine all the more. To make matters worse, I had lost the little pink plastic soap dish given to me by Clara. It just added to the sadness. Maybe I needed something to eat.

Rolling into a town where I thought we could stop for lunch, I pulled over and looked at my GPS. It was playing up. Instead of giving directions at each crossroads, it was just pointing in a straight line at the next waypoint, the destination we hoped to reach that evening. Even if there was a forest in front of me, it would point straight through it.

Then I realised that somebody had switched on the off-road setting, so it would always take us the route as the crow flies. What a relief. At last I knew why my GPS wasn't giving decent directions. Spotting Charley approaching, I flagged him down to suggest we take a break.

'Hey, Charley, somebody's set my GPS to off-road,' I said. 'That's why it's not been working.'

Charley didn't bother taking his helmet off. He just shook his head and shouted through it: 'The funny thing about you is you sit at the bottom of this road, just here, waiting for me to go past you and you go: "Somebody has put this to off-road setting. That's so infuriating." And you just switch it back without any thought whatsoever. Well, who's been fiddling with your GPS other than you? I just love the fact you always blame somebody else. I could tell in your little mind you'd been going: "Charley's been fucking with my GPS." I'm sure you were thinking that. Just makes me laugh. "Somebody's been fiddling with my GPS!" Hah!'

I wasn't quite sure if Charley was teasing me or genuinely pissed off but I was getting hungry and I'd become more interested in locating my next meal.

Under a greying sky and with mountains looming in the distance, we stopped for lunch at a roadhouse near Bojnice. I chased a great big hairy spider off my tank bag, which I took to be a sign of good luck, wrote some postcards and just enjoyed being with Charley and Claudio. After lunch we got out our cigarettes – I seemed unable to just have one cigarette after dinner and found myself back on twenty a day – and planned our journey ahead. We stopped at a castle near Bojnice, where we were surprised to bump into some English tourists, particularly when their daughter pulled out a *Down With Love* DVD and asked me to sign it. Then we booked into a hotel in the town, on the way to where the parents of Claudio's children's nanny lived.

CHARLEY: We left the hotel early, riding through the Slovakian countryside, at times in heavy rain. Similar to the Czech Republic, Slovakia was a little less manicured and dotted with allotments and vegetable gardens, the older people wearing traditional dress. There were few signs of tourism, but the people seemed accustomed to visitors, with almost everyone we met speaking English.

On two occasions we came upon motorcyclists waiting for us. They were sitting on the side of the road and, as we passed them, we waved. They immediately put on their helmets and chased after us. At the next traffic lights, they stopped beside us for a chat. It seemed very strange, but also very charming, that motorcyclists who had read about our journey now went out of their way to join us for a few miles.

Ewan was a bit low. He said his wife had been upset on the phone that morning and that he found it difficult to cheer her up when he was also missing her. I'd been through the same emotional wringer the night before, when I phoned Olly. I could hear in her voice that she was missing me and it immediately made me homesick. The fortune-teller in Prague had said I was missing home more than I realised and she was right. Perhaps I had dismissed her too readily after all. I was missing my kids. I was missing my wife. And I was just missing that routine of home, all that stuff you take for granted. I'd also spoken to Kinvara, my eldest daughter. She asked how long I was going to be away. Three months, I told her. 'It's a very long time. You've only been away a week,' she said and it really hit home.

We rode on for a while, turning south off Route 66 towards Turna, passing through villages in which the houses looked like they hadn't been painted or renovated since the 1920s, the whole place empty apart from a few drunks staggering down the middle of the road, their faces friendly but showing the consequences of living for decades in poverty and oppression. Some of the villages and towns were completely deserted, ghost towns built around a factory that had long been abandoned, the surrounding countryside parched by the sun in mid-summer, drenched by rain in spring and autumn, and frozen by ice and snow in winter. Where we did chance upon a few people standing around in the towns and villages, they all stopped whatever they were doing as we approached, staring at us as we passed by. 'It's as if we were from the moon,' Ewan said over the radio one of the times this happened. At one point, we came around a bend, emerged from some woods and it was as if the world had dropped away on one side of the road. To our right was the most magnificent view, valleys and mountains stretching away from us for tens of miles.

Late in the evening we arrived at Turna Nad Bodvou, a small town in a valley dominated by a massive cement factory, and were led by Claudio to the house where the parents of his children's nanny lived. It was a large terraced house backed by a garden overflowing with vegetables. Csaba Kaposztas looked like a silver-haired Jack Nicholson and Maria, his wife, had a kind face with a beaming smile and spoke excellent English. 'I learned it at school,' she said, 'but I never got the chance to travel and to use it.'

Completely self-sufficient, keeping chickens and a pig to make their own sausages and ham, they were an amazing couple. At last Ewan's black mood seemed to be lifting. 'It's lovely to be in this home,' he said. 'It's such a nice welcome difference.'

Ewan was very taken by the house and garden. He loved the atmosphere of the place and the warmth and sincerity of two people who welcomed two relative strangers into their lives.

Maria cooked a traditional Slovakian dinner of spicy tomato soup with paprika, pork from one of their own pigs and cake. 'It's my husband's favourite,' she said. 'Eat plenty of it. Breakfast isn't until the morning.'

'A good philosophy,' Ewan replied.

As we ate, Maria showed us pictures of her family, spoke of her five children, described their days working together at the cement factory, and told us about her seventy-year-old pen pal in

Edinburgh. They had been writing to each other for thirty years but had never met.

After dinner, Csaba, grinning mischievously, beckoned us downstairs and led us into the garage. Pushing his Lada towards the garage door, he uncovered a flight of steps beneath it. He led us down to the bottom, where we squeezed through a small gap chiselled through the concrete and entered a vast space that this most resourceful of men had hollowed out underneath his home. Along each wall, oak wine barrels were decorated with medals he had won for the red and white wine he made from his own vines. But that wasn't all. The vault was lined with bottles of homemade fruit and grain schnapps, brandy and apple brandy, all offered for tasting.

'Jesus,' Ewan whispered quietly to me. 'He makes every kind of alcoholic substance known to man. If you lit a match down here, the whole fucking country would blow up.'

Csaba proudly showed us a well he had spent five years digging with his bare hands to avoid having to walk into town with a wheelbarrow to collect water from the hydrant. Sunk 12 feet into the rock, it held about 5 feet of water that he used to irrigate his vegetable garden. Then he took us back upstairs and sat on the end of one of the beds, showing us pictures of his daughter Karolina, now Claudio's nanny, and telling us stories of when she was a child.

The next morning, after Maria had cooked breakfast, she and Csaba took us on a tour of the village by car, showing us where they went to school, proudly pointing out the frescos in the church and indicating derelict buildings, their windows and frames apparently stolen by gypsies.

'Slovaks work hard and want to make the country better,' Csaba said, his wife translating. 'But gypsies just play music and dance and want to do nothing,' he added dismissively. Ewan and I looked at each other in the back of the car. To us, it sounded like a good life, but it was depressing to see travellers facing the same intolerance in central Europe as at home.

We eventually bade them farewell and pressed on for the border, hoping the crossing this time would be less fraught. Several hours later, having taken two hours to cross the Slovak frontier, we were waiting to cross the Ukrainian border when Russ ran up with a message from Sergey, our Russian fixer.

'Right. Here's the deal,' said Russ. 'The customs officials will only accept original vehicle registration documents, but we only have photocopies. BMW and Mitsubishi have the originals. If we can't get through here, our only alternative is to turn back and head north into Poland, through Belarus and Russia to Kazakhstan.'

The detour would add thousands of miles to our journey, but, according to Sergey and Russ, the customs officials refused to bend the rules. We were sticky and dirty and the sun was beating down. Wedged between trucks spewing black clouds of diesel fumes, we were stranded in no-man's-land with nothing to eat and very little water, not knowing what to do next. Ewan was fed up and I was worried I'd said something that had irritated him. Needing to get away from the others to figure a way out of our dilemma, I ambled across the tarmac to a shabby toilet block. Behind the block I bumped into an old Slovak, who said he was an artist. He wore gold-rimmed sunglasses, was dressed in a stained nylon shirt and spoke a few words of German, a language of which I also had only a rudimentary grasp.

'*Ukraine nicht gut. Grosse Mafia. Viele probleme,*' the old man warned urgently. Holding up two fingers like a gun, he emphasised his point. 'Peng, peng,' he said, shooting in the air with his fingers and shaking his head. '*Mafia alles Ukraine.*'

Although he was unshaven, dirty and missing several teeth, there was no mistaking the sincerity of his warning. The Ukraine was clearly not a place a bunch of expensively kitted-out and obviously wealthy Western motorcyclists should consider visiting. I wandered back to the road where the crew were waiting and Ewan was smoking. I told him the bad news.

'Everyone stay calm and we'll be all right. Don't panic. Those mafia guys can smell fear,' he said.

'But the old man said they'll steal everything, then kill you,' I whimpered.

Fixing me with a cold stare, Ewan sucked on his cigarette, exhaled and sighed despondently: 'So what the fuck are we going to do?'

5
Little by little

ACROSS THE UKRAINE

CHARLEY: I spotted him shortly after midnight. I was tired, irritable and desperate to cross the frontier after negotiating with guards and officials for eleven hours, each time longer and more frustrating than the last. It was exciting at first, a confrontation with an unbending bureaucracy quite different from anything we were used to in the West. But now I wanted more than anything to get into the Ukraine just to be able to crawl into bed. Then I noticed him watching me.

He looked wealthy in that subtle way that usually means someone has been rich for a while. Expensive, understated clothes and a trendy haircut. A flat-top greying at the sides. About forty, he looked like a successful businessman, but his BMW had red number plates. Diplomatic plates, we later found out. And he knew all the guards, policemen and functionaries. But most intriguing of all, he was also interested in us. Chatting to the guards beneath the fluorescent lighting above the customs huts, he would occasionally stare at our small group. I was standing near Russ and David in the darkness, lit only by the lights of the trucks. Ewan was further away, wrapped in his sleeping bag on a patch of scrubland, trying to sleep while trucks belched diesel fumes around him. The Ukrainian businessman called up a Toyota that had been ransacked for drugs or some other contraband, I assumed, and, turning to me, he shrugged.

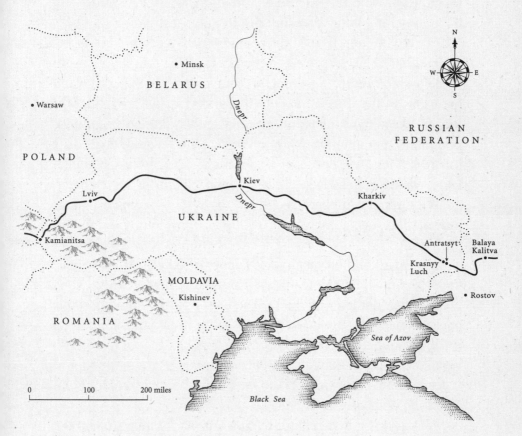

I shrugged back. 'Pffft,' I said, hoping the universal expression for 'What the hell can you do?' meant the same thing in the Ukraine.

'Yeah,' he said in heavily accented English. 'Import cheaper.'

I took it to mean there was less duty to pay on a car that had been ripped apart or damaged, and went back to discussing with Russ the only real subject of interest. Where were we going to sleep that night? We'd arrived at the frontier shortly after midday with the hope of reaching Uzghorod, about five miles into the Ukraine. Now, in the middle of the night, we'd abandoned any hope of getting into a hotel at our intended destination.

'I have a hotel.' It was the businessman, sidling over to us. 'Camelot. Not far from here. You stay with me tonight.'

He passed over a brochure. His Camelot hotel looked plush and luxurious in that Russian, new-money kind of way. I thought it looked like a knocking shop, a gin palace where rich executives, politicians and high-ranking civil servants would take their mistresses for long, decadent weekends of sex, caviar and vodka. But it was a hotel and we were in urgent need of beds for the night.

'Why don't you come and stay?' he said. 'It's nearby. Have dinner. Stay late tomorrow. Parking no problem. Garages no problem.'

I knew I should be suspicious. Plenty of other people besides the old man with the gold-rimmed sunglasses had warned us the Ukraine was riddled with mafia. There was nothing to suggest this businessman was a gangster. But surely he would have mafia links, I thought. If you owned a big hotel in the Ukraine, you would certainly be paying protection money.

I strolled over to where Ewan was trying to sleep and told him about the offer of a hotel bed.

'Why is this guy prepared to hang around for ages to help out a bunch of strangers?' Ewan asked. It was a good point. And if we ignored it we would be disregarding the first lesson of our training for surviving in a hostile environment.

EWAN: Jamie Lowther-Pinkerton could have stepped out of the textbook for English army officers. Tall, skinny, patrician and quietly authoritative, he ran a three-day course on hostile environments. He trained business executives, journalists, voluntary workers and government officials bound for the most dangerous places on earth, including war zones and countries torn apart by civil war and terrorism. And us.

We were convinced Jamie was a former member of the SAS, although he never confirmed it and usually changed the subject whenever special forces were mentioned. The walls of the farmhouse where the course took place were lined with pictures of Jamie with men he said he'd known when they were in 'the regiment' or 'at Hereford': Jamie and his mates in frogman's gear, or looking dishevelled and dangerous in a jungle, or standing behind the Queen Mother at an official function. They were the type of friends and colleagues who backed their cars into parking spaces for quick getaways. And Jamie's conversation was littered with anecdotes about 'great mates' who were 'built like brick shithouses' and 'were in the . . . actually, he's in the Agency', which we took to mean the CIA. We never managed to pin down exactly what Jamie had done in the past or even how he was currently engaged, other than that it had something to do with 'security'. Charley tried several times to get Jamie to talk about the SAS. 'What does SAS actually mean?' he asked. 'Doesn't it stand for . . .'

'Special Air Service,' I interjected, hoping Jamie might open up.

'Oh . . . yeah . . . er . . . Special Air Service . . . yeah . . . isn't it?' Jamie said in the faltering way he used to deflect inquiries. 'Yeah . . . or Scandinavian Air Services . . . or whatever it is.'

And then Jamie would return to the subject at hand. How to spot a bomb beneath your car, or evade surveillance, or take cover from automatic gunfire, or floor an attacker, or talk your way out of a kidnap threat, or retrace your steps through a minefield. His lectures were interspersed with medical training accompanied by some of the most gruesome pictures imaginable of gunshot wounds, machete injuries and limbs blasted off by personnel mines. It seemed there was no threat to life or limb that Jamie had not encountered and dealt with in his efficient and nonchalant way, including meeting bears in Siberia and Alaska, something we were concerned about.

'I had an encounter with . . . I don't know what sort of bear it was,' Jamie said. 'I'd like to say it was a grizzly but I wouldn't know one from the other, but it was in a river in Alaska. We'd just climbed McKinley and . . .'

'That's the highest mountain in North America? The one they use to train for Everest?' Charley asked.

'Er . . . yeah, yeah. Anyway, we had a few days off and I quite like the old fishing, you know. So I went down to the Seward Peninsula with a mate who's called Phil Bateyes because he's got one eye that's half-closed and he's about six foot ten, SAS guy you know and all the rest of it . . .' And Jamie launched into another of his intriguing anecdotes.

Over the course of three days, Jamie impressed upon us that there were several never-to-be-broken golden rules that governed travelling through central and eastern Asia.

'I'd say avoid travelling by night or early in the morning. It's when people – you know I'm talking about remote areas now – it's when the baddies will want to operate. To them it's a business transaction and if they are trying to rob you or whatever, they will want to get away with it. The best chance of getting away with it is under cover of nightfall, so I would say travel by day,' Jamie said.

'Dress down, don't cause offence,' Jamie advised us about border crossings. 'If you have to queue for an hour, queue for the hour. Don't try and jump. And never – this is absolutely key – *never* hook up with anyone else to cross the border.'

CHARLEY: After half a day at the border, our minds were entering emotional meltdown. The Slovak border had been a breeze in comparison with our attempts to enter the Ukraine. We had reams of documents and the British embassy in Kiev had been working on our behalf for nearly seven hours, but all to no avail. The Ukrainian authorities would only accept the original vehicle registration documents for the BMW bikes and Mitsubishi 4x4s. Our laminated photocopies were not up to scratch.

We called BMW in Britain, who e-mailed and phoned BMW headquarters in Munich, who rang BMW in Moscow, who faxed BMW in Kiev, who contacted the border and guaranteed that the motorbikes belonged to them and that they would not be sold in the Ukraine. Still no movement.

As well as Sergey Grabovets, the easy-going, muscle-packed former Russian special forces commando who was acting as our fixer, we'd been joined at the border by Vasiliy Nisichenko, a tall, laconic, chain-smoking Russian doctor. Both would travel with the support crew to assist David and Russ. Sergey immediately got to work, tracking down his brother, a chief of police who lived near Volgograd, to see if he could help us get through the border. We even heard that the KGB was on the way, travelling 460 miles from Kiev through the night to persuade the border officials to let us through. But still nothing.

'Don't worry. It will all be okay,' Sergey said.

'So are we moving then?' I asked.

'Yes. We are moving. Maximum ten minutes.'

Four hours later, having been called in half a dozen times to answer questions, we were still at the border. Then the news we had been waiting for arrived. Two generals, one in Lviv and one in Kiev, had authorised us to enter the Ukraine. Overwhelmed by the number of people calling on our behalf, the guards and officials relented.

Two hours later we were standing in yet another office block, watching the guards eat their dinner while they discussed what to do with us. The generals' authorisation had merely allowed us to pass through immigration and passport control. Now we needed to get through customs, run by a completely different set of officials who knew nothing about our predicament. We had to start again from scratch.

'We need the original documents for the bikes,' the customs officials chorused in what had by now become a familiar refrain. 'And would it be possible for Ewan to autograph two more postcards, please?'

Claudio, who had been filming using night-vision equipment, his camera poking out of a foul-smelling latrine block so that we wouldn't be spotted, had the best advice: 'There's nothing you can do but wait. They, too, will get bored after a time.'

Finally, when it seemed we had reached a dead end, the officials got bored and agreed to create a transit paper that would allow us to pass through the Ukraine. Having typed out ten copies of a document we were unable to read, a customs officer stamped each of them on the front, turned the pile over, stamped each of them on the back and handed us an invoice. David and I traipsed downstairs, paid a cashier, picked up a receipt, had it stamped and took it upstairs, where the customs official was working on the second set of ten copies of the document. Then the whole procedure started again. Back down the stairs with the invoice for the second set, pay the cashier, get a receipt and so on until we had paid for five complete sets of the documents, one for each of the three motorbikes and one for each of the two support vehicles. Then the five sets of documents had to be taken through four departments and stamped in each one. Finally, two and a half hours later, we were allowed to pass through the border. 'Ukraine awaits and then on to Russia,' Ewan trumpeted over the intercom, sounding like a conquering general.

It was nearly 3 a.m.

EWAN: We were dog-tired and hungry, desperate for bed, but, underneath it, thrilled to bits. I really believed that the delays and aggravations were what made the trip interesting. The journey was not solely about sitting on the back of a motorbike. The motorbike was just the means by which we had chosen to get us from one experience to another. I knew it would be the hold-ups and mishaps that I would remember for ever and this had certainly been one of them.

I loved every drawn-out minute of the negotiations. They fascinated me. And while Charley and David bargained with the officials, I watched a big old black Mercedes with darkened windows draw up at the border. The door opened and a man in a leather jacket, slacks and black leather shoes stepped out. Gaunt and narrow, with a cigarette pointing straight out of his mouth, he looked like a weasel. He was the hardest, most frightening man I'd ever seen. Skinny and weedy, but ball-shrivelling scary. He walked towards me, looked at the bikes with contempt, his cigarette wiggling slightly in his mouth, turned on his heels and walked back to the border crossing. The car's side window dropped down. Another guy looked out. He was the second most frightening person I'd ever seen. Something in their faces made me feel that killing somebody would mean absolutely nothing to them. To them, the act would just be an irritation.

The weasel-like man collected his passport and climbed back into the Mercedes. Just before he sunk into his seat, he turned round and gave the soldier, at whose beck and call we had been all day, such a telling-off. A complete dressing down. Really unpleasant. And the soldier upon whom we had been fawning all day suddenly looked like a little schoolboy. Head dropped, he looked frightened and subservient. The hard man with the cigarette clicked his car door shut and drove off. Everyone who had seen the incident sighed with relief. Totally scary men.

So when Roman, as Charley had discovered his friendly hotel owner was called, popped up again just as we were passing through the final checkpoint, I was torn between relief that a bed was in sight and great suspicion about his motives.

We climbed on to our bikes and, riding slowly in convoy with the support vehicles, inched our way through the last few checkpoints. Passing mile upon mile of trucks and cars that had been queuing for days to leave the Ukraine, we felt victorious. We'd worked well as a team. David and Russ's flapping at the

Slovakian border had given way to a quiet professionalism. Thanks largely to their efforts, we'd beaten the system. Our documents were not up to scratch, but David and Russ had persuaded the Ukrainian authorities to relent and let us enter. However, the thrill of our success was undercut by a much more basic emotion summed up by Charley: 'I'm so tired I could scream.'

Faced with the dilemma of whether or not to trust Roman, I thought back to Jamie Lowther-Pinkerton's parting words: 'This is the final thing,' he'd said all those months ago as we sat enveloped by the big sofas in his comfy farmhouse. 'Trust your instincts. First impressions are usually right and it applies particularly to survival in the cuds. I really can't stress it enough. If you've got any doubt at all, check and then move in the opposite direction. Whatever the context.'

Now, faced with what might be a critical decision, I was too tired to know what to do. What slightly worried me was that Charley had met a complete stranger in the queue, who was towing a car back into the Ukraine that had been ripped to pieces by the border guards. And lo and behold this wheeler-dealer said he ran a hotel, back to which he insisted we should follow him. How could we know he really owned a hotel? I thought it might be completely innocent, but I hadn't been asked for my opinion. Charley had made an executive decision. I didn't think we should have committee meetings every five minutes but it would have been nice to have been consulted, instead of being told what we were doing. But that was Charley for you.

Sergey advised us not to take up the offer of a bed for the night. David and Russ were unsure, but Charley had made his mind up. 'It's fine,' he said. 'I got a good vibe about it. Let's go.'

CHARLEY: We drove into the night, deeper and deeper into pitch darkness. Roman had said it would only be 9 kilometres, but it seemed like we had already ridden twice as far. The further we rode, the more nervous I became. It didn't feel right. My mind started playing tricks. Shit, this is not good, I thought. Jesus, he's going to take us somewhere, slaughter us and steal the cars and equipment.

Just as I was thinking we ought to bolt, Roman's car turned off the road to Uzghorod. I looked down at my GPS. It was indicating we should stick to the main road. I was convinced we should make a run for it, but Vasiliy, our doctor, was riding in Roman's car and we couldn't desert him. Following a twisting track for several long, nerve-racking minutes, we rode further and further into the forest. My stomach was in my mouth. We crossed a bridge and just as I was thinking we had driven straight into his trap, the lights panned up to reveal a huge pink hotel. Lit by floodlights and surrounded by chalets, it was decorated in a medieval style. So that explained the Camelot reference. Nearby was a row of garages: secure parking, just as he had promised. Roman jumped out of his car, all friendly, while three security guards in uniforms circled us. 'Come inside,' he shouted and ushered Ewan and me up the steps.

It was like walking into a castle, albeit one more appropriate to a theme park than the knights of the round table. It had ramparts, thick stone walls, arches and turrets. With our bags over our shoulders, we climbed a couple of flights of stairs to our rooms and bumped into David. 'You guys are not going to believe your rooms,' he said, his eyes wide with incredulity.

Ewan insisted I took the larger room, or rather a baronial suite of rooms. The dining room had a table that seated eight. The living room had a leather sofa, two leather chairs and a widescreen television which received all the porn channels imaginable. The walls were covered in replicas of Old Masters and the huge bathroom had a Jacuzzi and a power shower. It looked like a hotel, but I was still suspicious.

'Can you believe it?' I said as Ewan ambled into my room.

'I don't really believe it, no,' he said. 'One minute I was in my bivvy bag on the verge next to that row of trucks, listening to the voices and choking on the fumes. And the next minute, after some kind of weird video-game ride through the dark, we're here. Is it dodgy or is it just me? Is this a bit dodge or is it . . .?'

I was still convinced they were going to murder us before we went to sleep. Like Hansel and Gretel, they were fattening us up for the slaughter. Worried that we would be overheard, we crept into the bathroom to discuss our predicament.

'It doesn't really feel right,' Ewan said. 'But am I right to be so suspicious? Maybe I'm being too cynical and it's our first experience of generosity. But I can't stop thinking what's in it for him and wondering what we are letting ourselves in for.'

The good feeling I'd had about our generous host had turned into a nervous disquiet, but I reasoned that he had spent a lot of money on Camelot and maybe he just wanted to show it off. 'I don't know,' I said. 'But the upshot is you're no longer asleep on the grass verge with lorries going by and we've swapped border police for two or three security guards wandering around.'

'What if we go downstairs and he opens a door and we go down another floor and there's a huge casino, full of mobsters smoking cigars and women in tight green shimmery dresses, all playing craps?' Ewan said.

'Look, Ewan, there's his and hers towels,' I said, searching for something to reassure me Camelot was just like any other hotel.

'And he gave me a cuddle as well,' Ewan said. 'I put my bags down, spread my arms to say thank you and he just gave me a hug as if to say "you're home now".'

'Oh, did he? Maybe he knows who you are.'

'He's just a nice guy,' Ewan said.

Roman woke up his staff and insisted they cook us dinner. At four in the morning, we sat down for a three-course feast in his basement nightclub decorated like a dungeon but decked out instead with spinning glitterballs, flashing strobes and a psychedelic lightshow.

'This must be a one-off,' I said to Sergey, who looked exhausted, his eyes red-rimmed and baggy after all his hard work at the border. 'It's so wonderfully kitsch.'

'No, no, no,' he said, 'this is quite normal for Russia or the Ukraine.'

Roman insisted we all have our pictures taken with him, while Russ, who had had a few vodkas, was all for celebrating crossing the border. But I was suddenly overcome with tiredness. Still nervous about being bumped off in the night, I sloped off to bed. Back in the room, I scanned the light fittings and the pictures on the wall for hidden cameras, but found nothing. Then I opened a cupboard. There in front of me was a shoe-shine pack with a little shoe horn. When I saw it I realised the building was a hotel after all and Roman had simply been incredibly nice. Everything he'd promised, he'd delivered. Feeling guilty for being so suspicious, I switched on the television, watched it for a few minutes and dropped off to sleep in the armchair. Rest at last.

EWAN: I woke early and went outside. In the cold light of day, I could see that what in the wee hours of the morning had seemed such a vividly scary mafia hideout, where gangsters were going to slit our throats and take our money, was nothing more than a very innocent hotel. I felt slightly embarrassed that we had not trusted Roman's hospitality for what it was. The previous night the hotel had come across like something out of *Goodfellas* but perhaps I had been watching too many movies. I reproached myself for being so cynical. Maybe living in a big city like London had made me inherently wary of strangers. It was a habit I wanted to shake off.

Wandering through the empty hotel while Charley and the rest of the team slept, I came across a map of the world on a wall. It took my breath away. Compared with what lay ahead, we had travelled so little. We'd barely begun the journey and yet I felt that, if we had to return home that day, we had already travelled a long way and had a completely fulfilling holiday. Even now, I couldn't conceive of the scale of our undertaking. For months I had been talking people through the map. Now I was sitting on my bike riding it.

We'd been on the road for just over a week and I was getting a sense that we were gradually easing ourselves into the trip. It was like we were trying each day on for size, unsure if it was the right fit for the months ahead. But I still couldn't fathom the distance ahead. The secret, I felt, was to take the journey in little blocks. Morning till coffee break. Coffee till lunch. Lunch till mid-afternoon break. Hopefully by then we would have reached our destination. If not, then push on a bit further until dusk. By breaking it up into chunks, we'd make it manageable. But the moment my mind drifted to the bigger picture, that we'd reach Russia in a few days and then enter Kazakhstan a few days later, the journey became overwhelming and panic set in.

I was still missing home and wondering if the feeling would ever go. At least I was no longer riding with a lump in my throat all day and every day. A bike ride usually consisted of leaving in the morning and returning home for lunch. Or riding to a track day at Donnington and coming back the next day. It certainly always involved returning to the place I'd left. Now we just had a huge ribbon of tarmac ahead of us. It would just keep coming at us and we would just keep heading east, knowing that we would not return to the places we passed. It was quite a bizarre feeling. And every mile took us further away from home, further away from our families, and increasingly I felt the loneliness of not being with my wife.

But accompanying the moments that tugged at our heartstrings there were times of great wonder. And, every so often, flashes of magic. Like when we were riding at the end of the day and the sun, setting in the west, warmed our backs and threw our shadows ahead of us on the road. Just chasing our shadows as we headed east. All the way round the world to get home.

The magic continued when we set off that morning. Western Ukraine was stuck in a time warp. Nothing seemed to have changed in the landscape or the way of life for the best part of a century. It was deeply agricultural country with small villages, farms, horses pulling ploughs and lots of women working on the land, while the men seemed to have nothing better to do than sit at the side of the road, watching the occasional vehicle pass by. The roads were rough, gravel-strewn and potholed, a challenge at first but good fun once we got used to them. The Ukrainians appeared to have spent all their money putting up mobile phone masts and had forgotten the roads, but it was nothing the bikes couldn't cope with. Then came a call over the radio. It was David: 'We're approaching our first bit of drama.'

At the edge of a village, a barrier had been pulled down across the road. A guard was standing beside a hut. We didn't know if he was a policeman, a soldier, a government official or a local bandit.

'They just want to see our papers,' Sergey said with a resigned air. 'It will be okay.'

It was local police. They wanted to see our vehicle registration documents, and again photocopies would not do. It had to be the originals. I assumed it would be another twelve-hour delay, as at the border, and I rather hoped it would take that long. I needed a nap. How perfect, I thought: there are some trees at the edge of the road and I can go to sleep under one of them. We sat at the edge of the road, smoking to pass the time, waiting for something to break the impasse. From now on, it wouldn't be a case of hold-ups just on entering a new country. There would be delays and checkpoints right across every country until we reached the Pacific Ocean.

'What do you think?' I asked Vasiliy, our doctor. As usual, he had a cigarette on the go and a smile creasing his hangdog expression. This was a man who had decades of experience of Russian and central European bureaucracy. He knew how to wait, how to keep nodding, how to chivvy things along ever so gently, never threatening or cajoling the officials as we might in the West, just making sure that we weren't forgotten and that eventually we would get what we needed.

'You want to know what I think?' he said in his thick Russian accent. 'Nobody promised us this trip would be easy. But it will be okay. You have to be patient.'

While Ukrainian trucks, coaches and cranes passed through the checkpoint, we waited and explored the village. Except for the strip of tarmac passing through its heart, it had probably never changed. There were old peasant women, their heads wrapped in scarves, clutching babies. Children were drawing water from a well. Two young lads were driving a grey mare pulling a wooden wagon, its wheels clattering on the ground. Three women, dots in a huge field, were tilling the earth with large Dutch hoes while the local men in flat caps sat on a bench, doing what Ukrainian men in rural areas seemed always to do. Watching the world drive by.

A grocer's shop was well stocked with basic provisions such as sausages and chocolate, giving us a chance to exercise the few words of Russian we had learned during the months of preparation – *privet*, *sbasibo* and *chetyre*. I wished we'd taken the Russian lessons more seriously, but by smiling and pointing we managed to buy a few groceries.

The housewives in the shop asked us where we were from. '*Ingliski*,' we said. They gabbled back in Ukrainian. '*Russki*' was not good, they made clear. But not having a clue what they were saying, we could judge only by their body language, all nudges and lascivious giggles.

This unplanned stopover had been the highlight of the trip so far. Unencumbered by the trappings of fame and celebrity, at last I was meeting real people in their own surroundings. I just wanted to be quiet and wait to be allowed through the checkpoint, but Charley was rushing around like a blue-arsed fly again, so I took myself over to a well and sat down on the edge of it. A little old lady came out of her rickety wooden house and joined me; she fed her cat and started to chat in Ukrainian. I couldn't understand what she was saying but it didn't seem to matter. I just listened to her voice and then I told her about us. She touched my forehead and crossed herself several times. I got the impression she was saying that I'd been sent to meet her, but there was no way to know for sure. We sat for a long time, the old lady muttering sweetly all the while. I was so happy to sit and chat with her. I think she was trying to tell me about her life, talking about the war and how terrible it had been. It was amazing to think she had probably lived in that house all her life. At one point she said she would pray for me. I told her we were going a very long way and that it would be very nice if she prayed for us. It was beautiful and I'll never forget her. She really touched me. She was a gorgeous woman, with beautiful eyes. A real sweetheart. I could have listened to her all day. She didn't know what I was saying either, but again it didn't really seem to matter. I was so content just to listen to her stories and I was really disappointed when I heard that at last we'd been let through the checkpoint.

CHARLEY: We continued on through western Ukraine, bound for Lviv. It looked incredibly poor and indeed some of the Ukrainians were ploughing the fields by hand; I saw one man slowly pushing a hand plough over a long, thin field. It was a pitiful existence and the whole landscape looked black and white. No colour. Nothing.

Almost every little village we passed through was empty. The only people we saw looked very old and thoroughly worn out. They just sat in front of their fences, gazing at the road. A few young kids wore windcheaters that were too tight for them. Occasionally a blacked-out Mercedes would sweep through at 90mph. Mafia or gangsters, we assumed, who couldn't give a fuck about the state of their country. The poverty was quite staggering, particularly as it seemed so close to home. It had taken us only a week to reach the Ukraine, yet it was another world.

By the evening we had reached Lviv, another long day's riding of more than 160 miles on broken roads, interrupted only by a visit to a beautiful church in a small village and a coffee stop at a roadside hut. Wherever we stopped, the people were incredibly helpful, not least at the hotel in Lviv. Claudio asked where we could park our bikes safely and the manager said 'here', pointing to the foyer of his once grand and ornate, but now slightly down at heel, palace of a hotel. Ewan rolled back the carpets and we rode the bikes up a couple of stairs, through the double doors into the lavishly decorated hall, laughing at the ridiculousness of trying to turn the heavy bikes around on the slippery polished marble floor.

We washed, changed and walked around the city with Andrej Hunyak, a Ukrainian friend of Claudio's. Like so many eastern European cities, Lviv was a beautiful place. Classical buildings, big squares with old men playing chess, most of the roads cobbled and uneven. Over dinner, Andrej, who was studying linguistics at Lviv University while working as a database administrator, told us about the difficulties of finding a job in the Ukraine. 'Rome wasn't built in a day and you don't build a free market in just ten years. It's only been thirteen years since the Ukraine gained independence. It's nothing,' he said.

We asked him about the change from communism to democracy. 'It was pretty dodgy,' he said. 'All you could get was the bare necessities. You couldn't buy clothes. There was nothing on the shelves in the shops. Everything was just empty. It was ridiculous. Now we've got plenty on the shelves but we haven't got money to buy it. It's too expensive.'

We'd heard similar stories in most of eastern Europe. Passing through the Czech Republic a few weeks before it joined the European Union, we'd found many young people still living with their parents, unable to afford a home of their own and expecting property prices to rise even more once their country was part of the EU. Many people in the Ukraine spoke at length about the mafia but nobody would let us use this in the documentary. It was a potent indication of the hold the mafia had over Ukrainians and their country, possibly greater than the fear instilled by the communist regime fifteen years earlier.

EWAN: Facing a tough deadline, we left the hotel early the next morning. Three hundred and sixty miles to ride by three o'clock. We had an appointment in Kiev at a Unicef centre that looked after children affected by the Chernobyl disaster.

Charley was very quiet and I didn't feel much like talking. The pressure, not only of the long ride to Kiev, but of the journey further ahead, had begun to sink in. We were still waking up in the early hours, eaten up with worries. The stresses of the border crossing, the bizarre experience at the Camelot hotel and the poverty we saw in the Ukrainian countryside had given us a lot to contemplate and heightened our homesickness. For the first time we realised the scale of what we'd taken on. We'd seen so much, ridden so far and done such a lot. It had been physically exhausting and mentally demanding. Yet we were only on week two of fifteen. And this was the easy part. Kazakhstan, Mongolia and Siberia would be much more challenging. It was quite an awesome feeling, a feeling I didn't want to ponder on for too long.

We rode for an hour or so in silence, stopping for coffee at a kiosk at the end of a long right-hand bend beneath a massive Soviet-era communist sculpture of a clenched fist thrusting out from the side of a hill. The sculpture was cracked and slightly dilapidated, but very powerful and impressive nonetheless. As I pulled my bike around to the kiosk, I noticed I was doing a U-turn in the road around what had once been a dog. It had been hit so hard that it had exploded all over the road. It was by far the worst road kill I'd ever seen. I glanced at it out of the corner of my eye, not wanting to look too close but finding it very difficult not to stare.

Charley and I stood at the side of the road sipping our coffee in silence while Claudio filmed the sculpture. It was the first time since leaving London that we'd not had anything to say to each other and our introspection had been exacerbated by getting used to riding with Claudio since Prague. Claudio had been fantastic company, easy to get along with and full of interesting anecdotes, but the dynamics of a trio are quite different from the relationship between two people, and we were still getting used to the change.

We'd all seen the dog, but no one had dared mention it. 'That dog's all over the place,' I eventually said quietly over the rim of my coffee cup. Charley looked at me and we both cracked up. 'It doesn't know its arse from its elbow,' I added and we fell into a fit of giggles. It was in such poor taste, but just what was needed to break the heavy silence.

'You know what was the last thing that went through that dog's mind?' Charley said, almost unable to get the words out he was laughing so much. 'Its arse.'

For the next few minutes, we trotted out one bad pun after another, grimacing as passing trucks squished and splattered the poor dog flatter into the road. 'Nooooo, don't watch,' Charley shouted each time it was run over again, but we were in hysterics. The dark mood had been broken. Charley and I were back in good shape.

It got colder and colder as we rode on. Really cold for the first time since we had set off. Until then, we had been blessed with the weather, so much so that I'd given up wearing my thermal gear a few days earlier, when it had been really hot. A sucker for a good sales pitch, I'd believed what I'd been told about thermal underwear, that it would keep me cool in hot weather as well as warm in cold weather. Dressed as if heading for the Arctic, the sweat had been running down my back. But now, with the lining removed from my motorbike kit and nothing but a T-shirt and underpants beneath my jacket and trousers, I was freezing.

'Sorry, guys, I'm really freezing. We need to stop,' I called over the intercom. We spotted another coffee kiosk, pulled over and began the tedious process of completely unloading our bikes to get at our thermals tucked away at the very bottom of our kitbags. Standing at the side of the road, stripped to our underpants while we stuffed the thermal linings back inside the riding clothes, we turned to stone as a police car slowly pulled by and the rozzers inside stared at us, half-naked by the roadside. The patrol car disappeared out of sight. A short while later it returned, the cops giving us the same quizzical look as they passed around the bend. Another minute or so later, it reappeared, this time with the siren wailing. 'Here we go,' I thought as they pulled in front of our bikes.

We'd been alerted to the behaviour of the police in eastern Europe and central Asia. Every guidebook we'd read and every traveller we'd spoken to had warned us they were notoriously unpredictable. And Jamie Lowther-Pinkerton had told us to work out a drill. 'What's absolutely key with going through checkpoints is that although it might be the accepted thing in many parts of the world, never offer a bribe,' Jamie had said back in early January.

'No money? Ever?' Charley asked.

'Never, ever upfront,' Jamie insisted. 'The thing to do is to say is there an official toll? Do I have to go and pay it at the police station or can I pay it straight to you? Could you explain what the situation is here? Then he can say "Yeah, there's an on-the-spot fining system". And you hand it over.'

In some places, the accepted procedure was to offer to buy the policeman breakfast. They'd refuse it, but take the cash instead and let you go. But the secret, Jamie said, was never to initiate the bribe. 'Don't believe what you've seen in the movies. Money in the passport or wedged into your driving licence is a definite no-no. Otherwise they can go: right, you're nicked for trying to bribe a policeman. And it'll cost you four times as much, plus a night in the nick.'

With Jamie's words at the back of our minds, we had decided a strategy. 'When we get stopped by the police, because we undoubtedly will, I'll do the talking,' I'd said.

The one thing we knew when the rozzers pulled up and climbed out of the patrol car was that they couldn't book us for speeding. Mainly because when they had first spotted us, we were standing in a state of undress at the side of the road. 'Okay, will it be two or five or ten?' I thought as the rozzers approached us. 'How many shekels will it be?'

'Are you German?' one of the policemen said.

'No, British. He's English and I'm Scottish,' I said, pointing to the flags on our helmets.

'Arsenal!' the policeman exclaimed.

Not a football fan, I nevertheless realised that I should play along. After all, Jamie had told us there were two English words that were understood the world over: fuck and Beckham.

'Yeah, Arsenal,' I said, smiling and trying to look enthusiastic about a team of which I knew nothing.

'Chelsea!' the policeman said. I racked my brain. I knew Chelsea had recently played a team from somewhere in Europe.

'Three-one,' the policeman said. 'Monaco three. Chelsea one.' I was lost. Football, the male lingua franca, and I couldn't speak a word. I smiled while the policeman looked the bikes over. He shrugged, got back into his car and drove off. I'd been all keyed up, ready to hand over a bribe when the time was right. But our first encounter with the fearsome police of the Ukraine couldn't have been sweeter.

As we approached Kiev, we were met by a Unicef car that led the way to the Chernobyl Children's Project. We pulled up in a courtyard outside a slightly dilapidated four-storey building that had been set aside for children who had suffered from the effects of the nuclear disaster in 1986. Other children were at the centre because the radiation had caused psychological or physical problems and their families were struggling to cope. We met Victoria, whose mother had been carrying her at the time of the accident. Born two months after the reactor meltdown, Victoria had had leukaemia since she was eight years old. Because of her illness, she had never been to school. At the Unicef-supported centre, Victoria was able to learn how to use computers. Now eighteen, she was studying information management at university. Other children were at the centre because their parents could no longer care for them because the radiation had caused psychological or physical problems. We also met a little girl who'd recently lost her father. He was one of the liquidators who had gone in to Chernobyl, eighty miles north of Kiev, to do the construction work necessary to seal off the reactor. Like six hundred thousand other men and women involved in the fire-fighting and clearance operations, he went into the contaminated region around the reactor knowing he would become very ill and might even die.

The centre was set up by Katernya Novak, a remarkable woman who lived less than a mile from the edge of the nuclear power station complex in Pripyat, the town built to service the power station. The entire population, many of whom worked at the reactor, were evacuated after the fire broke out and the radiation escaped. Her first reaction was to set about helping children like her own whose health had been damaged by the accident. Many had thyroid cancers or leukaemia.

It was wonderful to visit the project. We looked at artwork that represented their problems. 'Children affected by radiation have very highly developed emotions,' the translator told us. We toured the computer room and participated in a dance therapy class with the children. It was difficult at first because we didn't know what to say. But I had found through experience with other charities that the first five minutes of meeting somebody who was critically ill, especially if it was a child, were always awkward and after that it got easier. You had to let children tell their stories and take control of the situation.

To break the ice, we told the children about the difficulties we were having speaking Russian. 'We didn't really concentrate as hard as we should have during our Russian lessons,' I said. 'I've been saying *chetyre*, *chetyre*, *chetyre*, to everyone I meet, thinking it was Russian for thank you. But one day someone said to me "Why do you keep saying four? Don't you know that's what *chetyre* means?"' The kids laughed. 'I don't really mind,' I said. 'I like *chetyre*. And I don't mind going round everywhere saying four. I like it.'

The children at the Chernobyl centre were fantastic and we were thrilled to be there and to be involved with Unicef. I was really proud to be able to do it. In Britain, we're very quick to knock people in the limelight whatever they are doing, but one of the great honours that comes along with doing the job I do is that you can be involved in raising awareness for charities or helping them raise money. I don't care what anybody says: there's no harm in it. I was extremely pleased to have built a link with Unicef that I hoped to carry on.

CHARLEY: The next day we took the bikes for their first service. After dropping them off, we went sightseeing. Kiev was beautiful. Unspoilt, laid-back and the first city we'd stopped in where Ewan didn't feel hassled. It was how I imagined Prague must have been before it became one of the most popular tourist destinations in Europe. Browsing through a flea market, we stopped to look at a stall selling fur hats.

'Do I know you?' It was one of the market traders, young and wearing a pair of wraparound shades. 'I know you.'

'Yes. Maybe you know me. This is Charley,' Ewan said, swinging his arm around the stallholder and slapping him on the back.

'Welcome to the Ukraine. Are you on the bikes?'

'Yes, we are,' Ewan said. 'How did you know about that?'

'Am I looking like I am stupid?'

'How did you know about the bikes?'

'I saw the TV. On satellite. Two BMWs, right?'

We'd come all this way and still couldn't escape the effects of the media. Then another stallholder wandered over. 'How you doing . . . Ewan McGregor?'

'Yes. How are you? Good to see you.'

'I watched your movie. *Big Fish*.'

'*Big Fish* is a nice one, isn't it,' I said. 'I loved it.'

'Not so nice,' the second stallholder said.

'You didn't like it?' Ewan asked.

'Not your best one,' the second stallholder said. 'You want to buy something? I make a special price, guys. It's my pleasure . . .'

The market was an eye-opener. Caviar was being sold by the bucketload, scooped with a trowel out of a deep barrel and shovelled into the type of bucket we would use to build sandcastles on the beach. A Russian 1950s bike was parked nearby and the streets were thronged with big Mercedes and BMWs driven by shifty-looking flash geezers, invariably with a very pretty, expensively dressed girl in $500 shades sitting beside them.

We stopped for lunch on the terrace of a restaurant. Chicken Kiev, of course. Then we visited a Soviet-era monument in a public park, a place of pilgrimage for newlyweds. Dressed in their white dresses and tuxedos, they were having their pictures taken beneath the arched monument. 'These Soviet statues and pieces of art really do inspire a kind of awe,' Ewan said. 'All those workers – they're such powerful figures. They must have given the common man a huge sense of strength and pride.'

But the day was overshadowed by a series of arguments I had with Russ and David. It started as soon as we met in the lobby of our hotel. My friend Fred Grolsh, who had recently moved to Kiev, had organised a sightseeing tour and booked our hotel, but the team were treating him with disdain. At least, so I thought. David and Russ were constantly late, they kept changing their minds, they kept talking over each other and they wouldn't commit to anything. I was embarrassed by their behaviour. 'Could you just stop and listen to what Fred has got to say and then we can get on with looking around Kiev,' I snapped at David. He said nothing, but it happened again when we dropped off the bikes at the BMW garage and I laid into David, who was still not paying my friend any respect.

'Don't you dare show me up in front of someone else,' David snarled at me.

'Well, you fucking listen to my friend who's trying to organise something,' I barked back. 'You might not like it that I snapped at you, but how do you think I feel? I'm tremendously embarrassed about the way you're treating Fred.'

The argument escalated, David and I ripping into each other, until Ewan stepped in. He was very upset. 'You've got to sort out this problem between you, Russ and David,' he said. 'Otherwise it's going to ruin the whole trip.'

I tried apologising to David, but he was having none of it. 'What's the point of saying you're sorry, when you know you're going to do it again?' he said. 'After a while it means nothing.'

That evening, when the rest of the group went out for a meal,

I cried off. I wanted to be alone. I phoned Olly, but didn't tell her what was going on. Concerned that Russ, David and I were facing a personality clash that could bring an end to the adventure, and knowing they probably felt the same way, I wasn't ready to tell my wife. At the end of the phone call she asked if I was all right. 'Yeah, I'm fine. Just a bit tired,' I said and rang off.

I sat in my room and thought about it. I knew it was make or break time. We couldn't head further east, where the stresses would be much greater, if we weren't getting on in Europe. Thinking it over, I realised I was the one who was creating the bad vibe and that I wasn't listening to what other people said. I was constantly jumping down Russ and David's throats, not letting them finish sentences and telling them what to do even when they knew better. It was a huge turning point. I realised Russ was just being Russ and Dave was just being Dave, and I was the one with a problem.

At the root of it, I hadn't faced up to the fact that I would be away from home for such a long time. It wasn't made easier when I phoned home to speak to my daughters and, like any young children, they didn't realise what I was going through. I could tell they were having plenty of fun, even though I wasn't at home. 'Yeah, yeah, yeah, Dad,' they'd say over the phone, 'whatever . . .' I missed my children more than I had ever imagined I would and I missed my wife, just cuddling up to her at the end of a day and having a proper chat. It was made worse by my constant worrying each and every day over where we were going to sleep, where we were going to go and what we would do when we got there. I had to face up to the fact that I was a worrier. I liked to know where we would be staying, but I needed to force myself to chill out and relax if my anxieties weren't going to ruin things.

I also needed to recognise that while Russ and Dave had their faults, they had done a fantastic job. They'd given their all to our trip, and they'd delivered on everything they'd promised. It wasn't a case of sorting it out with them and coming to a compromise. I needed to sit back, relax and let Russ and Dave – who were both being so professional – look after things. I'd been ignorant and selfish. I just needed to accept that everything was going to work out. Russ and David could be left to do their jobs. My kids and wife would be okay without me. And sadly, the frictions were mostly my fault. It was a hard thing to admit but once I did, I felt a whole lot better, relieved that the burden of the trip had been lifted off my shoulders. I was trying to control everything. I needed just to let things happen. Otherwise these 108 days were going to slip by and I would have missed it all.

EWAN: Charley and I set off the next morning on our own. Claudio had flown back to London to retake his motorcycle test. This time he had to pass.

I was sorry to leave Kiev and determined to return again soon with my wife. I'd had a fantastic time on my last afternoon in the city, when I'd returned to the hotel for a rest, but ended up wandering down the high street. I'd seen it was crowded and that there was something going on and I wanted to explore.

Wandering among crowds can be a bit awkward for me, not because I get swamped but just because it makes me feel very self-conscious. It's something that's very difficult to come to terms with, particularly as being well-known and successful is something that many of us strive for, and I'm well aware of the dangers of moaning about it. But the reality is that while being recognised can be very flattering, and I'm very happy to sign autographs, I find it a bit awkward to walk in crowded areas of cities. I end up just being stared at a lot. I understand why it happens, but if I'm on my own it makes me feel a bit shy and embarrassed.

So to wander down the high street in Kiev on a Saturday afternoon, as if I was walking down Oxford Street in London or Sauchiehall Street in Glasgow, and not be stared at was fabulous. It had been a long time since I'd done that and it was liberating. I really liked it. But with everyone we met telling us Kiev would soon be the new Prague, I felt it wouldn't be long before its fabulous atmosphere was spoilt and it would be a shame if this lovely city, full of life and vibrancy, was to be taken over by some of the things we had seen in Prague, such as the hordes of stag parties and hen nights wandering the streets in search of cheap alcohol. I vowed to return sooner rather than later.

Riding to Kharkiv, we were pulled over by the police several times. Each time, we phoned Sergey to translate and he helped us smooth things over. Approaching Kharkiv, Sergey's brother, Alexei, met us and led us to our hotel. The next morning, Alexei, or King Rozzer as we called him because he was the local chief of police, led us back out of town. With sirens blaring and the lights on the top of his car flashing, the traffic parted before us. Within minutes, we were out of Kharkiv, an industrial city of which we'd seen very little, bound for Krasnyy Luch. I had new knobbly tyres on my bike and a full tank of gas. Riding across a landscape of vast fertile plains dotted with occasional copses of trees, the BMW was running like a dream, the road was long and straight, and I was heading for Russia. I was happy as old Larry. I loved being on my bike. I loved being on the road.

The only impediment to our progress was the police. We rarely rode for more than half an hour without being stopped, mainly because they wanted to have a look at the bikes. Given that it was an unusual thing to see a couple of guys on motorcycles riding by, it seemed fair enough. But the third time it happened was not so lucky. Having seen the speed limit, we were keeping the speed down as Charley slowly inched past a very slow Lada. He didn't cross the solid white central line, but he was overtaking.

Almost immediately we heard the siren: a police car sitting in a lay-by. It flagged us down. A large policeman got out, walked over and asked Charley for his papers. Wanting to make it clear that Charley and I were in this together, I also handed over my papers and my passport. We'd been stopped so frequently by the police that I'd lost any sense of anxiety about it. And the knowledge that we could probably pay them off erased any respect we had for the rozzers.

Taking our papers over to the patrol car, the policeman beckoned to Charley to sit beside him in the front seat. Pointing at a diagram and some text in what we assumed was the Ukrainian highway code, he shook his head. 'It's not good, not good,' he muttered, pulling a ticket with a stamp on it out of his notebook. 'It's a big problem.'

Standing out on the roadside, I leaned in the side window. 'Is there a fine?' I ventured, remembering Jamie Lowther-Pinkerton's advice. 'Do we have to pay a fine?'

'Yes,' the policeman said, looking at me sternly. 'Yes, there's a fine.'

Taking my money out of my pocket, I heard the policeman ask me to get into the car. I sat in the back and pulled out some Ukrainian bills.

'No!' the policeman growled. I rummaged in my pocket for some more Ukrainian bills.

'No! No, it's no good,' he said. 'Problem, problem.'

Charley and I immediately clicked and spoke in unison. 'Dollars?'

A smile spread across the fat policeman's face. Charley removed twenty-five dollars in five-dollar bills from his pocket, just as Jamie had advised us. 'Have a crumpled-up dollar in the bottom of a pocket,' Jamie had said. 'Pull it out slowly. Make it look like it's the only one you've got.'

'Twenty dollars,' the rozzer demanded.

'Come on, fifteen,' Charley said.

'Twenty dollars.'

But Charley was sticking to his guns. 'Come on. Ten? Fifteen?'

The policeman was having none of it. 'Twenty dollars,' he said. Pointing at Charley, the rozzer looked him in the eye and said: 'You, twenty dollars.' Then he turned around to where I was sitting in the back, pointed at me and added: 'You, twenty dollars.'

There was no haggling. That, it seemed, was that. There was nothing we could do but say 'Aw, all right,' and pay up twenty dollars each.

We plodded back to our bikes. As I swung my leg over the saddle, I shouted over to Charley. 'I didn't even do anything wrong! I didn't overtake the car on the single solid white line.' We'd been completely fleeced by a rozzer in the cuds and we were crushed. It wasn't the money. It was the humiliation. We'd been powerless to do anything about it and the rozzer knew it.

Charley moaned about it for a wee while. 'I feel really disappointed in myself for allowing this to happen,' he said. But as far as I was concerned it was better than having our bikes taken away from us.

We rode on for a short while, then stopped for lunch by a field, pulling off the road and riding down a track a short distance. Just as we were settling into our bread and cheese, an orange van approached. It drove past us, down the hill, then stopped and drove back up. I was immediately suspicious. 'What's this guy want?' was my first reaction.

With countless warnings about the mafia and the crooked police, I had come to expect the worst. The driver stepped out of his van and just stood there, quite near, staring at us. Charley handed him a bit of chocolate. Meanwhile, I looked him up and down with mistrust as a large plough crawled up the field. Then it dawned upon me. He was just a farmer, waiting to speak to his farm workers and hanging out with us in the meantime.

Again I was annoyed at my immediate suspicion of strangers. It was obviously going to take quite a while to get over the feeling that everyone wanted something from us. I needed to learn to trust people. Not everybody was going to rip me off. This man out in the fields was just a farmer, yet I had various scenarios running through my head, all of them involving trouble. I needed to get over my hang-ups.

*

A couple of hours later and we were once again standing in front of a policeman like a pair of fed-up naughty schoolboys.

'Your speed was too fast. You were doing eighty kilometres an hour,' the policeman said. I had been in the lead, ticking along quite slowly on an empty road in wide open countryside.

'No, no. I was doing fifty miles an hour,' I said.

'Yeah, fifty miles is eighty kilometres. But this is a fifty-kilometres-an-hour zone.' It was ridiculously slow, particularly for a straight country road, but there was no way out. He had us bang to rights and we were going to get nicked. Again.

This time, however, we had learned our lesson. I phoned Sergey, explained what had happened and handed the phone to the policeman. He listened and gave the phone back to me.

'Sergey?' I said and listened as our fixer spelled out our penalty. 'All you have to do is take a photograph with him. He'll send you on your way, no problem. No fine. Nothing.'

I turned to Charley. 'We played the Ewan card and it seems it's going to work,' I said. Charley grinned.

The policeman introduced himself. His name was Vladimir. While Charley and I took it in turns to pose with him, he chatted away.

'Where are you staying?' he asked.

'We're going to Krasnyy Luch,' I said.

'No. Where are you staying?'

'A hotel.'

'No, no,' Vladimir said. 'You stay with me. You come to my house and you stay with me.'

'That's very kind,' I said, 'but there are more of us. There are several more coming.'

'No problem.'

We chatted for a while. Sweeping my hands in front of me to illustrate a point, I suddenly noticed that I wasn't wearing my wedding ring. It was gone. My heart sank.

I went straight to my gloves and looked inside them. My wedding band had come off once before, when I had been on a bike trip in France, and I'd spent hours combing the ground around a campsite searching for my ring, only to find it in my glove.

But this time the gloves were empty.

'Charley, I've lost my wedding ring,' I said. I felt sick. My stomach turned. It was a horrible feeling. We searched around the bikes, but we couldn't find it. Charley phoned the support team. Jim immediately checked the footage we'd shot at the hotel that morning. I'd been wearing my ring when I packed my bike, Jim said, so I'd obviously lost it somewhere along the road after that.

Only a fortnight ago, the night before I left home, I'd suggested to Eve that it might be safer if I left my wedding ring at home. 'I won't get laid on the trip otherwise,' I'd joked, but I'd chosen to wear it because I couldn't bear to be without it. Now that ring was missing. We'd stopped so many times, for lunch, for coffee and being flagged down by the police, that it could have fallen off anywhere. We climbed back on our bikes and returned to the previous stop, about five minutes up the road, where another policeman had wanted to give our bikes the once-over. It wasn't there.

We rode back to Vladimir, thanked him and took his number, then rode on. Charley was very understanding. 'Let's stop for five minutes and have a coffee,' he said.

I phoned Eve. 'Oh darlin', I've lost my wedding ring,' I said. 'I can't find it, my love. It's not on my finger and it's not in my gloves.'

Eve was sweet. 'Don't worry about it, darling,' she said. 'These things happen and it's part of the experience of your trip.'

Thinking we could stay with Vladimir, but that the support team would need a hotel, we rode on to Krasnyy Luch. The town had seen better days. It was shabby and there was no sign of a hotel. Charley approached a man standing outside a bank in the central square.

'We're looking for a hotel,' Charley said. 'Hotel. Somewhere to sleep. Is there a hotel here?'

'*Niet*,' the man said. 'Bank.'

'No, I know this is a bank,' Charley said, 'but I'm looking for a hotel.' He mimed putting his head down on a pillow.

'*Niet. Niet,*' the man said again. 'Bank.'

Charley tried a few more times, then gave up. We stood in the town square, while a grey-haired bearded man dressed in black trousers and a camouflage jacket shouted at us. Unable to understand him, we didn't know if he was insulting us or trying to help. A group of lads in leather jackets, hanging out on a street corner, looked us up and down, then came over to us.

'You're an actor?' one of them said to me.

'Yeah, yeah. I'm an actor,' I replied.

'You do porno movie,' the Ukrainian lad said.

I cracked up. 'Er, no,' I said and the lads all burst out laughing. 'We're looking for a hotel. Hotel?'

They laughed. '*Niet. Niet,*' one of the lads said as his mates scratched themselves all over. Bedbugs.

We ambled over to a large building with pillars, where a small crowd had gathered to stare at us. Among the crowd was a young guy who said he was a musician, a mother and child and a woman training her dog. I decided to get my tripod off the back of my bike to film them. As I pulled it out my wedding ring fell on the floor. Ting, ting, ting it went across the road. I can't describe my joy. I was so elated and suddenly it all made sense. The ring had slipped off my finger when I'd been stuffing my tripod back on my bike at lunchtime, when I'd been viewing the innocent farmer with such suspicion. I'd ridden for 180 miles since then and my ring hadn't dropped of its perch. That I hadn't lost it was a small miracle, one for which I was very grateful. What a relief.

By late evening, the fading sun casting horizontal light across the land as we followed Vladimir's Lada out of Krasnyy Luch, once again we were chasing the shadows of our bikes stretched out in front of us on the road. And once again I was questioning the motives of a friendly stranger. Vladimir had turned up at the arranged time and told us to follow him, but, try as I might, I couldn't keep my suspicions in check. For one thing Vladimir had suggested that we all go to a sauna. I thought it might just be a thing that Ukrainian men do after work, but other thoughts did cross my mind. If it was just a sauna, then I wouldn't have a problem with it. But it could mean so much more. And I really didn't want to find myself in that situation. No thanks.

Vladimir led us into a square in Antratsyt, a small town about five miles from Krasnyy Luch. As we pulled up outside a white building on a square in the middle of town, a large crowd of young, well-dressed men walked forward. 'Oh shit,' said Charley, 'I think there's a welcoming committee.'

They wanted nothing more than a few autographs. While we happily signed some postcards, I noticed a small, slight man, smart in a leather jacket and with neat black hair and a thick dark moustache, lurking at the back. This young Robert de Niro lookalike stepped into a brand new silver BMW M5 coupé, the only western car we'd seen in a town full of Ladas, and sped off in a cloud of dust. Pointing urgently in the same direction, Vladimir jumped into his police Lada and drove off in hot pursuit.

'What's going on?' I asked Charley. 'Is this cool? Is this all right?'

'Yeah, I think it's fine,' Charley said. 'I think we're staying with this other guy.'

We followed the dude in the silver BMW through the backstreets of the town. Judging by the way he was driving, he seemed to have the run of the place. Traffic lights, pedestrians and other vehicles were ignored. 'He's definitely the Dudemeister in this area,' Charley said over the intercom.

'I have to say I'm a little jumpy about this,' I replied.

'You nervous?'

'I just don't know what we're letting ourselves in for,' I said as we passed through a neighbourhood of shabby pavements and rundown houses.

'Look at that house! That beautiful one on the corner,' Charley shouted over the intercom. 'Look at that . . . oh my fucking God, it's his house and it's enormous.'

Solid steel gates parted in front of us. Behind a high concrete wall was a carefully maintained compound and, at its centre, a modern house the size of a small mansion. We drove in.

'You think this is going to be okay, Charley?' I asked over the intercom.

'Yeah, I think it'll be fine. They've obviously told a few people that you're coming. Looks like you've got a little entourage there. I think it's going to be fine . . .'

6
Mansion on the hill

ANTRATSYT

CHARLEY: Inside the compound, the dude with the BMW had already jumped out of his car and was directing us to park in a large, empty garage. As we climbed off our bikes, he threw an arm around our shoulders, introduced himself as Igor and beckoned us to follow him out to his driveway. Facing his front garden, an untidy expanse of dirt that was about to be landscaped, Igor stood like a general surveying his troops on a battlefield. 'My house,' he said. 'Your house.'

The big steel gates to the road swung closed and Igor introduced us to Gala, his wife, his teenage daughter and some of the other people standing around, and explained how he came to be there.

'So you were on the ships?' I said. 'Sailing around the world? A seaman.'

'Peru . . . Argentina. I'm three years submarines and twelve years seaman, industrial fisherman.'

'Submarine? Wow.'

'Yes. Atlantic. Soviet Union Atlantic patrol,' he said as he ushered us up a flight of marble stairs into his home. Gala stood giggling, a hand over her mouth, while we removed our stinking boots, embarrassed that we had to expose these complete strangers to what smelled like rotting fish smothered in vinegar. Igor led us up to the first floor and then climbed a spiral staircase to a large attic room where Vladimir, our first policeman friend, explained he had brought us to Igor after his wife had said we couldn't stay at his house.

'You sleep here. All your room,' Igor said. With wooden ceilings and floors, it was an impressive space that occupied the entire third floor of the house. There were a few pieces of furniture, some easy chairs and a chest of drawers, and, hanging from its strap in the corner, a machine gun.

'Great Voor,' Igor said proudly, pointing at the tommy-gun. 'Great Voor . . . two!' He pulled back the bolt and squeezed the trigger. The gun gave a clunk then a click. Ewan and I let out a quiet sigh of relief. It wasn't loaded.

Igor smiled and nodded at the gun. 'Partisans,' he said. 'Russian freedom fighters.'

EWAN: We changed out of our sticky motorbike kit, showered and went downstairs, where Igor was holding court in the large whitewashed kitchen. With his dark hair greased back, his bushy moustache and olive skin, Igor could have passed for an Italian. Dressed in black shirt and trousers with razor-sharp creases, and leaning back against a kitchen cabinet, he looked like a young Robert de Niro in *The Godfather Part II*, a look I think he probably cultivated.

'Sit down,' Igor said, gesturing to a kitchen table covered by a chequered green and white tablecloth. Wine, coffee and water were poured and photographs handed round as Igor recounted tales of his life aboard a Soviet submarine. A friend and his daughter had been summoned to fill the gaps in his broken English.

'Me in submarine,' he said, passing a photograph to me. 'With Kalashnikov.' All of the photos were of Igor. And in all of them he was holding a gun. The next picture showed Igor on the deck of a submarine, a rifle strapped to his back and an arc of water spraying from a hose held between his legs. 'Our submarine,' Igor said, laughing at the picture. 'Name: *Exxon*.'

While Gala cooked behind him, Igor explained his past. He had been a turbine mechanic on the Atlantic submarine patrols from 1981 to 1984. For three months at a time he was incarcerated in a nuclear submarine fitted with a top-secret sonar system, patrolling the Atlantic at the height of the Cold War. Then he joined the merchant navy, working for fifteen years in the Soviet fishing fleet. At some point, he'd been a miner and there had also been a year's unemployment when he first came back home.

Another picture showed Igor in a band. All the musicians wore sailor's uniforms of open-necked wide-collared blue shirts trimmed with two white stripes. 'Much drunk,' he laughed, rocking on his heels. 'Soviets . . .' he added as if no other explanation was necessary.

Then Igor showed us a photograph of himself standing in front of a Soviet propaganda poster. A gorilla-like American soldier was charging out of the picture, his bayoneted rifle thrust in front of him and his teeth gritted, yelling as he stamped on a globe of the world. The enemy, hell-bent on international domination, was quite clearly the message. 'Crazy times,' Igor shrugged. 'You eat?'

'Uh . . . do you want to eat?' we said, unsure of the correct protocol. 'Are you going to eat? Shall we all . . .?'

'It's simple,' Igor said. 'Are you hungry?'

'Yes,' Charley and I chimed in unison.

'Then eat.'

At that moment, the doorbell rang. Sitting with my back to the dark wood door, I turned around to be confronted by a broad, tough-looking man. He had a sleepy eye and swollen bruiser's hands, one of which he was offering to me. We shook hands. 'Vladimir,' he said, his deep voice booming.

'Ewan,' I replied, trying not to gulp. I turned back to the room.

Charley was sitting opposite me, his eyes widening, pupils dilating as he stared over my shoulder.

'He's taking off his gun,' Charley whispered.

'What?'

'He's . . . taking . . . off . . . his . . . *gun*,' Charley hissed. I was immediately frightened. I didn't know what we thought we were doing in that kitchen or even exactly where that kitchen might be. All I knew for sure was that I was in a house where I'd already seen a machine gun. Now a man built like a bull was taking off his handgun and putting it down right behind me. Resisting the urge to whirl around and stare at it, I sat absolutely still, waiting for an excuse to steal a glance.

More men arrived, all with bulges under their jackets or sweaters. Menacing men who would be even more intimidating in other circumstances, but who were on best behaviour in Igor's house. A small guy with a shaved head walked in. A real hard nut. I could see the butt of his pistol poking out beneath the hem of his sweater as he leant forward with a thin-lipped half-smile to shake my hand. As he turned to face Charley, I caught Charley's eye. We both glanced at the gun, then at each other, knowing what the other was thinking. A few hours earlier, we'd been on the open road, heading for the Russian border. Now we were in a room surrounded by men with heavy-duty weaponry, while the top dog's wife cooked us dinner in the background. I felt very ill at ease.

Vladimir sat down and cracked the seal on a bottle of vodka, the bottle tiny in his enormous hands. Pouring out a round of shots, he started to talk.

'We could show you around tomorrow,' he said. 'We could go hunting. You like to hunt? Or we could take you down a coal mine. I work in the mine . . .'

'Yes, you must stay here for two days,' Igor interjected. 'You must see the mine.'

I sensed that Charley was becoming as nervous as I was and I just wanted to get the fuck out of that house.

'We need to wait and see what our producers have to say,' I

said. 'They are on the way here. We have to cross the border tomorrow and we need to consult them.'

And there were plenty of troubling questions. We were surrounded by tooled-up men who said they worked in the coal industry, but why would a miner carry a gun? It didn't seem right. And why was Igor's house so big in a neighbourhood of shacks and small houses? What was going on?

'Let's start with cheers,' said one of the heavy-set men, lifting his glass. As we all raised our glasses, I seized the opportunity to look behind me. There, sitting on a stool, was Vladimir's holster and a 9mm pistol. And Vladimir apparently worked at a coal mine.

'So you used to be a sailor, Igor,' Charley said. 'What do you do now?'

'I met you by my shop,' Igor replied. 'I sell electrical appliances. Kettles. Fridges.' Judging by the mansion and its swimming pool, it must have been an extremely successful business. Igor certainly commanded respect from every man in the room. The more people arrived, the more he appeared to be the person in charge. The local big cheese. Maybe it was no coincidence that our search for a bed for the night had led us to his house.

'Do you know Madonna?' Gala asked.

'Erm, sorry to disappoint you,' I said, 'but no, I don't.' We couldn't understand a word of Ukrainian, but we soon picked up the vibe. Hollywood was mentioned several times. So was *Moulin Rouge*, and gradually I realised that maybe we weren't in quite as much danger as I had initially thought. Our arrival was quite clearly an event. Nevertheless, I couldn't dispel my unease. I still didn't really know what was going on. And although I found it exciting, I also felt very uptight.

Igor sat down at the table. 'Why you do this journey?' he asked. 'What for? Who for?'

'It's just to go round the world,' I said. 'To see something different. To meet other people. Like you.'

'You are interested in travel? You find it interesting?' Igor was perplexed.

'Yes, very interesting. Every day we meet new people. We met you today. We're in your house now. That's very interesting.'

'For me, there is nothing interesting in travel. I have done it enough.'

'Maybe when we've finished this trip, we will have had enough of travelling, too. I think we reach that point by the time we reach Magadan,' I said.

'You are going to Magadan?' Igor raised his eyebrows. 'That is very strong.'

'Because it's far away? Or because you have to be strong to get there?'

'No. Magadan very serious.'

'What do you mean? Very serious?'

'The weather is serious. The land is very serious. Magadan very serious place.'

Wherever we went, there was a sharp intake of breath from the locals whenever we mentioned the next destination on our itinerary. In the Ukraine, they said Russia was dangerous. In Russia, they said it was Kazakhstan. The Kazakhs warned us of the perils of Mongolia. And in Mongolia, as everywhere else, we heard the same refrain when we asked about Siberia: You don't want to go there.

'You come to coal mine tomorrow.' It was Vladimir, becoming more insistent with every glass of vodka and rekindling our unease about our host. We didn't want to cut our visit short, but the guns made us nervous.

'We'll see what our producers suggest,' Charley said.

'You are not here alone?' one of the heavies said, picking up on the conversation.

'How will others find you?' asked the hard nut with the shaved head.

'When are your friends coming?' another said.

'Have you spoken to them? How will your friends find house?' said Vladimir.

'The policeman will show them the way,' Charley said. 'You know, the policeman that brought us here.'

'How long have you known the policeman?' I asked Igor.

'The policeman? I don't really know him,' Igor shrugged.

His reply took us aback. How come the policeman had brought us to Igor's house when they didn't even know each other? 'You must know him,' Charley said. 'I thought you were friends.'

'No, I don't. Really,' Igor said nonchalantly. 'You know, it's small town and I know everybody and everybody knows me.' He turned to the other men in the room and spoke in Russian. They roared with laughter.

'What did Igor say?' Charley asked the guy who had been translating.

'He made joke about how they wouldn't have any problem finding the house because everybody knows what this house is,' he said.

Igor cut in. 'Everybody knows how to find this place,' he said with a flamboyant smile. 'It's mafia centre of town. Everyone knows how to find mafia house.' There was a brief silence and then the room filled with more raucous laughter while Charley and I stared at each other, trying hard not to show our nerves. 'We're just kidding,' Igor said. 'Just kidding.'

'And he,' Igor added, pointing at the hard nut with the shaved head and the gun poking out from beneath his sweater, 'he is in Ukrainian anti-terrorist squad.'

The laughter stopped.

Again I didn't know what to think. The longer the evening went on, the more I felt we shouldn't be there. Just as the tension was becoming too much to bear, there was a loud knock at the door and David walked in. The support crew had arrived. Charley and I leapt up and threw our arms around them, relieved to see Sergey, Vasiliy, Jim and David. We followed them outside to where the trucks were standing in the drive, looking reassuringly impressive. While helping them unload the trucks, we briefed them on what had gone on. 'You won't believe it,' Charley said to David. 'Igor's fucking amazing. And there are guns everywhere.' David just stared back as if to say: what have you let yourselves in for?

Ewan and Claudio on a fishing boat on the Caspian Sea. Claudio, our cameraman, was the unsung hero of the trip.

A caviar fisherman.

Charley and a curious camel.

At the Singing Dunes in Kazakhstan. Ewan is right at the top, in the distance.

A quiet moment and a
rare stretch of good road.

Ewan in Charyn Canyon, just past Almaty. By now we'd been travelling for four weeks.

Charley in Kazakhstan, nearing the Russian corridor that links Kazakhstan with Mongolia.

Near Gorno-Altaysk, Russia. This was the first night the whole team camped together, and it helped dispel the inevitable tensions of the previous weeks. From left to right: Vasiliy; Charley; David; our Russian 'fixer' Sergey; Russ; Ewan; second unit cameraman Jim, and Claudio.

The same night, relaxing by the fire.

Ewan crashes out on the Russian border.

By the time we reached the Mongolian border we were absolutely exhausted.

A change from the bikes.

Many Mongolian families still
live a nomadic life in gers
(also known as yurts in other
parts of the world).

Russ and Vasiliy were both in this support vehicle when it crashed – rolling over twice. Amazingly, no one was seriously hurt.

Another breakdown. Claudio rode most of the trip on a BMW, but travelled through part of Mongolia on a temperamental bike we nicknamed the 'Red Devil'.

(Above) Ewan arriving at White Lake. It had been our goal for ten days, over very rough terrain. There were times in Mongolia when we felt we couldn't go on, but in the end it turned out to be one of the most rewarding parts of the trip.

Then, excited about introducing the team to our new friends, and relieved to have some back-up, we went inside where Igor's wife had set up a huge dining table in the hallway, laden with bottles of vodka, bowls of rice, chicken and lamb, and a baked cheese dish.

Regularly punctuated by speeches and toasts, much of the dinner was spent on our feet, chinking glasses and throwing back shots of vodka, or in my case, water. Vladimir, who was drinking more than anyone else and was in charge of the drinks, had developed a tic on his lip. Meanwhile, Igor made a series of welcoming speeches. The hospitality was overwhelming, particularly as they had known us only a few hours. It brought home the bizarre randomness of the experience. As a result of being stopped for speeding, we were now in a mansion in the wilds of the Ukraine, being feted like long-lost family members. We were total strangers and we got a three-course dinner and beds for us and our four friends. If someone dropped in to my gaff in London like that, they wouldn't get the same treatment.

More people arrived, most of them men and all wanting to shake our hands and to examine the bikes in the garage. At the end of the meal, Igor, who had spent most of the meal taking phone calls or standing in the kitchen, talking intently with a squint-nosed man in a double-breasted suit, ushered us outside.

'When I was in navy, I dreamed of building house,' he said as we stood in his garden smoking cigarettes, 'and for ten years I have known people will come to this house from far, far away. Now you are here.' He paused. 'My home is your home. Is not my home. Is your home. I am guest.'

Our cigarettes finished, we returned inside where Igor showed us his wife's walk-in wardrobe with a wall of shoes eight shelves high and Vladimir related the tale behind a wild pig's head fixed to the wall. 'Three days I wait in tree for pig,' he said. 'Then I shoot it with Beretta.' It was his proudest hunting moment, he said, picking up another glass of vodka and draining it in one gulp. Turning to Charley, he said 'Watch this' and then balanced the empty glass on his lips. He jerked his head. The glass spun off his chin. Vladimir lunged to catch it, but missed. Tumbling to the floor, the glass smashed into tiny pieces, silencing the room. Vladimir looked embarrassed, swaying slowly while half a dozen of his associates scurried around him, tidying up the glass. 'Come outside,' he said to Charley, his voice slow and slurred. Charley followed him out of the kitchen door, a few of the other men trailing in their wake.

Dinner over, only a few of us remained in the kitchen, chatting and drinking. Charley, Vladimir, our doctor Vasiliy and a bunch of heavies were outside. Igor was nowhere to be seen. Hearing footsteps behind me, I turned around. My heart skipped a beat as I realised Igor was coming down the stairs, laughing manically, a guitar held aloft in his left hand and a Kalashnikov in his right. David had frozen in mid-movement, his mouth open wide. I knew what he was thinking: Igor is gonna fucking mow us down.

Igor swung the Kalashnikov around, snapping out the stock with a loud, metallic twanging sound. 'Ffffbbbbing' it went.

The room reverberated with a twang as the butt of the gun snapped into place, a sound I will never forget. Grinning wildly, Igor cocked the machine gun, shouted 'Please! Please!' and squeezed the trigger. I felt my guts churn. The gun clicked. The chamber, as far as I could tell, was empty. Or was that normal for a gun? Would the bullet follow with the next click?

'Welcome! Welcome!' Igor boomed. We all laughed nervously as Igor delighted in the sheer thrill of the spectacle. 'Here!'

And then I found myself with the machine gun in my hands. Sergey, who was sitting on my right, gently took it from me, glanced in the magazine and peered down the barrel, and, satisfied they were empty, handed it back.

'Oh yeah . . . oh yeah . . . made in Russia . . . nice . . . that's a nice gun,' I said, stuck for words. After all, what do you say to someone who's just come downstairs brandishing a Kalashnikov?

Pap! Pap! Pap! Pap! Four gunshots cracked in the garage just outside the kitchen door, the garage that Charley had entered less than a minute earlier. 'Oh my God,' I whispered. I looked at David. He was as white as a sheet. Not wanting to believe anything had happened to Charley, my first reaction was to assume there was an innocent explanation. Knowing I mustn't be seen to lose my cool, and telling myself Charley would be all right, I wandered as casually as I could out to the garage.

CHARLEY: Brandishing a Kalashnikov, Ewan burst out of the kitchen door, closely followed by David. For a split second, I thought everything was about to go horribly wrong: the heavies would assume Ewan, having heard the gunshots, had imagined I'd been wasted and had seized a loaded machine gun to shoot his way out of the compound. With so much armoury in circulation, the potential for unintentional carnage was enormous if anyone misread the situation.

Ewan scanned the area and spotting me, healthy, alive and not lying on the ground in a pool of blood, smiled and immediately relaxed. But David was another story. He looked like a cornered animal, caught between fight and flight. 'Charley, my heart stopped beating,' he said, throwing his arms around me. 'I thought you'd been fucking blootered.'

We'd been standing in a small group outside the garage, just by the kitchen door. Vladimir and some of the heavies had been showing off their guns. '*That's* not a gun,' Vladimir had said, pointing at one of his associate's weapons and pulling his pistol out of its holster. Doof! Doof! Doof! Doof! He fired four rounds in the air. To them it was innocent fun, but to us it was more telling than anything we'd seen so far. Igor and his friends clearly didn't need to worry about letting off their guns in a heavily built-up neighbourhood. Nobody went 'Oh my God, what are the neighbours going to think' or 'Oh shit, the police will come'. Nothing. To them, it was just a silly bit of fun.

One of the things that had slightly worried me before we set out was that maybe nothing much would happen We'd leave London, we'd go round the world and arrive in New York and that would be it. But since we'd left it had been one thing after another. Every single day. A border crossing that took fourteen hours. Now, a house full of guns and guitars. 'It's insane, man,' Ewan said, a broad smile cracking his face. 'We had dinner, usually people then bring in some coffee, but Igor brought in a fucking machine gun.'

EWAN: We went back inside to find Igor standing halfway up the stairs and waiting for our return. Lifting his left foot up one step, he stood askew, his guitar clutched to his chest. He then launched into the most dramatic folk song imaginable, clicking his fingers, wailing dramatically, plucking the strings, then strumming them manically. It was a *tour de force*, a passionate peasant song delivered at full throttle.

Igor had the most incredible natural, rich tenor. Quite wonderful. Watching him, I experienced a variety of emotions. I admired him for his chutzpah, his love of life and his hospitality. But at the same time he scared me to death. Igor was singing a beautiful song and I just felt all over the place. Ill at ease, but kind of safe. I wasn't scared that something was going to happen to us but I was uneasy about the true nature of Igor's activities. And I couldn't help wondering why all his associates were carrying guns. Jamie Lowther-Pinkerton had warned us that we'd come across a lot of locals carrying AK47s when we were out in the cuds, but somehow the Ukraine felt a bit too close to home for everyone to be tooled up.

At the end of the song, we all applauded, whooped, shouted and laughed. Igor promptly launched into the next song, a real tear-jerker. Although we couldn't understand the lyrics, we were carried along by Igor's passion and his fantastic voice. At times intense and powerful, then suddenly tender and soft, his singing was so overwhelming that we forgot to clap when he finished. Instead, Igor applauded us and handed me the guitar.

I felt too shy to sing. 'I don't think it's going to come,' I said. I wished I had Igor's balls. Mind you, he had a Kalashnikov when he came down the stairs with his guitar. Eventually it came and I sang a couple of songs, 'Running to Stand Still' by U2 and 'Famous Blue Raincoat' by Leonard Cohen. Afterwards, Charley and I went outside for a cigarette. We could hear Igor still singing inside. 'I'm feeling really good,' I said. 'On the one hand there's an element of not knowing what the fuck is going on, but at this point I don't know if that's because of me or them.'

'They're being incredibly friendly,' Charley said. 'I think they genuinely want to show us around tomorrow and I don't think we should miss the chance.'

We were playing the polite British card. Not wanting to cause any trouble and 'I'll have a coffee only if you're making one'. But I could see the respect in which everyone held Igor. He was in charge. He was the head of something, but we just didn't quite know what. And in the face of his incredible generosity, I was still unable to shake off that nagging doubt about what Igor might want from me. That stupid London suspicion that shuts out so much.

Charley and I watched our warm breath condensing in the cold night air. 'It really is freezing,' Charley said. 'Look, I've got goose pimples.'

'My mum would die if she could see us now. Out in T-shirts on a cold night and, behind us, a house jammed to the rafters with guns,' I said. 'She wouldn't sleep for months if she knew – "You were in a house with guns!" – "No, mum . . . it was okay . . . really . . . Charley was there." What a voice though . . .'

We were tired and ready for bed. The strain of living on our nerves all evening had caught up with us. As if on cue, the owner of that magnificent voice stepped outside.

'It's your house,' Igor said. 'Sleep when you want to.'

The next morning, at breakfast in Igor's kitchen, Charley and I discussed the route ahead and whether to take up Igor's offer of a visit to a coal mine. We were happy to see the mine, but at the same time felt an urge to get moving. In the cold morning light, there was still something unexplained and therefore uncomfortable about being in the company of armed men, most of them nursing hangovers. I wanted to get on the move, but Charley thought the mine visit was an opportunity we shouldn't pass up, especially as we were not scheduled to cross the border until the next day.

'We need to leave at midday,' Charley told Igor. 'If we can visit the mine and get away before noon, then fine.'

'Let's go,' Igor said. 'You ride in my car.'

I sat in the front seat next to Igor. I immediately wished I was in the back with Charley. Igor drove in a way that was as lawless as the display of firepower the previous night.

'Too fast!' Charley yelled. It was even more alarming in the front. By the way Igor was driving, I could tell there was no question he would be stopped. We sped through busy crowded areas, where children and women were milling in the street. The climax of this very arrogant display of power and invincibility came as we approached an old man crossing the road. As the man reached the curb, Igor swerved directly towards him. For a moment I thought we were going to hit him. I didn't know if the old man was someone Igor knew or if he was someone he was trying to frighten, but it freaked the living daylights out of me. And all the while Igor drove at breakneck speed, he said nothing. The silence made it all the more menacing. Again, I didn't really feel threatened. I just felt uneasy.

The mine was much larger than I had expected. It had dozens of buildings, several mineshafts and a web of conveyor belts crisscrossing the complex. Vladimir, the vodka king with the sleepy eye and swollen hands, was waiting to take us on a tour. First stop was the goods yard, where the noise of train wagons being loaded was deafening. Then Vladimir took us indoors. We followed him into a stark, boxy office, long and narrow with an empty desk and a large portrait of a politician on the wall.

Insistent that no one except Charley and me came into the room, Vladimir shut the door behind us. What the fuck usually happens in here? I wondered. Vladimir sat down behind his desk and rocked back in his chair, smiling. We didn't know what to do. Then the penny dropped. He wanted us to take some pictures of him at his desk. It was his office and he just wanted us to see him at work in it.

CHARLEY: Vladimir took us to a tiled locker room and handed us miners' outfits. White linen long johns and vest, dark gabardine jacket and trousers, Wellington boots and a helmet. 'Just so that they don't get blood on our clothes when they cap us downstairs,' Ewan joked. I thought it made us look like waiters in an Indian restaurant.

'This is a bit embarrassing with all the miners watching,' Ewan said. 'We're a bunch of tourists doing this for fun, and for them it's work six days a week. Year in, year out for twenty years and then you get a pension that barely pays for your phone bill.'

'Bit of a shock to see what real people do for a living,' I said.

'Do I look all right in these pants?' Ewan said, smiling.

'Does this helmet bring out my eyes?' I asked.

Our larking around was interrupted by the foreman. Miming writing on the palm of his hand, he said something in Russian. Sergey translated. 'They want your names,' he said. 'In order when they make your graves they know what to put on the cross.' Sergey snorted his deadpan laugh.

'That's nice,' Ewan said nervously.

'Wicked sense of humour,' I added.

Our steel- and rubber-soled boots clanked against the stone floors and the noise reverberated off the tiled walls as we clomped our way to the pit cage. For Ewan, who had played a Yorkshire miner in *Brassed Off*, the ritual was a familiar one. 'When you get in the cage, the door shuts and you just start to drop, it's the most peculiar feeling,' he said. 'It really is a very claustrophobic moment. I just hope I don't freak out. That'd be embarrassing, wouldn't it? In front of everyone. Help! Let me out!'

Instead of a lift, the mine had a cage on rails that descended a very steep incline for almost a mile to the coal face. 'Keep your hands inside the vehicle. Keep your hands in,' Sergey shouted as the doors slammed shut.

'Imagine my agent now,' Ewan yelled as the driver released the brake. 'If she could see me . . .' The cage plummeted into the earth with a roar which sounded like the afterburners on a fighter jet engine. Perched at the front of the rickety carriage, gazing into darkness, our ears popping as the cage picked up speed, we hung on for dear life. The cage tilted forwards as the descent became steeper and six minutes later we came to a shuddering halt.

The mine, we were told, had been well known throughout the old Soviet Union for the quality of its coal. Soviet bureaucrats had renamed the town Antratsyt, the Ukrainian word for anthracite, to commemorate its huge reserves of this most valuable type of coal. But underground, the pit was staggeringly primitive. Packs of a dozen men were pushing ten-ton trucks of coal along railway lines. There was no lighting except for the lamps on the miners' helmets. All around, tunnel walls had crumbled and their roofs collapsed. In western Europe, the mine would have been condemned but in the Ukraine it was business as usual, the black-faced miners dressed in the same outfits as us, albeit with leather shoulder and elbow pads for those pushing the trucks. With no ventilation, the lack of oxygen left us completely drained after a mere forty minutes, yet the miners endured six-hour shifts in the same conditions. Back at the surface, we passed a shower room with a dirty, black, stone floor, the pipes dripping and the tiles cracked. Dilapidation reigned. As with the agricultural scenes in western Ukraine, it was like stepping back into the nineteenth century. An unbelievable, overwhelming glimpse into a very different world so close to home.

*

EWAN: Back at Igor's house, Gala had made lunch. Again a massive spread. Again a lot of heavies hanging around. And again a long series of vodka toasts. 'We will always remember Ukraine with great fondness,' I said, my glass of water held high. 'So we toast you and we thank you.'

Igor got to his feet and delivered a long speech, culminating in a toast. 'They thank you for the chance to meet you,' Sergey translated.

I recognised a young guy in a black pinstriped suit with a striking face from when we had met Vladimir the policeman the previous afternoon. Then he had been wearing workman's overalls and driving an old rusty van. Now he was immaculately dressed and standing in Igor's kitchen. He made a speech explaining he had been on the way to hospital when we had last seen him. That night, as we were in the middle of our guns and vodka orgy, his son had been born. 'I will always remember you because I met you the day I first met my boy,' he said. And another vodka shot was thrown back. Later, as we were packing our bikes in the garage and signing autographs, he came over and told me he'd spent five years fighting in Afghanistan. Then he lifted his jacket to show me his gun under his beautiful suit. 'Oh yeah,' I said, 'very nice.'

One of the heavies from the previous night turned up. One of the quieter revellers, a judo and karate fanatic who seemed very sure of himself, he pulled two beautiful necklaces from beneath his clothes and gave them to Charley and me. Placing one of the chains and pendants in my hand, he squeezed my hand closed around it. It felt warm and worn, as if he'd had it around his neck for a very long time. 'This for you,' he said in broken English. 'This to give you good luck because your journey is so great, so big.'

It took us about half an hour to leave. Every family member, friend and associate of Igor had to be hugged and kissed. All the younger children begged to sit on our bikes and Igor's daughter and her three friends wanted autographs. Finally, Igor handed us pictures of himself impeccably groomed in a black suit with a black shirt and a black silk tie with a few thin white diagonal stripes on it. 'Which border crossing you go?' he said. 'I make call. You have no problems.'

We climbed on the bikes and pulled away. As we turned the corner out of Igor's compound, I sighed with relief. We'd made it.

We roared down the road, whooping loudly to release a day's pent-up tension. 'Fucking hell, Charley,' I shouted over the intercom. 'I don't know what that was all about, and part of me loved it, but doesn't it feel great to get away?'

But I'd spoken too soon. As we approached the outskirts of Antratsyt, I spotted one of Igor's heavies following us. It was the quiet guy with the big broken nose, driving a car with blacked-out windows. 'Fuck . . .' I shouted. 'Charley, why are we being followed?'

My mind went into overdrive. It was just like the movies. They'd wined us and dined us, now we were being pursued to the edge of town. Who knew what would happen there?

I watched the squinty-nosed guy in my rear-view mirror. Then another car appeared, driven by one of Igor's associates who had chauffeured the support team to the mine. Was he the back-up? He shot past us, pulled into the side of the road and flagged us down.

'You wait here,' he said. 'Igor wants to see you.'

And I thought: Oh God, what's going on now? Let's just get out of here before anything awful happens.

A BMW appeared in the distance. It was Igor. The seconds ticked slowly by while we waited for the car to approach and come to a screaming halt. Igor got out.

'You forgot this,' he said to Charley, handing him some photographs of himself at a family gathering and another of him holding the tommy-gun from the attic above his head. We'd left them on the dining-room table after breakfast.

'Thank you so much for all your hospitality,' I said. I couldn't stop thanking him enough.

Igor pulled his BMW out in front of us and raced off. I slotted in behind him, following in his slipstream. We drove about half a mile beyond the city limits. Then Igor sped ahead and swung his car into a 180-degree turn, blue clouds of tyre smoke and dust enveloping it. He came firing back towards us, horn blaring, headlights blazing. As he passed by, I stood up on my pegs, shaking a clenched fist above my head and shouted. '*Yeaaaaaaaahhhhhh!* Bye fucking bye!'

In one respect I was genuinely very fond of Igor. He'd been so kind to us. And I admired him for what he had been through on the submarines, as a fisherman and afterwards, when he had been unemployed for a year. But ultimately, despite his extraordinary hospitality, I was relieved to leave his house. For my liking, there had been too many guys showing their side arms.

CHARLEY: About an hour later we were at the Russian border. It took us fourteen hours to enter the Ukraine and only fifteen minutes to leave. We'll never know whether that was the result of Igor's phone call, but the border guards were waiting for us. Our passports and customs documents were given only a cursory glance. The guards were more interested in admiring the bikes, collecting autographs and having their pictures taken with us, insisting we wore their high, red-rimmed, gold-braided caps. It was more photo call than immigration check.

'You!' one of the guards said to me. 'You. Do this!' He revved an imaginary motorbike and lifted his hands. He wanted a wheelie. I was only too happy to oblige. I climbed on to my bike and hoicked a little wheelie on the tarmac in front of the guards' huts.

'No! Here!' the guard said, pointing through the border. I couldn't believe it. A member of one of the world's most uptight bureaucracies wanted me to wheelie across his nation's frontier. I swung the bike around, waved to the guards to clear the area close to the barrier and let rip. By the time I reached Russian soil, my front wheel was 3 feet in the air and I was doing 40mph. I banged the front wheel back down on the ground and looked back. One of the border guards was waving manically. Then he blew his whistle. Fuck, I thought, now you've really blown it, Charley.

The guard beckoned me to come back to the barrier. Slowly I rolled towards him, expecting to be torn from my bike and dragged into a dirty office for, at best, a severe dressing down.

'Again!' he said, smiling broadly and holding up his camera. He'd missed the shot and wanted another chance to take a picture. I revved the Beamer, a guard lifted the barrier and I roared through the border once more. It doesn't get much better than this, I thought as I popped an even longer wheelie into the world's largest country. First the night of guns and vodka with Igor; now in all likelihood I'd become the first person to execute a motocross stunt into the former USSR. Roll on Russia.

7

Death, war and pride

BELAYA KALITVA TO AKTOBE

EWAN: After a day and night in the company of Igor and his associates, it was a delight to be back on the road. The bikes greedily ate up the smooth Russian roads and we enjoyed every mile of the journey. Charley sat high on the luggage roll that he had strapped behind his seat, put his feet out in front of him and larked around, dispelling the tensions of the previous twenty-four hours. By early evening we were in Belaya Kalitva, riding through row after row of Soviet-era apartment blocks on the way to our hotel. With its concrete corridors, Formica-clad doors, *Titanic*-era plumbing and multi-coloured bathroom tiles, the hotel was an assault on the senses, but I loved it. My bedroom had pine panelling, patterned carpets and orange curtains, sixties furniture including a Bakelite radio and a big white television, a tacky seaside print on the wall, a lacquered wardrobe and an orange nylon eiderdown on the bed. I was chuffed. It felt as if we really were somewhere else. 'We're in Russia for God's sake, Charley,' I said. 'I'm so excited and I love my room.'

Charley was exhausted and that night, over dinner, the strain of the previous few days began to show. He was very negative, cutting off Russ, David and Sergey in mid-sentence and handing out opinions as if they were facts. Then, as we talked about whether the journey would change our lives, he stood up. 'Fuck life changing,' he snapped. 'We're just a couple of wankers riding around the world on bikes.' Then he stormed off.

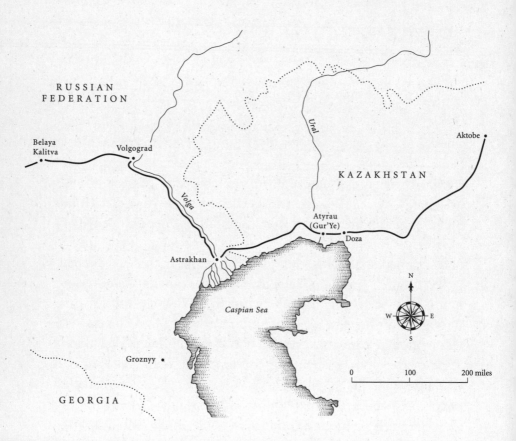

I certainly didn't feel like a wanker on a bike and the journey had already changed my outlook in many ways. I'd been touched by the lives of the many people we had seen and met. We were travelling through a part of the world that had experienced so much turmoil, where people's lives had been profoundly shaped by war and politics, and yet where they were still filled with so much pride, that I felt I couldn't avoid being affected by it. It had made me more aware than ever of my inherent suspicion of strangers and I'd vowed to shake it off. I knew similar emotions must have been running through Charley's mind. He was just letting his tiredness get in the way. The next day, as I watched Charley listen intently to a guide telling us about the Cossacks and their history of being persecuted and exploited by the tsars and the communists, I could see that he was moved by their attempts to rekindle a community. They had established a centre to give young Cossacks, many of whom were unemployed or had alcohol problems, a sense of their heritage. A young kid gave us a demonstration of Cossack riding skills, lying on his back on the horse as it galloped around an arena, making it bow and encouraging it to lift its front legs. There was an incredible affinity between the boy and the horse, and I could see it had made an impression on Charley. He even popped a little wheelie for the kid as we left.

We made for Volgograd, riding across a pancake-flat landscape, whipped by a harsh wind and harassed by the police. The police were only doing their job, but for us it was a hassle that considerably slowed our progress. Looking stern and sinister each time they walked towards us, the Russian police soon relaxed when we took off our helmets, smiled and spoke in English, showed our papers and used our maps to explain our journey ahead. Most of the time they weren't even interested in seeing our passports: they just wanted to have a look at the bikes and practise their English.

Even worse than the attentions of the police was the wind. With wide, open plains, there was no shelter and the gusts were exhausting. They buffeted my body and thumped my head, sending my bike veering sideways. Riding at a 45-degree tilt, the only relief came when we passed trucks. Then the wind would be interrupted and my head and neck were given a brief respite from being blown around until – boff! – the wind slammed back into us as we passed the front of the truck and we had to grapple with our bikes to make sure we weren't blown across the road. We were so desperate to reach our destination that we skipped lunch, which just made us all the more tired and the last forty miles a killer. I spent half the 170 miles to Volgograd riding with my eyes half-closed.

We stopped to fill up at a very primitive petrol station not far from Volgograd. Charley paid for 20 litres in advance but it wasn't enough to fill our two bikes, so he returned to the attendant's little hut to ask for the pump to be switched to free flow instead of a prepaid amount and continued filling his tank.

'Stop the pump!' It was Charley, beside me. I turned around. The fuel was pouring out of the top of Charley's tank, over his bike and along its blisteringly hot exhaust pipes.

'Fuck . . . the pump won't stop pumping petrol,' I shouted, watching Charley clamp his thumb over the top of the nozzle. A spray of petrol spurted out from beneath his thumb directly into my face.

'Aaah, my eyes,' I screamed as the fuel blinded me. The pain was immediate. Somehow I managed to grab a bottle of water. I poured it into my eyes. Fortunately, the support crew had pulled into the petrol station moments before this happened. Vasiliy grabbed me, checked my eyes and washed them.

'God the pain . . . I'm so sorry . . . It's just awful to see my mate . . . and your eyes . . . and pouring water . . . and it's something I've done.' It was Charley. In a flap. 'It's just horrible and I feel like, my God, it's my fault and what a fucking idiot I am. I'm so fucking clumsy and I'm fucking so stupid. You must be really pissed off with me and not only pissed off but the pain and . . . oh my God. I just didn't know what to do. And I'm completely freaked out.'

'Charley, it doesn't sting any more.'

'Oh . . . I'm really sorry, mate.'

'It's not your fault,' I said. 'I just got it straight in my eyes when you put your thumb over the nozzle. The Marx Brothers couldn't have done it any better.'

'Oh shit, I'm really sorry, mate.'

'Don't worry, it was an accident.' I'd been injured and I was having to console Charley.

'Well, at least the doctor finally got to do something,' he said. 'It was a tiny squirt . . .'

'Wasn't that tiny.'

'It was just so horrible for me.'

Horrible for him! I thought, still wiping my stinging eyes.

'I mean I was just panicking,' he continued. 'The petrol was just pouring out of my bike and all I could think about was what the fuck do I do to make it stop.'

'It's a lesson,' I said. 'If it happens again, we'll just throw the hose on the floor and let it pump petrol down there. It won't do any damage that way, will it?'

'Wasn't it fucking hard today?' Charley was changing the subject. 'The wind? It's like someone's pushing you in the side of the head all day long. It's given me a headache.'

'Ask the doctor for some painkillers.'

'I've got some Anadin Extra,' he said.

'Got any morphine?' I joked. 'Or maybe a pizza?'

'Phwoar! An American Hot from Pizza Express with extra cheese and a side salad.' Charley's tongue was hanging out.

'I'll take Pizza Express, too. Very good pizzas. A Margherita with anchovies and pepperoni. You can keep the salad. Just give me two pizzas.'

'I'm really salivating now,' Charley said. 'God that acid . . . my stomach . . .' And with that the incident was over and our minds refocused on the last few miles. When we reached Volgograd, Vasiliy took me to a clinic. We traipsed along several long corridors to the office of a female ophthalmologist. She put my head in a rig and told me to read some charts – not easy, considering the letters were Cyrillic. Afterwards, I waited in the corridor and rang a doctor in England. He had given me laser surgery to correct my short-sightedness so that I wouldn't have to wear glasses inside my helmet on the journey. He gave me some advice on the drugs the ophthalmologist had suggested and said that if I hadn't poured that water in my eye straightaway the petrol would have burned the cornea and I wouldn't have been able to ride my bike for a fortnight. It put the frighteners up me, although I was reassured that at a critical moment my instinct – to flush it out – had been right.

Vasiliy and I returned to the hotel, a former haunt of senior communist party cadres, the KGB and Politburo members when they were in town. Charley and I tossed a coin for our rooms, and having won, I found myself in a massive suite.

'I'm in the bed where Nikita Khrushchev used to sleep,' I told Charley, who had a tiny room.

'I hope they've changed the sheets,' he said.

We'd been allowed to stay in the hotel because it had secure parking, but it meant we were the only people in the building. The outside was shabby and decked in concrete tiles. Inside, however, it was amazing. Like many places in Russia and the Ukraine, it was stuck in a time warp, in this instance the late 1950s. There was a grand piano in the foyer, which I couldn't resist playing, and the telephones could have come straight out of *From Russia With Love*. We were shattered after the long, windy ride, so we ate early and went for a sauna across the road from the hotel in a *banya* used by generations of Russian leaders. Sweating in the steam rooms and being beaten with oak branches was just what we needed. We got back to the hotel to discover that Claudio had passed his motorbike riding test. Having failed the day before we left London, he'd flown back to Britain from Kiev, taken his test successfully and was now on his way to Volgograd. It was fantastic news. Now we could take on the most demanding part of the trip with a cameraman in tow instead of having to worry about how to film it ourselves.

The next morning we had a chat about the journey ahead. 'We're about to enter new territory,' I said, 'and it's where hotels won't be available. We are going to have to camp, prepare our own food and purify our own water. I just want to know if everyone's ready for that. Have we got the right stuff? Do we feel we're missing anything? Because, if we are, this would be a good time to replenish stocks.'

After breakfast we unpacked everything and repacked it. It was great. I'd long admired the BMW, but that morning I really fell in love with it. I was out in the car park with my iPod on, just tinkering with my bike, repacking panniers and fixing a minor breakage to my seat while the music played. I turned around as Charley came out. He also had his iPod and we had both had the same idea. It was lovely. Everyone was there. The support crew were checking the trucks and repacking them. Everything was shipshape and Bristol fashion. I couldn't have been happier.

I felt ready for the journey to get tougher. I was physically and mentally prepared, and looking forward to the challenge. My only concern was the relationship between Charley and me. At times it felt a bit strained, our special dynamic upset when we were with the support crew. The previous evening I'd looked at some footage of the three months we spent at Shepherd's Bush, preparing for the trip. I yearned for those easy days, when Charley and I laughed a lot. It felt so close then. But over the last week or so, things had changed. It felt as if Charley and I were standing apart, experiencing the trip separately instead of together. It was probably because of the stresses and strains of being away from our families and the growing realisation of the enormous undertaking that lay ahead. We'd been riding for two weeks and it had been relentless. Three hundred miles or more a day had become a regular occurrence. Stopping only to film or because we were hungry or because we were falling asleep on the bike made for long days. They were *great* days, but once we pulled on our helmets, they were *separate* days. It made me hanker after the 'bugger it' attitude that seemed to have been lost in the rigours and the sheer mind-boggling nature of being on the trip.

What worried me was that up until now it had been the easy

stuff. I knew we'd got some serious hardship ahead and when I thought back to the off-road training we did in Wales in February, when I had struggled behind Charley, I felt really frightened again. My spirits had been so low and I had lost my confidence on the training course. Already I could feel my stomach wobbling a bit at the prospect of the roads in Kazakhstan, Mongolia and Siberia. For me, those three names were at the heart of the experience and we'd only be able to relax again when they were behind us.

After preparing our bikes, we went sightseeing, taking a boat down the river, going go-karting and visiting the war memorials. We'd phoned our mothers the previous evening, and they both had something to say about Volgograd. My mother had done a geography project on the Volga for her Highers and at the time had wondered why because she thought she would never see it. She said I was seeing the enormous river for her, after all that time. Charley's mother, who is German, said she remembered teenagers heading off during the war to what was then called Stalingrad. She knew some of them and most didn't come back. The siege of Stalingrad was the bloodiest single battle in history. Up to two million people died, most of them Russians, but also a large number of Germans, Romanians and Italians. In the winter of 1943, prolonged street fighting and the destruction of 80 per cent of the buildings had reduced the population of Stalingrad to a primitive level of human misery and filth worse even than the First World War trenches. The Russians' only hope was to close in on the Germans and resort to hand-to-hand combat. The Germans called it *Rattenkrieg* – war of the rats. Even the sewers were fought over and close fighting went on for weeks inside the grain elevator, a huge silo where Soviet and German soldiers were so close that they could hear each other breathe. Starving, dehydrated and numbed by vodka, a platoon of the Russian army led by Sergeant Yakov Pavlov commandeered a three-storey building at the city centre. Surrounding it with mines, positioning machine guns in its windows and breaking down walls in the basement for supplies and communications, they turned it into an impenetrable fortress. Pavlov's masterstroke was to position an anti-tank gun on the roof of the building. Tanks approaching the building were unable to raise their guns high enough to hit the gun, which could pick off the Panzers with impunity. Pavlov held the building for fifty-nine days, when he was relieved shortly before the Russians launched a counteroffensive in the spring of 1943. The Germans were sent into retreat and for them it was the beginning of the end on the eastern front.

We stood beside what remains of Pavlov's House, a burnt-out corner of the apartment block that was a crucial turning point in the war, thinking about how the people we'd met along the way didn't seem any different from us, yet all the statues we'd passed in Slovakia, the Ukraine and Russia were monuments to battles or wars. There was always someone with a machine gun or a soldier or a working man toiling to arm the motherland. It seemed a shame that war was what we ended up commemorating both here and in the West.

CHARLEY: The next morning we left for Astrakhan. We passed a massive oil refinery and factories that stretched for hours along the route out of Volgograd, miles and miles of shitty factories and shitty rusting pipes giving way eventually to rows of small houses, allotments and then a smooth road across a wide open landscape following the Volga down to the Caspian Sea for the rest of the day. We stopped for a cigarette and a rest, watching a yellow-bellied black-backed snake shimmy across the ground at great speed. 'Isn't it lovely to cruise along, just gobbling up the miles,' I said to Ewan, while Claudio filmed nearby.

'I just can't get over that last piece of road,' Ewan said. 'Suddenly I was in the trip that I'd been dreaming about, I was riding along and I went: God, this is it, this is what I've been dreaming about all this time. Flat, flat, flat. No wind. A good road. It was phenomenal.'

The mood was great and remained that way even when we were stopped repeatedly by the police, Ewan playing the Obi-Wan card by showing them a picture of himself in *Star Wars*. They waved us through: bliss. The only downer came when we passed a car crash. Two guys, one with a bloodied head, were staggering out of an Audi that had crashed off the road into a ditch. The driver of the Lada, which was sitting in the middle of the road with a caved-in roof, was almost certainly dead. Passers-by were attending and we picked our way through the mess, hoping the drivers would be all right. It was a timely reminder of the consequences of the hazardous overtaking of which we'd seen so much. With drivers often trying to nudge us out of the way, it could quite easily have been one of us in that pile-up. I noticed we all tidied up our riding a little bit after seeing that.

The fertile plains turned into a sandy desert landscape, we spotted our first Kazakh faces and for the first time it felt as if we were really out in the cuds. 'Kazakhstan tomorrow,' I shouted to Ewan as we pulled up at the end of the day. 'The 'stan, man!' It was early evening and we were in Astrakhan, pulling up outside the hotel, where an attractive Russian woman was playing with her daughter, who with her Barbie doll clutched tightly in her little hand immediately triggered pangs of homesickness for our daughters. A man came out and spoke to the woman.

'I heard your voice,' Ewan said, 'and I'm thinking that sounds like a Scottish accent.'

'Och aye,' the man said. 'From Kirkcaldy.'

'Never. I spent a year at drama school there. What are you doing here?'

'Working on the oil.'

'Well, it's nice to meet you. We're doing a world tour. Northern hemisphere, that is.'

'Aye, I heard about it.'

'Did you? Well, we've made it this far.'

'That's excellent. It's the only hotel in town . . .'

'Is it?'

'Well, there's another couple of dodgy ones, but . . .'

'Well, I imagine this is our last hotel for a while. Do you know Kazakhstan?'

'I've been working in Kazakhstan for four years and we've just got a project here in the Caspian, so I'm really based in Kazakhstan, at Aralsk.'

'What's it like? We're heading down towards Almaty. Is it all right? I mean it's not . . . because you hear nasty stories.'

'It's like anywhere,' the Scot said. 'It's too big a place to be full of daft people. You can't have them round every corner.'

'That's good to know.'

'They're just getting on their feet and there's a long way to go, but they're nice people.'

'Well, it's been nice to meet you. Kirkcaldy boy as well. If I'm passing through Kirkcaldy, I'll let them know.'

'Cheers,' the Scot said. 'Hey, see ya later.' We'd ridden more than 2,800 miles and bumped into someone who, as Ewan put it, came from 'jooost arooond the corner'. Maybe the world was a smaller place than it seemed after long days in the saddle.

That night I watched a videotape that Claudio had brought from London and the first thing that struck me was that we'd lost the spark and fun that we had in the three months at Bulwer Street. Ewan could sometimes be very sensitive, taking things to heart a bit more than he should. I felt we just needed to lighten up a bit more. I knew it should be a part of the journey, having fun and joking around. But at that moment, with the stresses of riding long distances and missing my wife and my children, maybe it was more than either of us could muster.

The next morning we crossed the Russian border. As usual, we were not allowed to film at first. Then, five minutes later, the cameras were out and the guards were asking for autographs and having their pictures taken with Ewan, insisting that Ewan wore their high-rimmed caps and even signed their passports. We then had a five- or six-mile ride to a river in the Volga delta. There on the other shore was Kazakhstan. Just a short ferry ride separated Europe from Asia. The boat was large enough to carry two articulated trucks and us. On the European side there was a concrete purpose-built landing jetty; on the Asian side there was nothing. The captain powered the flat-bottomed craft on to a sandy ridge, opened the gate and we rode our bikes up the riverbank.

Already it felt very different. We passed through the Kazakh frontier, a row of shabby huts, and there in front of us was a welcoming committee. Eric, our local fixer, who we had met several times in London, was standing next to the mayor of the region. Two young women dressed in traditional outfits were holding trays of fermented camel's milk. It tasted fizzy, like carbonated goat's yoghurt. I struggled a bit to swallow it. Fortunately they also gave us little pieces of cake that took away the taste, but God it was horrible. The formalities over, a police car accompanied us from the border to lunch with the mayor, where they tried to force vodka on us. With ambitions of riding more than two hundred miles to Atyrau, we had no choice but to make our excuses and to ask for a quick lunch as we were in a hurry. While we waited, some folk singers appeared. A woman with a guitar, two more women in national costume and a man in a dark suit with a balalaika and a penchant for clapping kept us entertained. And then came the tea. Really good tea, just like British tea. It was glorious, like being at home. 'Is the tea always this good?' I asked the mayor.

Eric translated his reply: 'Tea for breakfast. Tea for lunch. Tea for dinner. If he doesn't have tea, a Kazakh man will die.'

'So how far is it to Almaty?' I asked. The town was our next major stop.

'More than three thousand kilometres,' said Eric.

'Wow. Three thousand kilometres to Almaty. Jesus!' It was two-thirds the distance we had ridden so far. We were closer to Prague than we were to Almaty, the former capital and the commercial heart of the country.

'For half the route, the roads are okay,' Eric said. 'But from Atyrau to the Aral Sea they're really bad.'

'Bad roads?' Ewan said. 'Bad roads are good roads to us.'

The mayor insisted we had a police escort all the way to Atyrau, our destination that evening. After a long negotiation, he gave in and we set off. We had a target of two hundred miles a day, but immediately the road turned into a rough dirt track, covered in gravel, a nightmare for motorbikes. There were short sections of tarmac, but they were so heavily potholed that they were at times worse than the dirt track. 'Look at the roads, man,' I said over the intercom. 'Careful on that sand.'

'Two hundred miles a day?' Ewan replied. '. . . Hmmm.'

If this was the way the roads would be ahead then, frankly, I was petrified. I had not expected the roads to be *this* bad straightaway. And according to Eric, these roads were good. They'd get much worse later. I felt overwhelmed.

'Jesus, this is gonna be absolutely exhausting.' It was Ewan on the intercom. 'We've gone about ten minutes into Kazakhstan and I'm already knackered. How is everyone? All right? Claudio? Are you okay, Claudio? You lead, Charley.'

'Beg your pardon?' I said.

'You go in front, please,' Ewan said. 'Do you want to?'

'You go ahead,' I said. 'I'm quite happy here.'

'Oh, go on . . .'

EWAN: We pressed on carefully. About fifteen miles into Kazakhstan, the road disappeared altogether and we had to bump down a slope on to a scrappy track, which we followed until the tarmac road reappeared several miles later. Jesus, I thought, we've got to cover large distances in this country and it's taking too long. We'd expected much better conditions. My stomach knotted with a sinking, sick feeling as I realised we were going to be in big trouble.

The landscape, however, was magnificent. An endless emptiness. We passed our first camel, standing in the middle of the road and staring at us as we passed by. It had a ring through its nose to signify that it was owned by someone and it was hobbled to prevent it straying. Not a pleasant way to treat an animal.

'Let's stop.' It was Claudio, as usual wanting to film. We pulled over. While Claudio got his camera ready, Charley and I larked around, pretending to be David Attenborough.

'Here we are in deepest Kazakhstan,' Charley whispered in David Attenborough's breathy manner. 'And right behind me is a very rare camel. *Camel camelodocus.*' Plop! The camel, unfazed by our antics, dropped some shit on the road.

'I scared it shitless,' I joked. We looked around. We were surrounded by desert. There were a few shabby buildings to one side, but otherwise there was nothing. Our bikes were parked side by side, the gravel road stretching into the distance. 'Jeez, doesn't that look great,' I said. 'It's like the cover of Ted Simon's book.' Ted's book, *Jupiter's Travels*, had been my inspiration for this trip. I'd read his tale of taking four years in the early 1970s to ride a bike around the world and it had made a big impression. The cover had a picture of Ted leaning over the handlebars of his 500cc Triumph Tiger on a dirt track somewhere in Africa. 'It's perfect,' I said, pointing at the bikes. 'It says it all. Let's take a picture.'

Claudio put down his video camera while Charley and I positioned ourselves in front of the bikes. 'You know, we should make sure we stay out here, just us alone,' I said. 'You, me and Claudio. No support crew. Always just us. By ourselves. It's much better this way.'

We waited for a lorry to pass. Then a white Lada appeared from behind Claudio and stopped right next to him. There were two men in the front and two in the back.

'*Zdravstvuite*,' we said – hello in Russian. The men inside the Lada smiled back. The driver opened his door, looked down at the camera and then up at Claudio. Just as I was about to launch into our spiel about going round the world on a bike, one of the guys who was hunkered down in the back seat, his jacket riding up around his shoulders, pulled out a gun, pointed it at Charley, then at me. I could see straight down the barrel. He held it there, pointed directly at me for what felt like ages. Oh fuck, I thought, oh no. I didn't have a clue what was going to happen. I thought they might want the video camera or they might want to rob us, or worse. Then the guy with the gun burst out laughing. I could see two rows of gold teeth. The driver slammed the front door shut and they sped off, leaving me shaking like a leaf. To that man, it was no more than a harmless joke. For me, it had been a threat to my life.

'*Jeeez . . . us.*' It was Charley, tapping his chest as if to say: that gave me a fucking heart attack.

'It was really weird,' Claudio said, laughing. He thought it was hilarious. 'He was pointing it right at you.'

'Fuck . . .,' I said. 'I could see right down the barrel.'

'No you couldn't,' Charley said. 'He was pointing at me. I was looking down the barrel. I could see right down the barrel. I mean, I don't know how you can look right down the barrel if someone's not pointing it at you.'

'Don't worry about it,' Claudio said with a shrug. 'He was just having a laugh.' Pragmatic as ever, for Claudio facing a loaded gun was nothing new. He'd been filming in war zones since the 1980s and had even interviewed Osama bin Laden, long before most of us had heard of him. But Charley and I were stunned, our enthusiasm for the trip ahead immediately drained. We feared Kazakhstan would be even more lawless than the Ukraine. Jamie Lowther-Pinkerton had told us that any self-respecting male in these parts would have a gun. It was a sign of wealth. To most people, it was no more significant than owning a dog. But knowing that did nothing to diminish its impact. It was still a strange thing to point it at a complete stranger for a laugh, wasn't it? We got on our bikes and I tried to put it to the back of my mind, but it stayed with me for several hours as we rode on. Only a few minutes earlier we had been talking about shaking off the support crew. But now, as I rode on, regarding every passing car as a potential threat, I wondered what the hell I had let myself in for.

The roads got worse. And worse. And when we thought they couldn't possibly become any more challenging, they deteriorated even more. At times it was like riding across a lunar landscape made up entirely of sand and gravel, two of a motorcyclist's three biggest fears. Only mud was missing.

We passed hundreds of nodding oil derricks – this was Kazakhstan's most oil-rich region – and countless camels, donkeys, horses and goats. Maybe it was the alien environment, but I found the sight of a mother with its young, such as a mare and her foal, affected me profoundly, reminding me of my two wee girls. Tears welled up in my eyes as I saw my youngest daughter Esther in a baby camel. I found it hardest to be away from her because she didn't really understand why I wasn't at home. My wife had told me that Esther had started looking for me upstairs, pointing into the bedroom and asking for her daddy. It was easier with Clara because I could speak to her on the phone and send her postcards, but there was no way to explain my absence to Esther.

Clouds covered the sun, the wind picked up, the temperature plummeted and I dreamed of a hot bath. We passed deserted buildings so thickly covered in dust it looked as if a giant bag of flour had been dropped on them. Forty miles short of Atyrau we were stopped by a policeman. Massively fat with a monster-sized cap, he looked like a big cuddly bear. Harrumphing, pursing his lips and shaking his head, he refused to let us go any further without a full police escort. Our attempt to negotiate with this particularly unbending force of authority was accompanied by a backing track of a blaring car horn. A little boy, about three years old, sitting in a nearby jeep was having a grand time parping the hooter. 'It's funny,' said Charley. 'Little boys are the same the world over.'

We rode into town with the police car ahead of us. With the Lada's lights flashing, siren blazing and the fat policeman bellowing through a megaphone, ordering the traffic to let us through red lights and crossroads, it wasn't quite the unannounced entrance we had planned, but at least we wouldn't have to search for our hotel. There was, however, something surreal about getting a full police escort through the outback of Kazakhstan, a country I'd never visited before, into a town about which I had absolutely no preconceptions. It was straight out of a David Lynch movie.

I spotted a crowd ahead, gathered in a lay-by. As we approached, a bank of lights was switched on and I realised I was staring at a pack of journalists, some of them toting television cameras. 'Oh my God, it's the telly,' I muttered over the intercom. 'Uh oh. Uh oh. Uh oh. A fucking tip-off to the old media. Just what we don't need.'

The police car pulled into the lay-by and the fat policeman jumped out. 'Stay here,' he instructed. It was a bewildering introduction to our first night in Kazakhstan – ordered by people we didn't know to stay somewhere we didn't want to, in the company of people with whom we didn't want to be, not knowing what was going on. I was too tired to think straight and I couldn't think of anything intelligent to say to the pestering cameras. All I wanted was a shower and some food. The police car moved off, we tucked in behind it and the journalists, who had jumped into their vans and cars, trailed in our wake. Once at the hotel, the bun fight started again, the cameras following us into the hotel and surrounding us in the lobby as Charley, Claudio and I tried to check in. Everybody wanted to shake our hands and get an autograph from each of us. That accomplished, they left us alone. Peace and rest at last.

CHARLEY: The next morning we boarded a boat for a short cruise down the Ural to the Caspian Sea to see caviar fishermen at work. The old pleasure boat smelled wonderfully of diesel oil and the captain was a real old sea dog with a raggedy white moustache, a battered old cap and one of those bulbous noses we suspected came from drinking too much vodka. While passing local fishermen rowing square-ended skiffs, dragging nets behind them through the dirty brown water and large tugs pulling barges up the wide river, we sat down to a delicious lunch of anchovies, dried fish, salad, a fish soup made with sturgeon, and piles of caviar. I'd never tasted caviar that good and I couldn't get enough of it, ironic given that we were on our way to find out about how perilously close the sturgeon, the fish that had produced the caviar, is to extinction. The caviar we were eating was considered the best in the world, darker and better quality than Iranian. When the local fishermen told us they sold it for only $100 a kilogram, a fraction of its price in London or New York, and that it was bought by some of the leading lights of Hollywood, I was tempted to hatch a plan to set up a large-scale import business. Over lunch, the sturgeon fishermen told us about a new method of caviar farming, equivalent to giving the fish a caesarian. It was slit open while it was still alive and the roe removed, then stitched up and put back in the water.

'I'm glad to hear that,' Ewan said. 'Because otherwise the sturgeon will become extinct.'

'Yeah, we have a saying,' I added, 'you wouldn't want to kill the goose that lays the golden egg. Oh, poor sturgeon. Another plate of caviar, please!'

The boat ride gave us time to assess our progress so far and make plans for the journey to Almaty. One day into Kazakhstan and we were struggling to keep on schedule. It wasn't surprising given that we had planned the route at Bulwer Street, blithely deciding we would cover a certain mileage each day without bothering to research the road conditions or the availability of petrol. Ewan was very concerned that we would arrive in New York weeks after our target date, something for which his hectic schedule did not allow. We also had to face the fact that the worsening road conditions made it more likely that one of us would fall off, or that we would damage our bikes, which might also delay our arrival. 'Its just the amount of it that's to come that frightens me,' Ewan said. 'All of Kazakhstan could be dreadful.

We just don't know. Then we're into Mongolia, where there are no roads, and then Siberia and the Road of Bones. I'm really concerned about how we are going to cope with it day in day out. The party's over in terms of tarmac, isn't it?'

'Yeah, but juggernauts go from Volgograd to Almaty,' I said. 'And if a juggernaut can do it, then we should be able to, shouldn't we? As long as the weather holds up . . .'

While we were talking, an official from the sturgeon authority came aboard. With a cigarette clamped in the corner of his mouth and wearing wraparound sunglasses, he pulled alongside in a flat-bottomed speedboat and leaped flamboyantly on to our boat's deck. It was a great entrance.

The official took us out in his speedboat, bouncing across the Caspian Sea in search of poachers. It didn't take long. Dressed in khaki parkas and tight leather caps with side flaps and chin straps, the poachers were bobbing on the sea in a boat that was overflowing with dead sturgeon. They were unrepentant. 'The sturgeon is our bread, our life,' they said. Believing they had a birthright to take from the sea as many fish as they could catch, the poachers used GPS to record where they had cast their nets, returning at night to haul in their booty. After a short search, we found one of their nets and in it, a sturgeon. It was a real thrill to liberate the scaly prehistoric fish and release it into the water.

EWAN: Hoping to evade a police escort, we got up and departed early the next morning, but it was pointless. A policeman had been waiting in his car since dawn, his sandwich and flask of tea packed and sitting on the seat beside him, and we rode out of Atyrau in the same manner that we'd arrived. At the edge of town, the policeman pulled over, shook our hands and told us to turn left at Doza. We pressed on, the three of us just happy to be on the road again, taking it easy and hoping for the best. After a short while we reached Doza, a scrappy town were the road had flooded and turned into a quagmire. In the middle of town,

Charley turned left on to a severely potholed track. 'I wouldn't have known to do that,' I said. 'Would you?'

'Yeah, my GPS told me,' Charley said. 'But fucking hell, if it's like this the whole way we're screwed.'

A short while later, the mud ended and the road returned to tarmac, albeit of the heavily potholed variety. 'So far, so good,' I said. 'But I can't help feeling this is lulling us into a false sense of security.' For about fifty miles, I enjoyed just gliding along, dodging potholes as if I was playing some kind of arcade game. I entered that tranquil space where everything slowed down and thoughts floated through my mind as we slipped along on a clear, crisp desert morning, making memories that would last a lifetime.

'Look at that truck!' It was Charley on the intercom. 'The last few trucks I've seen coming this way were plastered in mud. Absolutely covered in it. Don't quite know what it means, but I can't help feeling it might not be good.'

We got the answer a short while later when we arrived in another nondescript town. It was ankle-deep in sloppy, runny mud. Stopping to get our bearings, within seconds we were surrounded by men and teenage boys, each of them offering different directions to Aktobe. Having plumped for the instructions offered by a middle-aged man, we soon found ourselves at a dead end, mired in sticky, slippery mud beside a railway track at the edge of the town, surrounded by abandoned rusting trucks and the empty shells of concrete buildings. Claudio dropped his bike, then I slipped over. More locals came running, each armed with yet more widely divergent sets of instructions.

'These fucking roads,' Charley fumed. 'Jesus! If they're like this it's going to take us a very, very long time.' The mud was every biker's worst nightmare. The only way to get through it was to keep the speed up, standing on our pegs to control the balance of weight between the back wheel for traction and the front wheel for steering, but one tiny wobble and we slipped over. We'd thought we'd have it easier than a car, but you can't fall off a car.

We picked our way back to the centre of the town, got off our bikes and waited for the support team to arrive. But when the team turned up and got out of the vehicles, even Eric couldn't understand the directions. In the end, we let the locals lead us to the edge of town. We were out on the open road again. A few miles later, as we rounded a bend, Claudio lost control of his bike. He went down with a crunch, the back of his bike slipping wide. I could see it was a proper fall, the type that could hurt him and damage his bike. He got up slowly, clutching his sides. 'I'm okay,' he said. 'That hurt, but I'm okay.'

The roads became even worse. At times, the gaps in the road were more pond than pothole, so wide that we had no choice but to ride through them, the water reaching the BMWs' axles and washing over our feet. Charley, the most experienced off-road rider, led from the front. I followed scrupulously in his tracks. By following Charley's line through puddles, I could be sure I wouldn't plunge into a hidden deep hole.

'Fuck, this is daunting,' Charley said. 'If this is what Siberia will be like for the entire length of the Road of Bones, then we are totally fucked.'

I could hear Thomas Junkers's words ringing in my ears. 'What if I told you six weeks?' Maybe he was right. Touching the piece of wood I carried in my pocket to support my side stand on soft ground, I prayed for good luck. My grey and black riding trousers were sodden and brown with mud, our bikes were caked in dirt. We certainly looked hard core, but it was no fun.

But our problems went beyond the poor state of the roads. Our slow progress meant we would have to camp. I wanted to sleep in a tent, but Charley was less keen and our doctor, Vasiliy, had advised us against it. 'Is impossible now. Is very serious,' Vasiliy insisted. 'Now season for high activity of black widow spider. Snake never attack if you step on it, but spider will bite. Even narcotic not make this pain less. Very pain.'

That was enough to tip it for Charley, who at the best of times didn't like the idea of camping. 'The season for black widows? We never thought about that . . .'

'There will always be a reason not to do something,' I said.

'But Vasiliy said it's also too cold at this time of year. He said the ground's freezing . . .'

'Of course it's cold. That's why we've got thermals. You get in your sleeping bag and you've got a ground mat for insulation. Sure, it'll be chilly, but that's not a reason not to camp.'

'You know I'm not a big camping person. I quite like staying in hotels, preferably with a golf course attached. Plus I still can't shake that guy's gun out of my head. I keep seeing his face and I just worry that we're going to be camping and some nutter's going to come up and do us.'

'What? In the middle of nowhere? We'll ride a mile or two off the road. Nobody will be able to see us.'

'I can't help wishing we had a green tent now. Maybe we can hide it behind a bush or something, but that bright orange tent sticks out like a sore thumb. Just the idea of camping fills me with dread and worry . . .'

It was a good point, and I agreed with him. Our orange three-man tent was very visible, but Charley had always known we'd have to camp and now was the time to get on with it.

'You know I have seen people bitten by spiders when I was in Brazil and they were in hammocks,' Charley said. 'Spiders do crawl up into hammocks. Or they lower themselves down on to you from above.'

'It will be okay,' I said. But there was another reason: I wanted to lose the support crew, who, because we were moving so slowly, were catching up with us every time we stopped. I'd started to feel like we were on some kind of school tour. It wasn't what I had planned. 'What do you think, Claudio?' I said. 'You up for camping?'

Claudio was typically straightforward. 'I think the spider story is just to frighten us. You want to camp? Then camp.'

I looked around. It was early afternoon and we'd just lunched on some bread and a tin of pilchards. Amidst all the hassle, I could still appreciate the raw beauty of our surroundings. The empty landscape had a calming effect. I was absolutely knackered and fed up with the state of the roads, but the sheer magnificence of our environment made me want to press on and see more. We climbed back on our bikes and moved off, but it got no better. In fact, it got a whole lot worse. What was laughingly marked as a major road on the map was in such a poor state it became easier to weave between the scrub along the side of it than travel on the road itself.

Then, in the middle of nowhere, we spotted a small group of people standing stock-still in the wind. Yet another welcoming committee. More fermented camel's milk served by young girls in traditional dress. They gave me a little stone pipe, about the size of a golf ball, on which I managed to play a tune.

'We have been waiting a month for you to arrive,' said a gold-toothed local dignitary dressed in a suit and tie. The track-suited man beside him announced he was going to accompany us all the way to Aktobe, more than two hundred miles away. It was very touching to be greeted and shown such hospitality everywhere we went, but we wanted to pass through Kazakhstan unannounced. It wasn't meant to be a grand media tour, shaking hands with dignitaries and being given the red-carpet treatment. It was meant to be a holiday. Just Charley and me, on our own, meeting the locals like any other travellers and dealing with problems ourselves. By the time we roared off to the accompaniment of a round of applause, I was really fed up. It felt like our adventure was being snatched away from us.

In spite of relentlessly poor roads and intense winds, by late afternoon we had managed to ride another 30 miles, taking our total so far that day to 210 miles. It sounded good until Charley pointed out we had a further 218 miles to ride if we were to reach Aktobe. 'I think it's pretty fucking impressive considering the fucking roads we've had,' Charley said. 'Let's get some fuel here and push on a bit. I don't think this is a good place to camp.'

I agreed. For one thing, we were being watched by two policemen who had just pulled up in a van. Our minders again. However, I was worried that belligerence rather than dedication was motivating us not to stop yet for the night. Charley and I wanted to keep going just to prove to ourselves – and our various minders – that the state of the roads would not slow our progress.

A couple of hours later and we'd stopped again. It was getting dark, we were fed up and our bodies were tired. We'd put more muddy miles under our tyres than we thought possible and we were near a town. The nearest hotel, however, was at least thirty miles down the road. I didn't know what to do. We'd been told in Atyrau that it was three hundred miles to Aktobe, yet we'd ridden 290 miles so far and there were at least another 150 to go. My body wasn't used to this amount of abuse. My forearms were stiff and there was a sharp pain between my shoulder blades. My legs were wobbling like jelly after spending a day balancing the bike by standing on its pegs. There wasn't much sun left in the sky and I didn't want to push our luck.

We rode into town and asked if there was anywhere to stay. For five minutes we watched a bunch of locals discuss our dilemma, then one of the policemen who'd been watching us from the van stepped forward. Fifteen minutes later we were in his house and our bikes were in his garage, the policeman's friends taking shifts to guard them through the night. He showed us to our quarters. Never had a large bare room with a concrete floor looked more appealing.

While Claudio filmed the family watching television in their front room, Charley and I unrolled our sleeping bags on the floor. 'I'm going to need earplugs because of your snoring,' said Charley.

'And I'm going to need a clothes peg on my nose because of your feet,' I replied.

In the front room, the policeman introduced us to his family. His wife was putting their three-month-old baby to bed. We watched her swaddle the baby in white cotton, put a dummy in its mouth and strap it into a white cot to make sure it didn't fall on to the concrete floor in the night. In one corner, a television blared.

'Hey, look at this!' Claudio called out. 'It's you two.' There on Kazakh television was a shot of Charley and me bumping along the road that day. It cut to me singing in *Moulin Rouge*, then a scene from *Star Wars*. The policeman's family gave us a quizzical look. I could tell what they were thinking: Jesus Christ, what have we got here. We shrugged and smiled. They pointed at the screen and then at us. We nodded. It didn't feel as awkward as I thought it might. It seemed quite natural. We were going around the world, we were in their house and we were on television. It was as straightforward as that.

Back in our room, I stared out of the window at the full moon. It had been our first day off-road. This was only the beginning. There'd be many more days like it in Kazakhstan, Mongolia and Siberia, yet we were already falling behind. In sixty days, we were meant to be in Magadan on the Pacific coast. Four weeks later, on 30 July, we were meant to arrive in New York. If we continued as we had that day, we'd be more than a month late. Next to me, Charley slipped in his earplugs and lay back in his sleeping bag. Within seconds he was asleep. He had an enviable ability to drop off quickly. As I stared at the ceiling, wondering how long it would really be until I might see my wife and children again, I wished I could sleep as easily as Charley.

8

Free as an eagle

ROAD OF DEATH TO SEMEY

EWAN: Determined to put the previous day's problems behind us, we got up early and, after a breakfast of meatballs, eggs, bread and tea, set off with the ambition of reaching Aktobe by midday. After breakfast we checked our bikes, but even after the rigours of the first off-road day, there was no damage. Even the tyre pressures were correct after hammering through hundreds of potholes. What amazing machines.

The roads were no better that morning, but now we knew what to expect. We ground our way north-eastwards until, about fifteen miles outside Aktobe, we were stopped by a police car. Exhausted and wanting to make up for lost time, we gladly accepted the offer of an escort through town. Anything to make the journey easier. With its siren wailing and lights flashing, the ubiquitous Lada led us through the outskirts of Aktobe, turning suddenly left into a street towards a football stadium. We were shepherded into a car park where, like lambs to the slaughter, we were thrust in front of a bank of television cameras and several dozen reporters. Another impromptu press conference. It was getting ridiculous.

As I pulled up, the media pack crowded round, firing questions and poking lenses into my face. 'Could I just get off my motorcycle, please?' I asked. They stepped back a couple of feet and gave me a chance to dismount and pull off my helmet.

'This is the head of tourism,' a female translator said, ushering a man in a suit and tie towards me.

'Yeah, I bet he is,' I replied, wanting to give him a mouthful but knowing it would be best if I kept smiling. We were taken up a flight of stairs, shown the empty stadium and bombarded with statistics, all to the backing of a Cher track blaring out of the public address system. Promising a cup of tea, the director of football asked us to join him for the next two hours. I politely declined, saying we had to press on. Then we were led back downstairs and pushed in front of the waiting reporters.

'Do you think you are more Obi-Wan Kenobi or Mark Renton?' I was asked.

'I'm neither,' I said.

'What is the intention of your trip?'

'To pass anonymously through the countries, to witness how people live and to experience the world just like any other travellers,' I said.

'Huh,' the reporter scoffed. 'Impossible.'

'No. In fact it's not been impossible, thank you. It's been that way up until now.'

I appreciated how valuable any publicity would be for the Kazakh tourist authorities. If it helped, I was happy to give small, pre-arranged interviews. I also understood the excitement there might be about two actors travelling through a country that didn't regularly feature on most actors' itineraries. But I believed it would be best for the Kazakh authorities if they would leave us alone to let us get a true picture of their country instead of forcing us to see Kazakhstan through the distorting prism of a series of press junkets.

But the questions continued in the same banal and dismissive vein. 'This is madness,' Charley said. 'It's got completely out of hand.'

I phoned Eric. 'We've just been led by the police to a massive mediafest at the stadium. Cameras everywhere. It's been very well organised. Could you please come and help us get out of it without causing offence. And we need to have a chat about what's going on.'

I'd thought Kazakhstan would be a highlight of the journey, the place where we'd be able to get away from everything and travel anonymously. Instead we were trapped in a media celebrity tour, just the thing I had wanted to avoid. The generosity was welcome, but I felt used. If only we'd been asked we would have set aside some time for interviews and done anything to help promote the country. Instead the attention had been thrust upon us and we were getting a distorted impression of Kazakhstan. It was a great shame.

Eric turned up, spoke to the officials and assured us this would be the last unannounced intrusion into our trip. Eddie, his driver, led us out of Aktobe and put us on the road to the Aral Sea and we hoped that would be our last encounter with Kazakh police minders or the media.

Although it was cold and windy, the road was much smoother than anything we'd encountered so far and we made quick progress. The potholes were still the size of paddling pools, large enough to throw a rider from his bike if they weren't avoided, but, compared with the previous day, it was easy riding and we even managed to find time to stop for lunch.

By that evening, we were standing on a pancake-flat plain beneath a tangerine-coloured moon, our tent erected behind us and a warm supper in our bellies. We'd turned off the road and ridden a few miles across the scrub to a blue lake, the perfect spot for making camp. I was thrilled to be camping deep in the cuds at last, just Charley, Claudio and me. After the razzmatazz of the media attention and the hassles of the police escorts, I wallowed in the serenity and sense of independence. It didn't matter that we hadn't had a bath or shower for a couple of days. In fact, there was a little boyish part of me that was rather excited about it. Bad hair had never felt so good.

Charley, however, still hadn't shaken off his reluctance to camp. 'What are all those holes in the ground?' he said as we put up the tent.

'Nothing. Marmots or rats. Something like that,' I tried to reassure him.

'They could be spiders. Black widows . . .'

'Not that big. Those holes are for something big, like a marmot.'

'Maybe the spiders went in and killed a family of marmots in there. Now there's a cluster of black widows in there, hungry and waiting for something to come along that they can eat. And here we are.'

'Don't freak yourself out about the spiders, Charley. It'll be fine,' I said. 'I haven't seen one spider. Let's keep it that way.'

We'd been told Kazakh shepherds had three ways of dealing with black widows: ash, bleach or sheep fleece around your sleeping place. Apparently black widows were frightened of sheep because they could eat them with impunity. Charley, meanwhile, had devised an ingenious way of keeping spiders out of our boots during the night. He had stretched a sock across the top of each boot. 'One of your survival tricks?' I asked.

'No, I thought of it just now,' he said. 'Motivated by total fear and panic.'

But even Charley had to concede it was beautiful. We sat on a small hillock, eating chocolate, watching the crimson sun slip below the horizon and talking about the day. 'What a spot,' I said. 'Surely this is better than some anonymous hotel room?'

'Yeah, it's bloody paradise,' Charley said with mock misery as we threw stones into the river and the sun disappeared. 'Actually, it's not bad at all. Now that I've got a warm meal in my stomach and my sleeping bag laid out, I'm happy about camping.' He hummed the banjo tune from *Deliverance*. 'Squeal like a pig, boy . . .'

For the rest of that night, all the talk was of mileages. We were now two days behind schedule and it was clear we'd been hopelessly naïve in our projections. Our route was living up to its local epithet, the Road of Death, on account of its many potholes and its dilapidated condition. And if the roads continued in their current state, there was every chance we were going to arrive almost a week late in Almaty. And everyone we spoke to said the next stage would be the worst. I couldn't see how it was possible for the roads to be any more challenging, but the locals warned us that a twenty-mile stretch was often so bad it was impassable.

*

CHARLEY: I slept like a log. It must have been the fresh air. Maybe this camping lark wasn't so bad after all. The only downside was that I got bitten by a mosquito, smack on the middle of a bum cheek when I crawled out of the tent for a poo, just after Ewan had said 'Mind you don't get bitten on your arse'. Even Avon Skin So Soft, which an angler friend had told me was the best mosquito repellent, had failed to keep the little bastard away.

I sat outside the tent and thought about how I needed to stop worrying about everything. I needed to learn to let myself go. Enjoy the moment rather than worry about everybody and everything else. I had to learn that I couldn't control everything.

'Did you sleep well?' It was Ewan crawling out of the tent.

'Yeah. Really did.'

'You were asleep in seconds as usual. It's an uncanny knack. Three seconds after your head hits the pillow you're fast asleep. Never seen anyone fall asleep quicker in my life.'

'That's what my wife says.'

'Mind you, there was a bit of a snore there,' Ewan said. 'Just at the beginning. Did I snore last night at all?'

'No, only in the morning. I had to give you a poke, but you just turned over and went "aaaassssmmmmhhh".'

'A poke? I wondered what that small thing up my bum was. Didn't realise it was you,' Ewan laughed. 'Anyway, what did you think of your first night sleeping in the cuds?'

'Once I got used to the fact that I've never been this far away from McDonald's, I really enjoyed it.'

I'd surprised myself how much I'd liked camping. I couldn't quite shake off my fear of being bitten by a black widow – and Vasiliy's subsequent warning that it was the mating season for scorpions had almost finished any thoughts of camping for me – but I did feel much more relaxed about it. As we ate our porridge for breakfast that morning, I almost felt disappointed the night hadn't been worse and that I hadn't had good cause for a moan.

We packed up and climbed on our bikes for a short ride across the steppe to the road. Or rather, whatever passed for a road in these parts. As we bumped along the scrub, I realised it had been a relief not to have to faff around with fixers, dignitaries, hotel managers and the rest. And, much to my surprise, I'd been as warm as toast. My sleeping bag was insanely warm and I'd worn my thermals as well.

We rode for a few hours, stopping at a building sporting a bright green KAFFE sign for some water. A stone hut in the middle of nowhere, tumbleweed and dust devils blowing across the road. As I was taking off my helmet, a green Russian jeep arrived, driving straight towards us and pulling up just inches away from our bikes. Two men, both small and wearing leather baseball caps, stepped out. We smiled but they just stared back blankly at us. They walked slowly around the bikes, silently looking them over. Still stony-faced, they looked us up and down, then walked past into the café.

'They're a bit unfriendly,' Ewan said. I felt very uneasy.

While the two men were inside the café, another pair turned up: security guards from a nearby factory. Seconds later, the first two unfriendly men in the leather baseball caps emerged from the café, gripping two large kitchen knives in their fists. Fuck, I thought, we're going to get robbed. Then the shifty looking men with the knives spotted the security guards. Their eyes darted from us to the guards and back to us. Quick as a flash, they hid the kitchen knives behind their backs and sauntered casually over to their jeep. It seemed the security guards had arrived not a moment too early. The men slipped their knives inside the jeep, climbed in and drove off. Not a word was said. I didn't want to be overly suspicious, but it was hard to escape the feeling that we'd just avoided a potential hold-up.

But there was little time to consider what might have happened. 'Fuck, I'm exhausted,' Ewan said when we were ready to depart. 'We've only done thirty-eight miles this morning and already I feel like I've done a day's riding.' It had been a tough morning. A lot of sand and gravel. The only way to cope with it was to keep your speed up, just barrel through it and hope for the best. Several times, we found ourselves in deep sand, which made the front wheel buck left and right, and we'd both nearly fallen off. The secret was to fight against your instincts. If the front wheel slipped away on gravel, the trick was to resist the temptation to pull on the brakes, which would make the bike fall over. Instead, the thing to do was to open the throttle. It made the bike sit up and straighten, and offered a chance of regaining control.

Ewan was in low spirits by the time we stopped for lunch at another café. There was a beautiful Russian motorcycle with a sidecar outside, but he took little interest in it as we sat under an awning and he brooded.

'Tough day,' he muttered. Sipping tea out of a little porcelain bowl with roses on it, he gazed out at the sandy desert while the café owner hovered by the table, looking awkward and picking up on his dark mood. At times like this, it was best to let Ewan work it through. If it got really bad, I'd try to find the right words to pull him out of it.

Ewan sipped the tea. 'Ah, that's good . . .' Then he spotted something at the bottom of his bowl and frowned. 'Funny tea . . . what's this shit?'

Ewan had a tendency to impose his moods on everyone surrounding him. One minute he was up, the next he'd hit the bottom of a deep trough. We all had our ups and downs, but Ewan's depressions seemed deeper than anyone else's I had experienced. When he was in a dark mood, he became highly sensitive, unable to let silly things slide. It made it quite hard to judge his character or to gauge his true feelings. I'd learned the hard way that there was little point in trying to take him on when he was in a dark mood. The best thing was to accept it and wait for him to get over it. He could snap out of a bad mood as quickly as he entered it. But it was a pain in the arse.

EWAN: I was really missing my wife and my kids. Every time I opened my top box, I saw them. Three pictures in a row, stuck to the inside of the lid: Eve, Clara and Esther. My beautiful girls. I couldn't wait to get back to London to see them. It was the biggest incentive I had to push on. With such a wonderful gift waiting for me at home, I felt like the luckiest man in the world, pushing eastwards day after day just to see my gorgeous family. But it also made the long journey ahead more daunting. Every mile we rode was both a mile closer and a mile further apart from them.

It had been a tough morning, the third in a row. I was hot. I seemed unable to get the thermals right. I'd take them off, it would turn cold and I would freeze. The next day, I'd put them back on, the sun would beat down on me all day and by lunchtime I'd be swimming in sweat. I also found the roads very challenging. That morning, I'd had two scares where I really thought I was going to fall. And with at least two hundred off-road miles to ride by the end of the day, I found it difficult to raise my spirits. I had that sick feeling in the pit of my stomach that I'd not had since the training days in Wales, when I'd thought I might not be able to cut it and when I thought I would let Charley and everyone else down.

We set off again and within a few miles I had dropped my bike. 'That's one-all today,' I shouted to Charley as he helped me pick it up. 'Not that there's any competition going on.' Another few miles later, the road became a bog. We rode across the desert, away from the road for several hundred metres, searching for a gap in the mud and puddles, my heart beating like a drum in my chest. It took a while, but a little later we were back on the road and it was Claudio's turn to drop his bike. 'Don't get despondent,' I told him. 'We've done ninety-five miles so far.'

Fed up with riding at the back, unable to see anything in the dust clouds thrown up by Claudio and Charley's tyres, I insisted on taking the lead. Suddenly I found my rhythm. I was back in the zone, reaching a decent speed on the sandy stretches, imagining I was in the Paris–Dakar rally and picking the fastest line through the potholes. The next thing I knew, I was on the ground and the sun was beating down on me. Overconfident, I'd lost control and fallen again. We ploughed on, riding an emotional and physical rollercoaster. One minute I was having a good time, just happy and content. The next minute, I was totally tranquil, not thinking about anything, just riding along. And a short while later, I would be grouchy and grumpy.

Our communications systems had been shaken apart and we could no longer speak to each other on the road. The silence and the long hours in the saddle gave me time to retreat into my mind and let my thoughts drift. My job had always been very important for me, but now I felt divorced from it. I'd spent a lot of last year dreaming of getting away – at least for a while. And because the casting of most films is finalised only at the very last moment, I had nothing lined up for when the trip was over. I felt as if I was in limbo, unsure of which step I should take next. I'd joked at the press launch in London before we set off that I might not return to acting. It was just a throwaway quip that was taken too seriously by the reporters present, but there was an element of truth at the heart of it. I didn't want to give up acting, but I was genuinely questioning the best way forward. Should I spend a year working in the theatre? Or was it time to direct a film or a play?

Nothing was stopping me from doing these things. I just needed to take the decision. I'd never been a great careerist. I'd always been driven more by seeking out interesting projects than thinking what would be good for my career, but maybe now was the time to take stock and decide how to move forward. I was also worried about what people were thinking about me taking off the best part of a year to travel around the world. Would it mean I'd no longer be sent the best scripts? I felt out of the loop. And in my job, when you are out of the loop, you really are out of it. There was no halfway house. You were either in directors' and casting agents' minds when they were putting a film together, or you weren't. Having worked almost non-stop since drama school, this was the first time I had nothing lined up and in the middle of nowhere I didn't know what to make of it.

The trip was also giving me the opportunity to contemplate things that had happened to me and to lay them to rest. I was carrying a lot of emotional baggage – guilt, fears and resentments – that needed time to be worked through and left behind. I'd done something similar when I trekked through the Honduran rainforests with Ray Mears. As we climbed mountains and hacked through the jungle, I had been conscious of discarding things that had been bothering me for years. Hiking for eight to ten hours a day, I had plenty of time to think things over. And it worked well for me. No, I'll leave this in the jungle, I'd think about a particular issue; I don't need to be carrying this any more. And now, I was again discarding things that had festered at the back of my mind for a long time. It was amazing what came into my head. At times I was completely lost in thoughts about people and things that had happened at school or in the years since. Relationships and fights, things I was proud about and things I regretted. Thoughts I had not considered for many years, but which I now realised were still unresolved. I knew that learning from your mistakes was part of growing up, but I seemed to have made a lot of them. I also contemplated the good things that had happened, like meeting Eve, getting married and having children. But most surprising of all was that I seemed to have no control over the thoughts; they just popped into my head as if to say 'Remember me? We go back a long way'. And if it was an uncomfortable thought, I had no choice but to sit with it and work it through. I couldn't run away from it. If it hurt, I couldn't dash out of the house saying I needed to buy some new shoes in Carnaby Street. I had to sit with my thoughts and my feelings on my bike and wait until they passed. And that was a good thing.

At other times, I just switched off and settled into the rhythm of the bike and the road. Amid all the physical exertion and mental introspection, there were moments of great beauty. That morning, as the Platters' 'Red Sails in the Sunset' played on my iPod, we spotted a herd of animals bounding across the steppe. They looked like antelope or gazelle. They were a long way away and we couldn't clearly see what they were, but Kazakhstan has large herds of mid-Asian ibex, Asian elks, Saiga antelope, Persian and black tail gazelle and Siberian roe deer. These were quite large animals with unique markings. On other occasions, we came across convocations of fifteen to twenty eagles sitting by the side of the road or perched on the tops of road signs. They were just hanging out and, as we rode past, they would all take to the air. It was stunning. Such beautiful creatures. It made me feel like I was in the Highlands of Scotland.

By that evening we were riding almost entirely on soft golden sand and my legs were again shaking from standing on my pegs all day. Charley wanted to sleep in a hotel. 'I just want a bath,' he pleaded. But having failed in our ambition of reaching Aral, we camped in the desert among some old mud-hut ruins. Charley heated up our sachets of vacuum-packed food for supper. Lancashire hotpot for him, chilli con carne for Claudio and me. With the birds twittering nearby and the mosquitoes buzzing around us, we scoffed our dinners hungrily, watching the sun come down on the hardest day's riding we'd ever experienced.

CHARLEY: The next day was no better. I awoke to find Manimal sleeping beside me. A mosquito bite had swollen into a massive lump stretching right across Ewan's forehead and on to the bridge of his nose, making him look like Neanderthal man with a huge, red, jutting brow. His arms were just as bad: puffy and red, the skin tight and sore around a string of mosquito bites. I felt sorry for him, and even more so a few hours later when he got petrol in his eyes for the second time. Fortunately it wasn't my fault on this occasion. The pump hadn't switched off when he had finished filling his tank. The petrol sprayed right across his face, into his eyes and ears. To have it happen twice was very bad luck.

The roads that morning were just as awful as before. You couldn't have made them worse if you had bombed them. So much for the promise of only twenty miles of really dreadful roads, I thought. For more than one hundred miles we'd been riding across atrocious surfaces, the road often splitting into five or six parallel tracks, all of them muddy and boggy. We had spent days at a time standing on our pegs, weaving between potholes, bumping through puddles. There had been hardly a moment in the previous few days when we'd been able to sit back and just ride along.

It hadn't helped that I'd slept badly the previous night. We camped so close to the road I was convinced someone would steal our bikes. At about 5.30 a.m., I heard a really loud car approaching us. It sounded as if it was careening across the steppe and was about to crash into our tent. I unzipped the tent, climbed outside and looked around. Nothing to be seen. Bewildered, I got back into the tent and zipped it closed. As soon as I lay down on the ground, I heard the car again. I jumped up, unzipped the tent and looked outside. There, on the road, was a car, passing very slowly but making a huge racket because its exhaust had fallen off.

The only two consolations were that we were on BMWs – I was convinced now that the KTMs would have struggled – and that we had allowed for just eighty to one hundred miles a day in Mongolia. We had vastly overestimated the distances we would manage in Kazakhstan, but given that we'd managed more than 250 miles the previous day, I was encouraged that we'd be able to make up lost time in Mongolia. Surely the roads couldn't be any worse there. It didn't seem physically possible.

And amid all the anxiety about the journey ahead, one golden light shone through: Claudio. His bike skills were astounding, defying all the laws of nature. With no training whatsoever, and experienced only on a scooter, he was putting Ewan and me to shame on the most treacherous roads imaginable. Time and time again, Ewan and I would cautiously cross an obstacle, Claudio often filming us falling over in the process. Then Claudio would pack away his camera, get on his bike, rev up and casually bump across the same obstruction, faster and more smoothly than Ewan or I had managed. It was fucking irritating, come to think of it.

We reached Aral around lunchtime and rode down to where, twenty-five years earlier, the waterfront had been. What was once the world's fourth largest expanse of inland water was nowhere to be seen. Since the 1960s, when the Soviet government redirected the Syr Darya and Amu Darya rivers to irrigate cotton and vegetable fields in Uzbekistan and other parts of Kazakhstan, the Aral Sea had been in retreat. Without its main water sources, the water level had fallen by about 50 feet and the Aral Sea had split into two much smaller lakes containing water that was now three times saltier than sea water. The water was now unfit for drinking and the once abundant stocks of sturgeon, roach, carp and other fish had died out. Aral had once been a thriving sea port supporting ship-building and fishing industries. Now it was a desolate inland town relying on the railway station for its trade. The only sign of its maritime heritage was a line of rusting fishing boats lying like beached whales on the sand, the sea now out of sight, over the horizon.

We pressed on without pausing for lunch. A short distance beyond Aral, the mud ended and we were riding on tarmac for the first time in three days. I was so pleased I got off my bike, lay down on the road and kissed the surface. It was such a relief to be back on what was almost a proper road. We took full advantage of the better conditions, putting as many miles as we could under our wheels as the temperature plummeted and a downpour made the surface of the dusty roads as slippery and dangerous as an ice rink. Thirty-five miles from Qyzylorda, the yellow low-fuel light flashed on my instrument panel and I didn't think we'd make it to the town. We rode on, praying our fuel would last, thinking we would be stranded in the cold and the dark, waiting for petrol while the rain pissed down on us. Half an hour later, Ewan and I were standing in the foyer of a hotel. We'd just made it.

'I hit the wall out there,' Ewan said. 'I couldn't ride another mile.' We'd put nearly four hundred miles behind us and we were both physically finished and emotionally drained. Shivering uncontrollably as I waited to go to my room, I was overjoyed not to be camping again. After forty-eight hours of dusty roads and living in each other's pockets, I wanted a bit of privacy. More than anything I wanted a shower. I stood under the hot water for half an hour, washing my hair three times to get it clean and slowly thawing out as I watched the brown water wash down the plughole, leaving a scum of oil, mud and sweat around the side of the bath.

EWAN: The sun burst into my bedroom, waking me up. I drew the curtains. It was a cool, crisp morning, but it was clearly going to be a beautiful day. I immediately felt much better than the previous night. We had four hundred miles ahead of us and I couldn't wait to get back on my bike. The weather was having a profound effect on my mood. I wasn't very good in the cold, but if it was warm and dry I was up for anything.

Of course we had the obligatory Kazakh police escort out of town, but with our track record of getting lost on the way out of cities it was actually a blessing. We were back on a tarmac road, floating along at 80mph and it felt fantastic. I was in the best mood I'd been in for a week, singing in my helmet and wittering away to myself, just having a laugh. The landscape changed. It was still quite flat, but the desert gave way to more fertile plains, dotted with lines of cypress trees. We came across a little yurt, the first we'd seen, so we piled in. It was beautifully decorated with brightly coloured fabrics but a bit smelly. 'I think they let the camels sleep in here,' Charley said. We had some tea and got back on our bikes, itching to move on.

It was at times like this that I was glad to be alive. Good roads, good weather, good bike, goodbye. The swelling around the mosquito bite on my forehead had gone down and I felt like I could take whatever was thrown at us. We passed a sign: one thousand kilometres to Almaty. After what we'd been through, it seemed a pittance. Two days' easy riding. I put some Beatles on in my pod and rode along listening to the music. When 'The Long and Winding Road' came on, I couldn't help but think of my wife and children and sing along to the tune. Blasting out the words inside my helmet, I felt fantastic.

We stopped in the town of Turkestan on the edge of the Kyzylkum Desert to visit Kazakhstan's most important building, a turquoise-domed mausoleum to Kozha Akhmed Yasaui, the first great Turkic Muslim holy man. It was a most beautiful, tranquil building inside and out. The main dome, apparently the largest in central Asia, had fifty-two ribs to symbolise the weeks of the year and a frieze of original tiles that dated back to the fourteenth century. Chatting to a young girl who showed us around, I realised I was no longer thinking of the trip as a journey between London and New York. I wasn't even thinking of it as a trip across Kazakhstan. I was living for the day, riding along, watching the world pass by and meeting people along the road. To have forgotten about the whole trip and to live in the here and now was a tremendous liberation.

After the mausoleum visit, we were promised a swift lunch with the local head of tourism. 'Remember what that guy Graham who we met at the hotel in Atyrau told us,' I whispered to Charley as we sat down in front of a platter of what looked like a tubular piece of thickly sliced meat. 'He said be careful what you eat because some of it is horse penis.'

'What? . . .'

'Look at it, it's fatty around the outside and cut in rings. It could be the sliced horse member that Graham warned us about.'

Charley bit softly into a piece. 'This is called cock-in-mouth . . .' Charley and I dissolved in giggles just as the dignitaries walked into the room. 'Shit,' said Charley. 'They've just come in and seen us playing . . .'

'Just put it back,' I said. 'Shit, I've dropped the penis. We should put it back until . . . don't put it in your . . .'

'Stop worrying. It's just horse meat that's been made into a sausage, so they won't take any offence,' Charley said. 'Although I did notice a little vein running down the middle bit.'

'And it's slightly bigger in your fingers than on the plate, don't you find. It swells a bit when you pick it up.'

We never did find out what the strange meat might have been, t the meal was, as promised, quick and delicious. Afterwards, we were given a police escort that surpassed anything we'd experienced so far. We'd got into the habit of overtaking the escort if he didn't pull over at the edge of town, but that was impossible with this particular police Lada. Forcing oncoming traffic off the road, he never slowed below 75mph. No part of the road was safe from him. He veered from one side to the other, barging cars out of our way. Truck, motorcycle, Lada or Mercedes-Benz, it didn't matter what they were, the policeman forced them out of the way. It was madness, particularly as we were comparatively narrow and could quite easily get to Shymkent without squeezing every other car off the road. And it was nerve-racking. Every five minutes or so, the policeman would narrowly avoid a head-on collision. We later discovered the policeman had driven so aggressively because he was concerned we would arrive in Shymkent after it was dark.

Shymkent was the venue for a demonstration of goat polo, the national game, played in a purpose-built arena and attracting teams from as far afield as Switzerland and Sweden. It involved two teams of four players on horseback, dressed in large hats and wearing leather boots, scrapping over the carcass of a headless goat. While folk music blared over the public address system, the players grabbed the 35-kilogram carcass, hauled it up on to their horse, galloped up the field and attempted to hurl it through the opposition's goal. Anything seemed to be allowed; the players spent much of the match trying to wrestle opposing players off their horses. It was a phenomenal spectacle, mainly because of the Kazakh's incredible horsemanship. After the match, they demonstrated another game, a Kazakh version of kiss chase in which a male rider chased a woman on horseback, lifting his hat every time he managed to kiss her. Then they turned around and galloped back towards us, down a long track towards the stadium, the girl raising her hat every time she managed to whip the male rider. At the end, they asked if I would like a ride. We weren't insured, but riding a horse for a few hundred yards was nothing compared with riding 1150cc motorcycles around the world on the shittiest of roads. I thought 'fuck it' and didn't need any encouragement. I was up on the horse in a flash, Charley following immediately afterwards. We galloped off down the track, a long, straight stretch of grass flanked by trees, getting used to the high saddle. At the end of the straight, I stopped and turned, waiting for Charley to catch up. 'Race you back!' I shouted, gathering up the horse's reins and digging my heels into its sides.

The horses were fantastic animals, hardier and faster than anything I'd ridden before. I got a head start on Charley and thought I'd left him for dust. Then, slowly, a horse's head appeared beside me and there was Charley. We were side by side, nudging elbows and knocking shoulders. Charley was not going to concede the race without a struggle. He had to be in front, even if it meant he had a heart attack. We galloped on, riding closer than I had ever done before, reaching the finish line neck and neck. It was a dead heat. I looked over at Charley, a smile like a Cheshire cat on his face. It had been exhilarating. A brilliant moment.

We left the polo arena and drove into Shymkent. As usual, there was a welcoming committee. A few local dignitaries and some young girls in traditional dress holding trays of koumiss – fermented mare's milk – and bread. We'd just finished shaking hands and were climbing back on our bikes when a young guy on a Ural motorcycle rode up. Dressed in leather jacket, jeans, shades and a Stars and Stripes bandana with a star positioned smack in the middle of his forehead, he looked like a real greaser biker. The bike, which was belching black smoke, had been fitted with high handlebars, like a chopper. As he came to a stop, he raised his right hand, gave us the finger, jumped off the Ural, relying on a bystander to grab it instead of using the side stand, and whipped out a camera. It was a professional paparazzi camera, the type I'd seen too many times before, with a long, fast lens. He hosed us down with the camera, laughing as he did it. Charley and I jumped on our bikes and rode off. The paparazzo gave chase, riding down the street behind us. Pulling level with Charley, he let go of his handlebars and snatched his camera out of a holster on the side of the bike. Firing off another couple of dozen shots, he shouted 'Is good, is good, is good,' then zoomed off. We had to admire his style.

CHARLEY: We left Shymkent early the next morning on a mission to reach Almaty, 450 miles away, in time for Eric's daughter's first birthday party. It was a glorious ride. The landscape had completely changed. After days spent on open plains, we were riding through valleys, over hills and past lush fields dotted with trees. Riding under a clear blue sky towards the Tien Shan, a line of snow-capped mountains that stretched across the horizon separating Kazakhstan and Krygyzstan from China and forming one of the world's longest borders, the air smelled fantastic and I felt great. This was really what it was all about.

It was a long ride, the last section spent battling tiredness, my eyelids heavy and my brain slowing. We spent the day riding in front of or behind a police car with flashing lights, which pissed off both of us. We hadn't ridden all this way to be mollycoddled and for Ewan to be treated like a celebrity. Every time we stopped for a break, the policeman got out of his car and prevented passers-by from approaching us or asking questions. I could see it was really winding up Ewan. 'What the fuck are we doing here in the first place,' he said, 'if it's not to meet people and let them ask questions and let us ask them questions. Balls! Balls! Balls!'

I felt like we were being wrapped in cottonwool. We didn't want to miss Kazakhstan and it was very likely this would be the only time we ever passed through the country, but heavy-handed bureaucracy was preventing us from experiencing it. We came to resent every moment of having a policeman fussing all round us, making sure everything was all right. That afternoon, Ewan was leading as a police car approached on the opposite side of the

road, its lights flashing and siren howling. The driver pu
to the side of the road, got out and waved to flag us down,
just gave him a thumbs up and continued riding at 80m
pretending we didn't understand that he wanted us to stop. It wa
naughty but we'd had enough of police escorts.

About fifteen miles outside Almaty we stopped to meet the KZ
Motorcycle Club, a gang of about ten bikers all dressed in biker
leathers except for one big guy with a bushy moustache who was
wearing a black cowboy hat and chaps. They accompanied us into
Almaty on their sports bikes and Harley-Davidsons. It was a
bustling, cosmopolitan city, thronging with Hummers and big
BMW and Mercedes 4x4s, customised with lots of chrome and
dark windows. 'Kazakhs like the best horses and the best cars,'
Eric said. After a week in the outback of Kazakhstan, it was quite
a culture shock to be riding through a comparatively wealthy city
of two million people. Nearly all the roads in the city centre were
lined with mature trees, the buildings standing some way behind
them. It gave a charming impression of driving through a thick
forest, the long tree-lined avenues hiding expensive designer
clothes shops, glitzy nightclubs, good restaurants and high-class
hotels. I was delighted to be back in civilisation.

We spent four days in Almaty, recuperating, servicing the
bikes, eating well and going out late, and visiting a Unicef project.

I spent an afternoon at the Tamgaly climbing centre, a mountain
gorge in the Tien Shan range about two hours from Almaty. With
funding from British Airways, Unicef had set up a project that
provided climbing lessons and facilities for 22,000 seven- to
fourteen-year-olds in Kazakh schools, providing an alternative to
hanging around on the streets with little to do. Social problems such
as drug abuse and crime among disaffected adolescents had
avalanched since the collapse of communism, but I could see from
the children at the climbing competition that the climbing clubs had
helped them build up confidence, adopt a healthy lifestyle, make
friends and increase their social skills. Unicef had found that those
schools that had climbing walls installed experienced less truancy.

The next day, Ewan and I visited one of the best climbers, Akmaral Doskaraeva, a fourteen-year-old girl who lived in a shanty town on the outskirts of Almaty and went to Shanyrak school, which had come second in the previous day's competition. It was heartbreaking to visit Akmaral at home, where her mother, Gulbashim, told us about her family's struggle and their hopes. As we listened through the interpreter to Akmaral and Gulbashim's remarkable story, I was overcome with emotion. Gulbashim and her husband had moved from the countryside, taking an enormous risk in coming to Almaty to find a job. For six months they searched for somewhere to live, not knowing if they would ever see their children again. When Gulbashim told the story, I could see in the face of Ismeral, Akmaral's seven-year-old sister, the absolute terror that still haunted her. It wasn't uncommon for parents never to return for their children, simply because they became trapped in the city, were paid a pittance and could not afford to travel back to their home village or to bring their children to join them.

They lived in a tiny house. One room was a kitchen and bathroom, the other was the living room and bedroom. Both were smaller than the bathroom in my Almaty hotel suite. Akmaral's youngest sister was all dressed up and reminded me of Kinvara. I felt so thankful and fortunate not to have had to face that kind of life. On the morning of 12 May, when we rode out of Almaty bound for the Charyn Canyon, I looked at the picture of my daughters taped to the inside of my windscreen and thought about home. I'd been away from them for only four weeks, yet I missed them terribly and I wished I could see them now. I couldn't imagine what it would be like to walk away from your children in search of a better life, not knowing for sure whether you would ever see them again. Akmaral was a survivor. When I saw her climb across the roof of her school gym, I could see the pride and self-belief that the sport had given her and her classmates. Teaching children to climb seemed such a simple idea, but it had changed the lives of the young people at that school.

As usual, we had a pesky police escort to the canyon. It would have been foolish to expect otherwise. Within twenty minutes, we were on the outskirts of Almaty, leaving its blatant prosperity, car dealerships and fancy restaurants behind. Another couple of hours further east and the lush, irrigated farmland serving the city had given way to a flat, arid desert. We took a turning off the main road to the Russian border and followed a valley towards Charyn Canyon. It looked not unlike southern California, except that we were periodically stopped by shepherds riding mules, their flocks of sheep and goats roaming all over the road. Eventually, when it seemed there was no chance of us getting lost, the police Lada pulled aside and waved us in the direction of the canyon. We rode on for a while, past disused checkpoints that twenty years earlier had controlled access to the highly sensitive Soviet-Sino border. Such a vast frontier was thought to be almost uncontrollable, prompting jokes in the Soviet era that the Chinese had instructed their troops to move only in small units of ten thousand soldiers or less.

Then, suddenly, there it was in front of us. The Valley of the Castles. Formed by the Charyn River, which flowed rapidly down from the nearby snow-capped peaks of the Tien Shan, the canyon sank more than 300 metres beneath the desert plain. As soon as we stopped to look at this spectacular gash in the ground, a police car rolled up, looking all the more ridiculous in this majestic and empty landscape. With ambitions of camping at the bottom of the canyon, amidst the red weathered rock formations, we followed a track that led downwards. It was a big mistake. We followed the track down steep slopes for several miles, only to find it ended abruptly with a sudden vertical drop to the canyon floor. We had no choice but to turn back. But we soon discovered that getting our bikes back up the steep, rutted track was impossible. It took us three hours to unload our bikes, cart all our luggage, piece by heavy piece, up the narrow track, and then ride up the path. Carrying it up the hill one piece at a time made me realise just how much weight the bike was carrying. It gave me a new respect for the BMW, carrying all that weight and us in comfort for long distances every day. We both fell at least four or five times, the bikes taking quite a battering against the rocky sides of the track. It really freaked us out, but we learnt a valuable lesson: don't go down a track if you don't have to and especially one as steep as that one.

We camped, cooked some steak we had bought at a market and slept in our bivvy bags. Having forgotten to seal my inflatable mattress properly, I woke in the middle of the night with nothing between me and the hard, stony ground. Inside my bivvy bag, only a mosquito net separated me from the night sky. I could see millions of stars. The Milky Way, which I had never seen so clearly before, stretched across the sky like a smeary band of fairy lights.

As I stared at the night sky, wishing I'd done something about my mattress before the night became too cold for me to get out of my sleeping bag and inflate it, I realised we were already a month into the journey. With two and a half months to go, I suddenly had the feeling that we hadn't got that much time left. It was like being on a fortnight's holiday. The best times were always the first couple of days because most of the holiday was still ahead. By the third or fourth day, I would start to think about going home and I'd started to think the same way about this trip. With eighty days to go, it was probably a bit premature, but I had an overriding feeling of wanting it to go on for ever. I just wanted more and more.

The next day was just as good. Warm air blew through our jackets as we made our way north to the Russian border, riding through a golden desert flanked to the east by the four-thousand-metre peaks of the Tien Shan. By dusk we had passed Lake Kapshaghay, a sixty-mile-long reservoir that served Almaty, and were riding along a dusty track towards the singing dunes, Ewan and Claudio ahead of me, silhouetted in the clouds of dust, the setting sun throwing long shadows ahead of us. We set out to climb the eighty-metre-high dunes, which rose like a small part of the Sahara in the middle of the rocky Kazakh Desert, but it was harder than it looked. The slope was steep, the sand was slippery and I was exhausted after a long day in the saddle. Ewan made it to the top, disappearing out of sight, then reappearing as the ridge of the dune twisted, but I turned back less than halfway up. The sun was setting as Ewan descended the dune and we camped nearby. Having woken at six, it had been a long day.

Early the next morning, we waved goodbye to Eric and Eddie the driver, who had stayed at a hotel about twenty miles away, and pushed on towards Russia. With more than one thousand miles to the frontier, we knew we had several long days' riding ahead of us if we were going to cross the border by the end of the week. Still behind schedule, we were relying on making up lost mileage in Mongolia. We stopped in a village for lunch where we met a young boy, no more than eight or ten years old, riding one of the largest horses I'd ever seen. 'Go on, give it some,' I shouted. The boy immediately understood, tucked in and galloped off across the scrub: an incredible little horseman. At lunch we were served by another small boy. Taking our orders from a point-at-it photographic book showing plates of food, he served a fantastic meal. Even in a tiny rural backwater, Kazakh hospitality ensured a big effort for visitors. We camped again that night, Ewan and I sleeping in our bivvy bags to spare the effort of having to put up the tent and Claudio in his one-man tent, untroubled at sleeping on the bare floor without a mattress.

'Oh, you better be careful of scorpions,' Claudio announced, 'because one's just run under my tent.'

That just completely fucked it for me that night. 'But once we're zipped inside our bivvy bags, it's all right, isn't it, Ewan?' I said.

'Yeah, it's fine,' Ewan said. 'I'm pretty sure if you don't bother these things they're not going to bother you. You just have to be careful to look around when you get up. Anyway, it's just so nice, it's so hassle-free and quick in the bivvy bag. You just roll it out on the ground, cook a little something to eat and then go to sleep in it. In the morning, you wake up with the wind blowing in your face, get up and roll up the bivvy bag and go. And I get a real kick out of just being in the middle of these vast open spaces.'

Unconvinced, I hunkered down into my bivvy bag and dozed in a light sleep that was soon interrupted by the sound of flapping all around me. It was only the wind ruffling the outer layer of the bivvy bag, but I was convinced there were scorpions everywhere. I had premonitions of waking up in the morning and Ewan shouting: 'Charley! Don't move! The whole outside of your bivvy bag's covered in scorpions.' I lay there, knowing it was ridiculous, but petrified all the same. Maybe I'd watched too many bad movies. It was 1.30 a.m. before I managed to fall to sleep. Then I woke at about 3.30, needing the toilet. I slithered out and crawled a decent distance away from the camp. Just as I was squatting down, a spider the size of a dinner plate crawled past me, freaking me out. Dear God. Some of us were born to camp and some of us just weren't.

EWAN: Determined to reach the Russian border within thirty-six hours, we rode from dawn to beyond dusk across heavily potholed roads. In all the planning at Shepherd's Bush, I had never considered it might be as hot as it was under the midday sun in Kazakhstan. We guzzled litres of water to keep ourselves hydrated and awake. At six o'clock that evening, we were close to Usharal, where we could have stopped for the evening. Instead, we egged each other on to Ayaköz, the town beyond Usharal, once again chasing our shadows as we headed east. It was beautiful and I was in a trance. At times like this, riding to central Asia seemed so effortless. 'Ewan, where you going?' a conversation played out in my mind.

'I'm just going out on my bike.'

'You gonna be long?'

'Nah.'

'Where you going?'

'Thought I might go to central Asia.'

It was so exhilarating that I would forget where I was. I'd drift off and then realise with a start that I was in the middle of a desert, piloting a huge bike towards the Russian border. I felt totally in my element, as if I was born to ride that BMW around the world.

We arrived at Ayaköz at ten o'clock, long after the sun had set and Claudio had hit a large pothole full pelt in the darkness, denting his front wheel rim. We'd put 470 miles under that wheel since breakfast and I was worried it might not make the same distance again. But we had no time to stop and worry about it. Desperate for a bed and a shower, we stupidly let our good old friends the rozzers take the lead. 'Follow us,' they said and we were too tired to argue. Signalling that we needed to sleep, we asked them to take us to a hotel but instead they led us to the town square, where a stage had been erected and some entertainment was laid on. Once again, we were caught in the hospitality dilemma. The extraordinary effort to which people went was incredibly flattering and kind, but we wanted to be allowed to travel anonymously, particularly when we were dog-tired at the end of a long ride. It was our last night in Kazakhstan and it would have been churlish to refuse, so we watched the entertainment: a bloke with a balalaika who sang a few songs in a style not dissimilar to Billy Bragg or a protest singer, two sisters in long dresses, a young man in a grey suit performing what sounded like Kazakh techno, and another man in a turban. A small crowd turned up as the show progressed and we ended up signing autographs and having our pictures taken with them.

We were then taken on a wild-goose chase round the town in search of somewhere to sleep, eventually ending up in a house that we believed belonged to the local Governor, although we never did find out for sure. Struggling to make ourselves understood, we tried to impress on four plump Kazakh women who were fussing around us that we just wanted to change out of our motorcycle clothes and go to bed. But as we were led from room to room, more and more people turned up to have a look at us.

'Where are we sleeping?' Charley asked one of the women. 'If it's possible we would like to get changed and wash.'

'Your clothes?' the Kazakh woman said.

'Yes. We've been wearing these all day,' Charley said hesitantly. 'I'm not sure I understand.'

'Please wait a moment. Please wait a moment.' The woman walked off, then returned. 'You want to sleep here? Your bags don't worry.'

'But where will we sleep?' Charley asked patiently. I admired the way he was politely ensuring the women did not forget our quest for a bed.

'You're doing a great job, Charley,' I said. 'You're like a diplomat. Like Prince Charles.' The women chattered among themselves in Kazakh. 'This is your room,' the woman said.

'Okay. Brilliant. Thank you very much,' Charley said, nodding vigorously and bowing.

'Thank you,' the woman said. 'Now you have sauna.' It was shortly before midnight, but we didn't have the heart to argue. We got changed and were herded to the sauna, where the three other Kazakh women stood waiting. It was entirely innocent. They were just being good hosts, but having not washed for three days we wanted a bit of privacy.

'I'm going to close the door now,' Charley said to the women outside the sauna. 'Bye bye.' There was some giggling outside the sauna and then we were left to perspire in silence.

We emerged from the sauna to discover that a four-course meal had been laid on for us. I was ushered to the centre of a long table, with a middle-aged man in a very smart suit to my left. 'I think he's the Governor,' Charley whispered.

The table was laden with the kind of food we'd been eating all the way through Kazakhstan: shashlik, a mutton stew, caviar, smoked fish, lots of salads and a mountain of bread rolls. Just as I was thinking that we were about to get through Kazakhstan without ever having to eat sheep's head, a door swung open and a woman carrying a large platter walked in. The head had been

Charley at White Lake in Mongolia.

Ewan surrounded by a crowd of curious onlookers.

The extraordinary beauty of Mongolia.

Riding into Ulaanbaatar with Ted Simon (foreground left). Ted's classic book *Jupiter's Travels* was one of the inspirations for our own trip and it was a real treat to meet him.

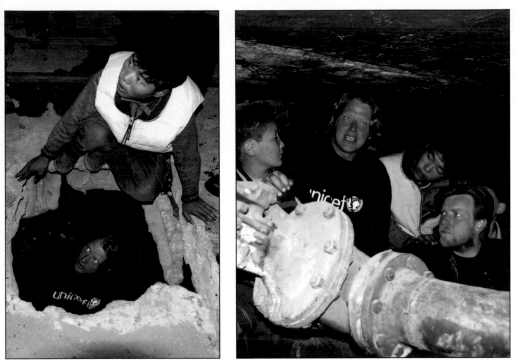

In Ulaanbaatar scores of orphans live under the streets in appalling conditions. We visited some of the children and a nearby orphanage with Unicef.

© Claudio Planta

On the border between Mongolia and Russia.

At the shores of Lake Baikal, which holds a fifth of the earth's fresh water.

Posing by a crashed truck in Siberia. The driver was still in the truck, having a snooze. When we asked if he was okay he just shrugged and said '*Normalya*', and went back to sleep.

Many of the roads in Siberia were flooded. It was exhausting, freezing and unrelenting hard work.

Another day, another bridge.

Charley cooks dinner on one of our many river crossings.

Taking a break as we neared the end of the Road of Bones. After many gruelling days, it was almost over.

One of our final river crossings in Far East Russia. We cut through dozens of rivers on our way to Magadan.

We couldn't have done it without our partners David (far left) and Russ (far right) . . .

. . . but in the end it all came back to the two of us, and two BMW 1150GS Adventures.

boiled, leaving a thin layer of greyish mushy flesh on it that looked like overcooked fat. I didn't know what to do so I proposed a toast.

'It's our last night in Kazakhstan and it's a night we certainly won't forget,' I said, raising my glass of water. 'Thank you very much for your hospitality and for allowing us to meet you and stay in your home.'

The Governor offered a toast in Kazakh, downed his glass of vodka and then, turning to me, offered some of the sheep's head.

'What do you do? I don't know what to do,' I said. 'Maybe you could show me.'

Turning to Charley, I said: 'Well, we didn't make it out of Kazakhstan without the sheep's head. I thought we might make it out . . .'

I thought it was quite funny and I was intrigued by the strange delicacy, but Charley looked worried. 'I want to see them eat it first to make sure that they're not making a joke of it,' he said.

'It's like . . .,' I said, slipping a sliver of the greasy meat into my mouth. 'Actually, it's fine.'

'You're making lots of noise chewing it. You sure it's okay?'

Our hosts were ripping the sheep's head apart. Everything came off it, even the insides of the ears. Charley smiled and nodded politely, but wouldn't eat it. Fortunately, our hosts weren't offended. They thought it was amusing rather than rude.

Eventually we got the sleep we needed so much before the final leg of our trip through Kazakhstan. The next day, we rode, via a gold mine that we visited in the morning, to Semey, close to the Russian border. Better known as Semipalatinsk, the Soviets used an area a few miles to the south-west of the city as the site for more than 450 nuclear warhead tests. Not somewhere in which I wanted to spend much time.

As we pushed on, I realised I didn't have a care in the world. I was drifting down a hill, marvelling at the sight of the hills and fields in front of me bathed in a beautiful golden light from the setting sun, the air fresh and heavy with the smells of the countryside and the acrid dust of the towns we were passing through, and I realised it was a perfect moment. I'd stopped worrying about the schedule or about how many miles we had chipped off the grand total each day. I was no longer worried about when or where we would have lunch and I'd managed to flush out my concerns about bigger issues, such as my future. For the first time in a long, long while, nothing was troubling me. I'd discarded the things that had been bothering me as we battled with the Road of Death, buried them in the deserts of Kazakhstan and entered a blissful worry-free state.

In spite of the police escorts and the media attention, I loved Kazakhstan and I was sad to leave. I didn't know if I would ever return, but I would always remember it fondly. Strangers had welcomed us into their homes and everyone we had met had been remarkably hospitable. Those three hellish days on the Road of Death and the other days spent riding vast distances across almost empty landscapes had banished my fears about what lay ahead and bedded us into the journey. The anxieties and the overexcitement about the whole thing had slipped away, leaving the experience of just doing it. We were covering huge distances. Four hundred and seventy miles that day. Another three hundred miles ahead of us the next day. Just riding from morning to evening. And as we followed the road, I came to feel that I belonged on that big motorcycle, rolling around the world. It was meant to be. And it didn't matter where exactly we were headed. We'd get there. We'd find somewhere to stay. Something or somebody would turn up. And if they didn't, we'd camp. It was that simple. At last I was living for each day, free as the eagles that lined the roadside, and I had the land of caviar, oil and gold to thank for that.

9
Little Red Devil

BARNAUL TO ULAANGOM

EWAN: We rolled up to the Russian border not expecting to pass through quickly. The support crew were waiting, Russ bursting to tell us that we'd arrived in Russia smack in the middle of the high season for ticks.

'Apparently one of the biggest sports stars in Russia just got bitten by a tick,' Russ said. 'They took him to the best clinic in the country. They did everything they possibly could for him. And he died.'

'Yeah, but we've been jabbed against tick-borne encephalitis,' I said.

'It's not one hundred per cent guaranteed,' Russ countered.

'Yes it is.'

'All right, go ahead and camp.'

'Russ always has the good news,' Claudio said, but Russ ignored him.

'Yeah, go and camp,' he said. 'It'll be good for the TV show. It's nice and progressive. At first you're paralysed, then you lose your sense of smell, then you can't hear or speak. But you're still alive in your body and the doctors just have to leave you like that until eventually you go. So if you want to go camping tonight, guys, just do it.'

'I'm going to the hotel, man.' It was Charley. 'Moto GP's on and we've missed every race this season.'

'Right. That's it settled then,' I said. 'Let's hotel it tonight, not because of the encephalitis, because we're going to camp – first it was spiders, then it was the snakes, then it was the bears and now it's ticks – but because we want to see the Moto GP and World Superbike, and more than anything because I want a cup of good Russian coffee.'

Greeted by a tall Soviet-era monument of a red star on the top of a massive white column, we rode into Russia. Everything immediately looked different. It was staggering, just like someone had abruptly switched channels from a black and white movie to a colour one. The landscape, the people, the houses, the roads, the fields had all changed. How did it know to do that? How did everything this side of the border know it was meant to look Russian, and how did everything a few miles before know it had to look Kazakh? I was pondering this when Claudio came to a screeching halt. We all pulled over.

'So what's happening, Claudio?' I said.

'I nearly had a head-on crash,' he said. 'That was nearly it for me. I was nodding off. These roads are too easy.'

It was baking hot, more than 110 degrees Fahrenheit, and we had all stripped down to our vests, Claudio riding with the sides of his trousers unzipped and flapping in the breeze. 'Funny that,' I said. 'I was just thinking about how much smoother the roads are in Russia.'

'Yeah, I was just thinking how it looks a bit like Mongolia, actually,' Charley said.

'How do you know it looks like Mongolia?' I said. 'We haven't been there yet. And anyway, it doesn't.'

'Well, it's a bit like Kazakhstan.'

'No. It doesn't look anything like Kazakhstan. How can you say that? Kazakhstan? It's amazing how different it looks from Kazakhstan.'

'Well . . . yeah . . . it's greener, but it's as flat.'

'It's completely different.'

'It's a different flat then,' Charley said. 'But it's still flat.'

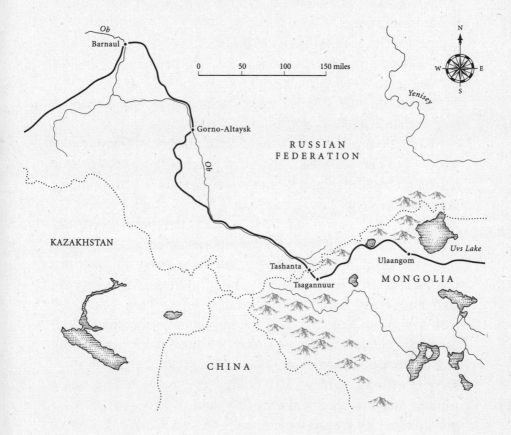

'Don't know about you, but I crossed the border and it didn't look Kazakhstan. There's a line on a map, there's a barrier and you go into Russia and it doesn't look like Kazakhstan any more. First thing that struck me. But you think it looks the same, Charley?'

'Well . . . I mean . . . but . . . yes, there were more trees and there are probably more Russians here than there were in Kazakhstan because we're in Russia.'

'But it's different grass and everything. Look, the fields are really green because they're irrigated.'

'It is different,' Charley said. 'You're right. You're right. You're right. It *is* different.'

I turned to Claudio. 'How are you feeling?'

'The roads are flatter,' Claudio said. 'No potholes.'

'You're not happy? You want potholes?'

'Yeah, because it gives me something to do. I had to concentrate,' Claudio said. 'I need a focus in life.'

Standing bare-chested at the side of the road, Charley was playing with his stomach. The only difference he would concede between Kazakhstan and Russia was the frequency at which his pot vibrated. 'This was Kazakhstan.' Charley shook his stomach violently. 'This is Russia.' Charley said, thrumming his belly gently. 'And this will be America.' No movement at all.

It was great to be in Russia, which seemed so easy and civilised after Kazakhstan. By late afternoon we were in Barnaul, a crazy place with the feel of a turn-of-the-century gold rush town. It was full of reckless drivers piloting right-hand-drive cars because of the proximity to China and Japan, and we passed several accidents on the roads into the centre of town. Despite having stripped off completely beneath our riding jackets and trousers, we were hot and sweaty, our boots a potential health hazard when we took them off. We showered, brushed up and set off for a restaurant called Rock and Roll in the hope of a wild night. After long, arduous days in the saddle, it was time for a laugh. We needed to let our hair down and have a big night. Barnaul was a vibrant, sexy place, most of the local women dressed in very skimpy clothes because of the hot weather.

'Fuck . . . look at her!' Charley said, watching a young Russian girl saunter past. 'Man, you could stand here any time of the day and you'd see twenty stunning women walk past in three minutes, all of them in tiny miniskirts with long, long legs. Unbelievable.'

Barnaul was a fun place to be. Reunited with the support crew for the first time in a week, we ate a Mexican meal under the fairy lights of a restaurant terrace, told stories and had a great night. Charley and I hadn't got on so well for a long time, just having a laugh and being silly. 'The cuds serve their purpose,' Charley said, 'and that's okay, but this has just made me realise how much I love cities.'

Unfortunately for Charley, we were straight back into the cuds the next day. He was very quiet as we made our way to Gorno-Altaysk, riding at the back. 'I just feel things are not going my way and I need some time,' he said, but it may have been the argument we had leaving town, when I had insisted on leading and had got lost. Charley had a tendency to want always to lead. I was happy with it most of the time, but there were times when I had enough of traipsing along at the back. 'I don't want to spend this trip being led around the world,' I said. 'That was never the idea.' But it seemed that whenever I took over, we'd get lost and then immediately Charley would go into a petrol station to get directions and take over the lead, without giving me the chance to sort things out myself. The riding, however, was glorious, across hot plains and through cool pine forests. Everything felt as if it had slotted into place. Riding through forests dotted with lakes, we arrived in Gorno-Altaysk in the late afternoon and spent the night in a four-storey dacha. It looked like an Alpine chalet and apparently once housed the secret police. We had little idea of where we were or who we were staying with, but it was something I had grown to love: just turning up, being told where to park our bikes and shown where to sleep. No prior arrangements and no fuss.

We rode higher into the mountains the next day, the twisty road climbing through thick forests and lush fields, and winding along meandering streams through mountain valleys carpeted with pink-purple heather. We'd always dismissed this part of the journey when we had been planning the route, but it was the best day's riding I'd ever had. 'We'll just nip through a bit of Russia between Kazakhstan and Mongolia,' we had said, not expecting the Altai Mountains to be a scenic highlight of the trip. I was in paradise, marvelling at how the landscape changed at every bend. It was staggeringly beautiful, with little wooden settlements beside rivers. Children and old ladies were collecting water in buckets from the river and carrying it home to irrigate their gardens, and lumberjacks were felling trees.

Like the previous day, it was stiflingly hot. Even though I was wearing nothing under my jackets and trousers, rivulets of sweat were pouring down my back. Spotting a mountain stream, we stopped, stripped off and went skinny-dipping.

'Aaaagh! Where has my penis gone?' I screamed as I stepped into the river and my body recoiled at the cold. Only just above freezing, the water came from melted snow a few hundred metres higher. It was having an alarming effect on my genitals.

'Fuck, I'm not going in there,' Charley shouted from the bank. 'It's too fucking cold.'

I managed to lie down and slip completely beneath the water, washing off half a day's sweat and cooling down immediately. 'Aaaagh! My feet are so cold! Complete penis disappearance!' I shouted.

Claudio strode into the river, wincing slightly at the cold but not making any fuss. 'The feet is the worst,' he said, splashing water all over his torso. 'Maybe it's because they get hottest in the boots.' Eventually Charley summoned up courage. Stepping gingerly across the stones, he suddenly ducked under the water and shot back up, yelling at the cold.

'This is so liberating!' I screamed, running naked along the riverbank back to my bike. 'Three nude men in the countryside. We should have some drums and bows and arrows.'

The best part of the impromptu skinny-dip was that we had shaken off our obsession with keeping to the schedule. We wouldn't have stopped at that river a week or so earlier, when there was an overriding feeling that we had to keep going, come what may. But we'd come to realise that keeping to planned mileage was pointless if we didn't experience anything along the way. We were three and a half days behind schedule but it didn't matter any more. The days were merging into one another. The experiences felt deeper and just as intense, but less pointed. I was taking fewer photographs and talking less about what we had seen and done each day because I no longer felt like a tourist or a traveller. The journey had become my life.

By late afternoon, realising that because of the winding roads we would not make it to the Mongolian border before it closed at seven o'clock, we stopped to camp beside another river. We contacted the support crew via the satellite phone and arranged to camp with them for the first time. David, a virgin to the glories of a night under canvas, liked to say 'Homey don't camp', but when he arrived, we discovered he was extremely well equipped with every camping convenience necessary to make a night outside as comfortable as possible. Homey did camp, it seemed. There were two large fold-out chairs for Russ and David, the producers, and little ones for everyone else, a really nifty metal table with a corrugated top, and a two-ring gas stove on a kitchen unit. It was quite unlike the hard-core camping to which we had become accustomed.

While the others collected a massive pile of firewood and made a supper of tuna and sweetcorn pasta, I got my fishing rod out for the first time. I cast a few lines, but caught nothing. Then we ate together, sitting around the huge campfire, gazing into the flames, telling ghost stories and chatting until one in the morning, taking turns to sing songs beneath the starry sky. Vasiliy, who led with a Siberian folk song, was followed by Jim, who sang something Czech, and I followed with 'Flower of Scotland'. It was a great night and exactly how I'd envisioned working with the support crew from the start – meeting up with them every five or six days to exchange experiences and tell tales of our travels but spending the rest of the time apart. It worked perfectly that way. We'd gone through a lot together, and Dave, Russ, Jim, Vasiliy and Sergey now felt like the best of old friends.

We continued climbing the next day, up mountain passes with snow-capped peaks. We crested the top of a hill to see the road stretching out in front of us straight as a die, the vast expanse split by a narrow tarmac ribbon running down the hill, across the valley floor and back up the opposite hill, not a kink in the road for as far as we could see. Ahead of us was Mongolia. The riding was beautiful, but after the late night around the campfire, the monotony of that long, straight road made it difficult to stay awake. By the time we reached the border, I was desperate for sleep and crumpled into a heap on the concrete floor, leaving Charley and Claudio to deal with the guards.

Two hours later, we were in no-man's-land. Behind us, the Russian border, all brand new gleaming concrete and steel buildings. As we rode down a hill towards a string of shabby wooden huts that looked as if they hadn't been painted for fifty years, the tarmac ran out beneath our wheels and the gravel began. Ahead of us stretched the Mongolian border, a frontier we'd been repeatedly told was not open to westerners. This crossing was strictly for local Russian and Mongolian goods vehicles, and it certainly looked like it was rarely used. But thanks to the tireless efforts of our office staff in Shepherd's Bush, we'd got special permission to enter Mongolia from the west, and make our way to Ulaanbaatar, in the east of the country, along a route rarely travelled by tourists. The formalities quickly dealt with, we rode into Mongolia, turned a corner and ran straight into a herd of yaks. Fifteen or twenty of the big, hairy monsters. We pulled into a clearing, where our local fixer, Karina, had been waiting for four days. She was very excited to see us and tied blue ribbons to our bikes, a Mongolian shaman tradition used to bestow good luck on babies and vehicles. I was determined to get off on our own, and as soon as we'd had a cup of tea we whipped off, telling the support crew we'd meet them at White Lake in five or six days.

Within minutes, Charley was on the radio. 'Fucking hell, look at these roads,' he said. 'This is like going back to the fucking Stone Age. What have we let ourselves in for?' We'd been told to expect dirt tracks, but we'd expected better than this.

'Sand would be preferable to this loose gravel,' I said.

'I'd even take mud,' Charley replied. 'Some dried mud would be nice, but this rocky gravely stuff is a nightmare.'

The roads were atrocious. They were cut into the landscape and we could vaguely follow them, but there ended any similarity with roads we had previously known. These were no more than tracks made by the nomads' trucks and animals. As we rode in parallel across sludge-coloured plains, an immense sky threw shadows in a million shades of brown across the rolling hills and mountains and five or six tracks cut across the steppe, making it difficult to judge which one went where. A couple of hundred yards to my right, Claudio was riding on one track, trailing a cloud of gravel dust. Leading our little pack, Charley was in the centre, at the tip of our little arrowhead, and I was on the far left. I'd hoped we'd be able to make up lost time in Mongolia, but even our target of one hundred miles a day was going to be hard work. It would test us and it would test the bikes.

Crawling along at about 20mph on the rutted tracks, we came to our first Mongolian town. 'Talk about poverty,' Charley said. 'There's nothing here.'

The buildings were crumbling ruins. A man and a child appeared. Both of them looked terrible, the child filthy and barefoot with a snotty nose and sores on his arms and face. 'Oh my God,' I said, shocked at what lay in front of us. We'd expected Mongolia to be our Shangri-la. It looked like it was going to be hell.

We rode on until we came to a patch of greener ground beside a river. It was past nine o'clock, the sky was darkening and a storm was brewing, so we decided to camp. Within minutes of putting up the tent, a truck pulled up. Two construction workers in blue canvas jackets and caps jumped out and came bowling down the slope to our camp. They looked over the bikes cautiously, fascinated by the dials and switches. We showed them our route from London to New York on the maps stuck to our top boxes. They ran back to the cab of their truck and returned with a bottle of vodka.

'That's very kind,' I said, shaking my head, 'but not for me, thanks.' It was obvious they wanted to sit down and share it with us, but after the shock of our arrival in Mongolia and a long day in the saddle, none of us was up for it. I pulled a piece of paper out of my pocket and scanned it for suitable Mongolian conversational phrases.

'*Sain baina uu?*' I said – How are you?

The smaller of the two construction workers shook his head. '*Kazakh.*'

'*Sain baina uu?*' I repeated.

'*Kazakh.*'

'Uh, you're from Kazakhstan?'

'*Ia. Kazakh,*' the construction worker said. Yes, he was Kazakh.

'*Rakhmet,*' I said. Unfortunately the only Kazakh I could remember was the word for goodbye.

The two Kazakhs cracked up. '*Rakhmet. Ia, Kazakh.*' They pressed their bottle of Mongolian vodka on us, making it clear they would not accept a refusal. Even if we weren't going to drink it with them, they wanted us to have it. I felt we had to give them something in return, so I dug out some Johnnie Walker miniatures I'd been carrying in my pannier for just such an occasion.

'These are from my country,' I said. 'Scotch whisky.' They raised their eyebrows as they looked at the tiny bottles in their palms. I hoped it was the golden colour of the liquid rather than the small size of the bottles compared with the litre of vodka they had given us. We shook hands, they departed, and we settled down to cook our dinner. The water was just coming to the boil when I looked up and saw a dark figure approaching on horseback, silhouetted against a triangle of stormy sky between two mountains. A young kid, no more than fourteen, he stopped about 50 feet away, and watched us warily.

'He's not coming any closer,' Charley said.

'Maybe we should approach him,' I said.

We walked up to the kid on the horse. The horse was small, a chestnut with a bushy black forelock and a white star on its snubby nose. I stroked it. 'Hello. Nice horse,' I said. The kid stared back, holding a stick that formed the rear part of the reins. He had dark, suspicious eyes. Maybe he was scared. We shook his hand in turn. He watched for a while, then turned his horse.

'Well . . . bye then,' I said. The kid click-clicked and cantered off, giving us the biggest beaming smile, all white teeth. We returned to watching our meal packs warm up in the boiling water. Then another horseman turned up. Dressed in a blue zip-up top and wearing a green khaki cap, he was older and taller than his predecessor, but his white horse was just as small. Again, he stopped about 50 feet away and just stared.

I walked up. 'I'm Ewan. This is Charley. What's your name?'

Holding the horse's reins, he tapped his chest. 'Limbenik,' he said. At least that's what it sounded like. He jumped down from his horse, showed the animal off to us as if he was offering it for sale and then indicated to me that I should mount it. I climbed up into the saddle and held the whip, a piece of cord on a stick. I sat on the horse for a couple of minutes while Charley went through the usual spiel – '. . . from London to New York on these motorbikes . . .' – and Limbenik nodded and smiled. I jumped down and Limbenik climbed back up, turned the horse and galloped off, leaving us to ponder on our first contact with the locals.

CHARLEY: We slept late, broke camp late and left late, but it was good to get a proper night's sleep. Setting off with the intention of reaching Ulaangom, a market town about 130 miles east, we rode across a landscape built for giants. It was baking hot and, with no vegetation in sight, the ground and surrounding mountains glistened like gold. The sheer beauty of it took my breath away. We followed the track into a gorge that led to Bohomoron. It was a small town, but without signposts or proper roads it was impossible to work out which track to follow out of it. We asked a few bystanders the way, but they couldn't understand us, so we turned around and rode back to a petrol station. Within minutes, we were surrounded by crowds of people wanting to look at our bikes. They were incredibly friendly but no help with directions. Then an old boy in a suit turned up, riding pillion on the back of someone else's motorbike. I thought he looked as if he might be able to help us.

'Ulaangom?' I said, pointing to a map in my other hand.

He shook his head and wiggled his hand to indicate a river. Then, pointing at my bike, he indicated the river was too high for a motorcycle to cross.

'Ulaangom?' I asked again. He held up his crossed hands in the shape of an X – the universal sign for road closed.

I shrugged. The man tapped my bike, grabbed my map and, with his finger, sketched out a route around a large lake shown on the map.

'I think he's saying the river's too high and we have to go round Lake Achit to get to the other side of it,' I told Ewan.

'Shit. What do you think?' he replied.

'It's a long way. Must be about a hundred-and-fifty-mile detour.'

'You know, Charley, he's wearing a suit and he looks like he knows what he's talking about. If he's telling us the river is too high, I think we should just take his word and get on with it.'

So we did. The man got back on the motorbike and with his friend led us a few miles out of town, where they stopped and pointed ahead, indicating that we had to follow the track around a large mountain in the distance. I was overwhelmed. Having turned up in a town that was little more than a collection of shacks, I couldn't believe that we were now meant to follow what appeared to me to be the least used of all the dirt roads leading back out of the town. I felt completely out of control and I could barely cope with it. The main roads, which were shown as thick red lines on the map, were only dirt tracks at best. But this route, which was used even less than the minor roads, was quite likely to disappear altogether at some point, leaving us stranded in the middle of Mongolia. There was no other traffic; the only thing we could do was trust our GPS navigation equipment, without which we would have been completely buggered.

Lo and behold, the track soon disappeared, leaving us to ride across wide open plains of stone and gravel, one eye on the GPS screen to check we were riding in the right direction. We stopped in a village of light-coloured mud buildings. Children came running out, giggling at the sight of us, their hands all over the motorbikes, wanting to have a look. They pointed us in the right direction and we pressed on. Occasionally we would come across a track and follow it for a while, feeling reassured, but then it would split in two or three directions, one track heading over a hill, the other disappearing around the hill, and the third taking off across the prairie, and we were plunged into uncertainty again. The riding was harder than I ever imagined it could be, much worse than the three days on the Road of Death in Kazakhstan because there was no road and because the terrain alternated between sharp rocks, deep sand and mud. There was no let-up, no short section of compacted mud or tarmac. It was just so hard. More than once I thought: what the fuck am I doing here? Why am I doing this? Who thought this would be a good idea? I just wanted to go home. For the first time, I really hit a low, my mood all the worse for not having eaten since breakfast.

We came to a stream running across the prairie. The stream was not that wide, but it was edged by 20 to 30 feet of mud. I took it steadily and just got my bike through. Ewan fell over and had to be hauled out of the mud. Claudio, of course, took his own course and effortlessly made his way across. A few miles further on, we came to an exceptionally muddy section, Ewan's bike sinking up to its axle. Claudio and I were straining to lift Ewan's bike out of the mud when a blue flat-bed truck pulled up. Like something out of dustbowl 1930s America, it was laden with what looked like the contents of several houses, including caged chickens and a goat, all wrapped in brightly coloured tarpaulins. From deep within the bundle came the sound of barking. That heap, we assumed, was a packed-up ger, the round, white felt and canvas tent or yurt that many Mongolians call home. Buried deep inside it was a dog. About ten men and several young boys clambered out of the truck cab and emerged from under the tarpaulin. They gathered around, lifting and pushing Ewan's bike until it was out of the rut. Ewan gunned the engine, sending a spray of mud flying over our Mongolian helpers. He was mortified. 'I'm so sorry. Really sorry,' he said as the Mongolian who had come off worst gave him a filthy look.

I made my way gingerly through the mud without falling. Claudio, typically, took it full pelt, just managing to grab control of his bike before it slipped away underneath him. 'I don't know how he does it,' Ewan said. 'It's fucking irritating.'

We saw few other people for the remainder of the day. Whenever we did meet someone, we stopped them to ask directions. Essentially nomadic, the Mongolians seemed to know exactly how to get around their country. And whenever we didn't know if we were on the right track, we kept riding, hoping we wouldn't get lost. Towards the end of the day, we passed through Hotgor, a mining town in which we had hoped to find a bed. But as the locals all appeared to be extremely drunk, we kept going, eventually stopping for the night and pitching a camp on a dry riverbed about 400 metres wide. With an eagle circling overhead and a huge black cloud approaching, we pumped water through our water purifier and wished we were anywhere else but there.

The day had been soul-destroying. The detour around the lake meant we'd made no progress further east. 'It's like wanting to cross Leicester Square and having to go via Wales,' Ewan said.

We'd also failed to make up lost days. At least four days behind schedule now, we still had half the lake to circumnavigate. The riding had been exhausting and the slippery conditions meant we could never look beyond the ground 10 metres ahead of the front wheel. It sapped all our energy, it was demoralising and we had no idea when it would end.

'Fuck, I'm knackered,' I said. We hadn't had a day off since Almaty and the constant riding was starting to take its toll.

'I'm just a bit homesick tonight,' Ewan replied. 'I'd quite like to be at home, getting into my bed at the end of the day with Eve.'

EWAN: Packing our bags after a hasty breakfast the next morning, we discovered the luggage frame on Claudio's bike had cracked on the left side, underneath one of his panniers. It was the first serious damage to any of the three BMWs. We set off determined to focus on the positive, the sheer madness of riding across a country where a swollen river can send you on a 160-mile detour. We rode back into Hotgor to stock up on water from a tanker, dropping a couple of purification tablets into it, and then began the first of three long climbs over mountain passes. It was hard work on fully laden bikes, but we kept at it, determined to make Ulaangom that evening and feeling as if we were in the pages of a *Boy's Own* novel. The track was treacherous. Boggy, rocky and muddy, it was bigger and rougher than anything I'd ridden on before and it was made all the worse by the knowledge that Claudio's frame was cracked and might give way at any time. At the top of the first pass, we came across a nomad on horseback with three camels and a couple of dogs. He was a stunning man, fine-featured and handsome, proudly sitting bolt upright on his horse. In the traditional garb of pointed leather herdsman's boots, a Mongolian hat and several layers of heavy woollen clothing, he was grazing his camels at the top of the mountain. He looked so perfect and so at home in his surroundings it could have been a hallucination. We rode past him, then stopped to look back in wonder. He rode over slowly, climbed down from his horse and stood at a distance, watching us. It appeared to be the Mongolian way, just taking your time to suss out strangers. Slowly he walked over and we shook hands. He circled around the bikes, looking them over and talking softly in a beautiful lilting voice. His skin was deeply tanned and you could see he'd spent all his life outdoors. As we chatted, not really understanding each other but still managing to communicate, I had an idea. That morning, as I was packing the tent on to my bike, I'd come across my binoculars and I had realised I would probably never use them on the trip. Up on that mountain, I immediately knew what to do with them. The nomad had a rifle on his back and probably often had to watch out for wolves, so I handed him my binoculars, letting him look through them at the mountains. Turning slowly, he told us the name of all the mountains he could see. Pointing at a mountain in the far distance, he made it clear that it was on the other side of the lake and that we would be back on the main road by the time we reached it. The mountain was still a long way off, but it was a relief to see the end in sight and I thanked him. He put the binoculars back in their case and handed them to me.

'No,' I said. 'I want you to have them.' With both hands, I pushed the binoculars towards him. 'You'll make better use of them than I ever will.'

He looked unsure. Then he smiled broadly and took them, making a little sign of blessing and thanking me. It was a lovely, spontaneous moment. I was struck by the beauty of this man's life and it felt really nice to give a present to somebody who lived at the top of a mountain, on a horse, sauntering along watching his camels graze and looking at the mountains, all of whose names he knew. He was so at home in his surroundings and so friendly to us, and at that moment I fell in love with him and the mountains and Mongolia.

We said our goodbyes and set off back down the mountain. It was a hairy ride, the bikes slipping on the sand and mud, but we coped well with it. Charley was riding slightly ahead and we were making real progress, buoyed by the feeling that we were returning to the road.

'I've had a fall. I've had a bad one.' It was Claudio on the radio. There was a quietness in his voice that made it sound very serious. Shit a brick, I thought, this is bad.

'Which side? Which side of the bike did you fall on?' Charley said. Then he immediately corrected himself: '. . . I mean, have you hurt yourself?'

'Oh yeah, Charley, it's "Have you hurt yourself" first, isn't it?' I said, angry that Charley seemed more concerned about Claudio's bike than Claudio's wellbeing.

We turned our bikes around and climbed back up the mountain to find Claudio's bike lying on its side and Claudio standing beside it looking concerned. He had clipped a rock with his right pannier, which had sent the bike spinning, and he had tumbled over on its cracked left side. Charley jumped off his bike.

'Fucking hell. You've just got to be so careful . . . it's really . . .,' Charley berated Claudio. 'You know we've said this before about your recklessness, Claudio.'

Charley stood over Claudio's bike, shaking his head. 'Anyway, it doesn't really matter. What's done is done. Your pannier's ripped off on the good side. The bad side looks a little bit worse, which is a shame.'

Claudio, who had fallen far fewer times than Charley or me, stood beside the bike, looking contrite. 'The thing is that you're okay,' Charley said. 'But I think from now on you should stick close to one of us and just take our route. Yeah?'

'Okay,' Claudio said.

'We both have more experience of this kind of gravel and . . .'

'Certainly have . . .' Claudio said, his head bowed like a naughty schoolboy being told off by a teacher.

'. . . and that way we can show you the easiest route,' Charley went on, 'which, I hasten to add, is not necessarily the smoothest route.'

'Sorry.'

'Nice place to crash, though. Beautiful place.'

'Sorry.'

'Don't apologise,' I said. 'You all right? That's the main thing. Did you hurt anything?'

'No, I didn't. I just slowly, slowly smashed my bike. That's the problem.'

Charley had been on the phone to Howard at BMW in England. Pointing at the Touratech frame on Claudio's bike, Charley said: 'The biggest problem from your crash, Claudio, is that this crack was not anywhere near as big as it is now and according to Howard we can't ride on without fixing it.'

The section of frame that was previously cracked had now split in two. Howard suggested to Charley that we strap it together somehow, then get to the nearest town where we could get it spot-welded. The welding, he said, was often fantastic in the cuds because so many of the vehicles were very old. Practice made perfect.

'Did Howard say anything else?' I asked.

'He said you're probably feeling pretty low at this stage. Just remember to smile. Look at each other and smile.'

I set about trying to hammer Claudio's pannier back into shape, while Charley did the most incredible botch job, using about forty cable ties to strap two tyre irons as splints across the split in the frame. It amazed me that he just got on with it, working almost in silence but knowing exactly what to do. When he had finished, he stepped back. 'That should hold it,' he said, 'with a bit of luck.' It looked like a work of art.

We took off down the track. Again the riding was very difficult. By lunchtime, concerned that we weren't making enough progress, I had sunk into a dark mood, not helped by the fact that there was no prospect of eating all day. Eventually, a day and a half after we started the detour around the swollen river, we made it back to the main road. It was easier on a proper track, but I was at the back and there was so much dust that I spent the next few hours eating the dirt thrown up by Claudio's and Charley's bikes. Climbing to the top of the third pass of the day, I was struggling to stay awake and fed up with having to carry some of Claudio's equipment, which made my bike so top-heavy I couldn't steer it. Getting it around some of the rocks was like trying to pilot a whale.

We reached the top of the pass and stopped. I immediately laid in to Charley, barking at him for throwing up so much dust, for riding too fast and for a dozen other things, all the criticism completely unwarranted and brought on by my bad mood. I walked away, sat down on a rock on the side of the mountain and surveyed the scene. I couldn't believe my eyes. It was the most incredible sight. I could see the track that we were going to take winding across the valley floor and twisting up the mountain beyond. I closed my eyes and sat there for five minutes, breathing the mountain wind blowing in my face. Every now and then, I would open my eyes to that magnificent view, take it all in, close my eyes again, let the wind rush over my face, then open my eyes again. It just blew me away every time I saw it. No man could be in a bad mood up there for very long. I apologised to Charley and we set off again, bumping down the mountain and across the valley floor until, a few hours later, we were overtaken by a couple on a two-bit yellow Russian bike that was moving much faster than ours. As it passed, I looked up and saw a little Russian jeep with a trailer racing along parallel to us. He's not bouncing around, I thought, and there's no cloud of dust behind him. Then it dawned on me: he was on a road. I'd forgotten they existed. I'd assumed we'd be riding on gravel and sand to Ulaanbaatar. The world was immediately a better place.

CHARLEY: We arrived in Ulaangom, a windswept town of a few thousand people, and stopped outside the police station. The botch job on Claudio's frame had held, but we needed to get it welded. We'd found most Mongolians to be quite blank-faced when first approached and this was no exception. I didn't know whether they got the message, but by miming and showing them the breakage I seemed to make myself understood. Suddenly one of them stepped forward, jumped on a motorbike and beckoned us to follow him. He took us to a welder sitting in the dust at the corner of two streets. The welder's equipment was dented, rusty and made a worrying buzzing noise, but it was our only choice.

'What do you reckon?' I said.

'He's the welder, isn't he?' Ewan said. 'He's got welding rods and a welding mask.'

Wearing a threadbare cardigan, the welder took a look at Claudio's bike while I got on the phone to Howard. We'd attracted quite a crowd of locals, all eager to look at our bikes and see what was going on. 'Don't let him do anything until I've spoken to Howard,' I shouted over the mêlée. I was worried that one wrongly placed weld would inflict more damage on an already handicapped bike. But there was no stopping the welder. He'd spotted the break and donned a pair of wraparound sunglasses, the type you'd get free from a petrol station. As I heard Howard's voice at the other end, the welder was preparing to touch his welding electrode to the bike.

'Stop!' I shouted. It was too late. The welder had already made contact with the bike, just after Howard had told me to make sure the battery was disconnected.

'It should be all right,' I said. 'He's only just started. Howard says we need to disconnect the battery.' We uncoupled the positive terminal of the battery and the welder went to work.

'Wow, wow!' I said when he was finished. He'd done a fantastic job. 'You are a great man. Excellent. You're the man!' With the bare minimum of tools, the welder had bonded a bolt across the break and added a second strip of metal to brace it. The break was repaired.

'How much money?' I asked the welder. He just shrugged and smiled.

'Give him five, Charley.' It was Ewan. 'I'd give him five dollars.' It was worth every cent.

I took the bike for a short test ride on a patch of dirt in front of a row of empty cargo containers. The frame was fine, but in the process of welding it we had wrecked the anti-skid braking system. Claudio's brakes worked, but only just. The bike would not have made it over any of the mountain passes we'd crossed that day. We needed brakes not just to slow down and stop but to help guide us round all the bumps. I got back on the phone.

'Shit,' I said after speaking to Howard. 'He said we should have disconnected both terminals.' We were stuck in the middle of Mongolia, nearly one thousand miles from Ulaanbaatar, three men with two working bikes. There was nothing for it but to strip the bike down and see if I could fix it myself. But an afternoon and evening of working in one of the unlit empty containers made no difference. The brakes were beyond repair.

A couple of Mongolians who were hanging around tried to sell us a Russian bike as a replacement, but it had no working brakes whatsoever. There was no cable attached to the brake lever. Then, out of the blue, in the wastes of Mongolia, an American guy turned up. His name was Kyle and he worked for the American embassy, surveying Mongolian military radio installations. He had cropped hair and looked very fit. We immediately thought he was a spy working for the CIA, but Kyle had a simple explanation for his curious job: Mongolia had no money, so the American government provided its border guards with free radio equipment. It sounded reasonably plausible and we didn't want to question it too much because Kyle had done a deal for us with a policeman and a couple of Mongolian men to get the broken BMW to Ulaanbaatar for $300. He also put us in contact with Todd, an American peace worker and the only other westerner in Ulaangom, who was going to take us to the market the next day to buy a new bike for Claudio.

'Kyle's clearly the man to know in Ulaangom,' Ewan said. 'In the Ukraine, it was Igor. Here it's Kyle. He sorts everything out.'

The next morning, Todd took us to the market, a row of stalls, concrete huts and shipping containers, their doors opened to display their wares, that sold just about everything, including bikes.

'So how does the market work here, Todd?' Ewan asked.

'It involves the exchange of goods for monetary value. People give money and then they get goods in exchange.' Todd had a dry sense of humour.

'You wouldn't be a teacher?' Ewan said.

'I am a teacher,' he said. 'I teach English at the local school.'

Todd proceeded to explain that Mongolia was split into eighteen administrative provinces, called *aymags*. Ulaangom, the regional capital, or Aymag City, of the Uvs *aymag*, was the local transportation hub and market town. With Todd's help, we found a stall selling brand new motorbikes, but we wanted one a year or so old, which we thought would be less likely to break down because of teething problems. But when we saw the bikes the locals claimed were a year old, we soon changed our minds: the brakes didn't work, the tyres were worn, and they belched blue smoke. Todd agreed the price of a new bike in 'Americ dolla' with a Mongolian woman who haggled down to the last cent. The $1,034.48 bike was unpacked from its crate and prepared for the road, and, an hour or so later, Claudio had a new bike. With its red tank and frame, and the longest chrome-plated exhaust pipe any of us had ever seen on a bike, we christened it the Red Devil. I'd been against the idea of buying the bike. It had a pretty rough ride ahead and I was convinced it wouldn't be able to keep up with our BMWs, but Claudio was dead happy. Determined to carry on, he really wanted it.

By mid-afternoon, the Red Devil was ready, we had packed up and Claudio's wounded BMW had been strapped to a truck to be taken to Ulaanbaatar. Ewan was desperate to put some distance between us and the support crew, even though we'd arranged to camp with them that night. He rode ahead without asking for directions. Before we knew it, we were lost. We hadn't even left Ulaangom. Meanwhile, Claudio was trundling along as happy as could be on the little Red Devil, quite unaware of where he was going. I raced past Claudio and took the lead, until we came to crossroads where the roads skimmed off in every direction imaginable.

'How the fuck are we going to find anything in this fucking place if we can't find the fucking right road?' I shouted. 'There's dirt tracks going off every-fucking-where.'

Eventually we found our way out of town in the direction of Uvs Lake. It was a hard ride and we fell over repeatedly on tracks of soft sand and mud. With dark clouds rolling across the sky, we stopped beside some gers to camp for the night. For the first time, I was really down in the dumps. We were back in the cuds and I was missing being in a town with a hotel. I felt overwhelmed by the roads, and had serious doubts as to whether or not we would survive Mongolia.

That evening we were invited into the ger by the nomads. The support crew, our Mongolian fixers, Ewan, Claudio and I accepted. Following Todd's instructions to enter the ger from the left, to say hello and to accept the offer of a cup of a tea, we sat in a circle around a large pot bubbling on a fire at the centre of the tent. Ornate carpets covered the bare ground; tapestries and intricately patterned fabrics lined the walls.

'Would you like to eat nuts?' our Mongolian fixer asked.

'What do you mean nuts?' Russ demanded.

'Bollocks,' Ewan said. 'Bull's testicles. I saw them castrating some animals behind the ger only an hour or so ago.'

'Noooo,' Russ said. 'No, no.'

The Mongolian woman who had invited us into her cosy ger lifted the lid on the bubbling pot. Inside was a brown liquid with a white foamy scum and what looked like lumps of gristle floating in it. She spooned the liquid with a ladle, lifted some up and let the lumps plop back into the cauldron. It was unmistakable. They were testicles. About two hundred of them. Lamb's, bull's and goat's testicles. A feast for Mongolians, but a nightmare for us. David had pulled up the neck of his tracksuit top so that it covered his mouth, Ewan was nervously stroking his beard and I had broken out in a sweat.

'Well, go on,' Russ said to me. 'This is something you do. You come from a farming background.'

'Why don't you do it?' I asked. Russ had turned pale. He looked very peaky. 'Russ is very particular about his food,' I explained.

'Just cheese, bread and tea for me. Simple tastes,' Russ said. 'Go on. Have a bull's nut. Have a look at it.'

The woman ladled out a single testicle for each of us and handed us bowls to put on the little Formica-topped tables in front of us. 'Oh my Lord,' Russ said, looking wide-eyed at his portion. He started to jitter. Ewan continued stroking his beard. I hummed a tune.

'I don't want to eat something that makes things,' I said.

'We'll all do it,' Russ said. 'We'll do it together.'

'I guess we should try,' Ewan said. 'But it does worry me slightly what it's going to be like to eat.'

'Only *slightly*?' David said.

'I'll tell you what it'll be like,' I said. 'There'll be a big lump of fat around the bollock. Inside it'll be gristly and full of semen. The last two nuts they put in there were swinging from an animal five minutes ago.'

'But there are two hundred others you could choose from . . .,' David said.

'I don't think I could do it,' Ewan said quietly.

I skewered a testicle on my fork. It was all veined and bulging. 'Me neither,' I said. 'This thing used to have feelings.'

'Why don't we do rock, paper, scissors?' Russ suggested. 'Whoever loses goes first.'

'No,' Ewan and I chorused.

'I can't,' I said. 'I will puke. It'll come straight back up.'

'I'll do it.' It was Ewan. He'd changed his mind. 'I'll eat a small one, but just a small one.' Without any fuss, he took a testicle out of his bowl, popped it in his mouth, chewed, swallowed and smiled. 'Suddenly I feel like I want to make love to every woman in the world,' he said. I knew I had to follow. The camera was watching.

'I'll try one,' I said.

'Just one each. One small one each,' Ewan said.

'Whoah, whoah,' said David. 'How did we get into the "each" thing?'

'C'mon David,' said Russ. 'They're fresh. They've come off today.'

'This one's twitching,' said David, scrutinising the ball in his bowl.

I looked at the testicle in front of me. A clear liquid was leaking out of it, dripping down the tines of my fork. I didn't want to think too much about what I was about to put in my mouth. I slipped it in, chewed once, but I couldn't swallow it. I spat it out.

David popped one in his mouth, chewed quickly and swallowed it straightaway. 'Hmm, it's very good,' he said, nodding. 'I think I've acquired a taste for them. It's given me the horn.'

'Have another then,' Russ chipped in.

'No, you have one, Russ,' David said.

'Go-on-Russ. Go-on-Russ. Go-on-Russ.' It was Ewan. Now, surely, Russ couldn't refuse.

'Okay, let's do it,' he said. His skin was mottled and damp. He was twitching slightly. Looking pasty, with his head bowed down and his eyes clamped shut, Ross closed his mouth on the testicle. He chewed quickly, running his hands across his face and through his hair as he tried to swallow it. Then he lurched forward and gagged.

'I can't do it,' he said. The testicle was back in the bowl.

EWAN: We left the ger and returned to our tents. It rained all night and most of the next day, turning what had been treacherous conditions into a nightmare. We slipped, we skidded and we fell. But I was still determined to break away from the support crew. We'd made our way this far without them or a police escort, relying on the people we met along the way. Charley, however, felt otherwise.

'It's just so difficult,' he said. 'I know you're dead keen on breaking out on our own, but I think it would be safer with the cars nearby. I'd rather be following them. It's just so tough otherwise.'

'C'mon, Charley,' I said. 'We survived the first few days in Mongolia like big boys. And didn't it feel satisfying? I don't want to go back to being watched over by minders.' I was determined not to let some mud get in the way of experiencing Mongolia the way I wanted. There was a whole different dynamic when the support crew were around, and, much as I loved them all, I preferred it when it was just Claudio, Charley and me.

Riding on mud, however, was no fun. We averaged less than ten miles an hour and our bikes were caked with great lumps of dirt. Several times, Charley and I fell over only to watch Claudio approach, his little Red Devil's engine backfiring and buzzing like a wasp. 'Slow down!' Charley would shout. 'Very dangerous!' But Claudio kept going at the same speed, dropping into ditches and sliding across mud without wobbling at all, and passing us by as if it was the easiest thing in the world.

But Claudio's bike was not as reliable as its rider. We'd just eaten some sandwiches for lunch and were bumbling along, when Claudio pulled over. His bike would not go into gear. 'Christ, what do we do?' I said.

'I've got no idea,' Charley replied. 'Absolutely none.'

While we were standing over Claudio's bike, trying to work out how to repair it, an orange Russian jeep with a canvas top pulled up. It didn't seem to matter where you were in Mongolia: if anything went wrong somebody would soon turn up. Two old boys in the obligatory blue canvas baseball caps got out of the jeep. Like most Mongolians, the first thing they did was offer us a smoke. Then, cigarettes lit and clamped into the corners of their mouths, they set to work on Claudio's bike. While they were removing the gasket cover to the gearbox, two more Mongolians turned up on horseback with a herd of horses. They also lit up and crowded around the bike, one of them offering advice while the other lassoed one of his horses and pulled it over. Between them, they mended Claudio's bike, even giving it a test ride around the prairie after they had tightened and tuned the gearbox. With just a couple of simple tools, they'd done major surgery and got the bloody thing working within half an hour. It was amazing. Claudio climbed back on to the Red Devil and we rode off, the Mongolians giving us the thumbs up as we bumped off down the track.

We pressed on, my anxiety growing with every fall, every rut and every ditch we got stuck in. Even at petrol stations, there was no respite. The petrol had to be pumped by hand, a long and arduous task when there were three bikes to be filled. 'You can get real bad blisters from this,' Charley complained. 'Blisters to add to the blisters from riding.'

And then Claudio's bike broke down again. As before, we didn't know where to start. And again, as if from nowhere, the Russian jeep turned up and our old friends, the Mongolian gearbox menders, climbed out. Cigarettes were shared around as before and then, while our Mongolian mates got to work, I took a look at the map. My first reaction was one of shock. We should have been covering whole pages on the map every day; instead we were struggling to accomplish just a few inches. We still had about a thousand miles to go to Ulaanbaatar and we were struggling to ride more than forty miles a day. I was fed up with falling off my bike every few miles. I was dejected and depressed. I'd run out of energy. I was scared of the roads and what lay ahead. And I was very concerned about the time it would take us to reach Ulaanbaatar. Then I had a brainwave.

'Listen, Charley. Let's get out. Let's go to Russia. Look how close we are to the border,' I said, pointing at the map. We were only about sixty miles south of the frontier. 'Let's turn north and we'll soon be in Russia again. We'll be back on proper roads. We can get Claudio's bike fixed and then ride directly east to Lake Baikal. It'll take us two or three days and then we could just drop south to UB if we wanted to. It's tarmac all the way and we'll get to Ulaanbaatar on time.'

Charley jumped at the opportunity of ending the misery. 'Fucking hell. That's a great idea. I've had enough of this,' he said. 'If we have much more of this, one of us is going to break an arm or a leg. I tell you, if a helicopter was to land right here right now and offer to take me home, I'd jump in it straightaway. No questions asked. No regrets. We've accomplished a lot, but this is too fucking hard. I'm not enjoying myself any more. Let's get out.'

I turned to Claudio. 'What do you think?'

'I don't think,' he said. 'You decide. I follow.' Claudio, as ever, would not get involved. The choice was ours.

'Let's call Dave,' I said. 'See what he says.' I unpacked the satphone and, a short while later, I got through to David.

'Hello?' It was David. 'Yes, Ewan? You okay?'

'Yeah, I'm fine, David. Listen, I've had an idea . . .'

'Shit . . . Ewan . . .,' Dave had that terrible sound in his voice that people have when something awful has happened. '. . . Ewan can you just stay by your phone? Can I call you right back? . . .' Dave was speaking in that vague, high-pitched monotone that you hear when you speak to someone who has just lost a relative or when there is an emergency.

'. . . We've got a problem with the . . . oh shit . . . oh shit . . . oh shit . . . Russ has rolled his car over . . . *holy* shit, holy . . . let me call you back.'

The line went dead.

10
Snow in my ger

BARUUNTURUUN TO CHITA

EWAN: For half an hour we waited for David to call. All the beauty around us, Claudio's broken bike being fixed and our other problems didn't register. Suddenly they meant nothing at all. I just wanted to know what had happened to Russ. And all I kept thinking was that for some stupid, stupid reason, Russ never wore a seat belt. I'd mentioned it to him several times. 'You won't notice you're wearing it and it could save your life,' I'd said. But Russ had always brushed it off. Then I asked Charley who else would have been in Russ's pick-up truck, what they called the Animal.

'Vasiliy,' he said. 'Vasiliy always rides in the Animal with Russ.' And Vasiliy never wore a seat belt either. For all I knew, the two of them were now dead. As we waited for David to ring, dozens of thoughts raced through my mind. But one stood out: Russ, Vasiliy, David, Jim, Sergey, Claudio, Charley and all the people who had helped us along the road were here all because of me. All because I'd had a dream. Because I'd wanted to get away from my life for a few months and experience some adventure. And now, as we struggled to cross a vast country with few proper roads, using a Russian bike that didn't seem to work, our support crew taking risks that might mean two of them were now dead or severely injured hundreds of miles from a hospital, I wondered if it was all worthwhile. If anything happened to any of these guys, I would never be able to forgive myself this indulgence.

Then the phone rang.

It was David. 'Hey, yes, everyone's okay . . . Jesus Christ, it's a mess . . . You have no idea. The Animal was on its fucking roof. But they're both okay . . . shaken obviously, but okay. Vasiliy's holding his back, but I think he's going to be fine.'

David explained what had happened. One of the rear tyres on the Animal had blown as Russ was driving up a bank. The back of the truck had swung around and it had overturned twice before coming to rest on its roof. David had come across the brow of a hill to see the Animal with its wheels pointing at the sky. He, Jim and our Mongolian fixers had pulled Russ and Vasiliy, who had actually hurt his back badly, out of the pick-up and lain them on the ground nearby, where Vasiliy had told a different story. Russ had been driving too fast, Vasiliy said, and had lost control. It didn't really matter. All that mattered was that they were okay.

'So what's Russ going to do now?' I asked.

'The dude just asked me to help him get his car back on the road, like he wants to drive away or something.'

And then David let the shock show: 'I mean . . . fuck. You know? Fucking . . . the whole problem is, you know . . . I could see the whole thing happening.'

He took a deep breath. 'So why did you call me in the first place, Ewan?'

Our problems seemed so trivial now, but I still needed to consult David on our proposal. I told him we'd thought of cutting our losses and heading for Russia. 'I'd hate to look back on it and think that we ballsed it up and pussied out of it,' I said. 'But at the same time we're achieving twenty-five miles an hour at the best of times – really at the best of times – and we've got about a thousand miles to go to Ulaanbaatar.'

'Russ and I won't take any part in your decision. It's your call,' David said. 'But let me just say this: this could be something you regret for the rest of your lives . . . I just want you to think about it very carefully because when we scheduled the trip we didn't speak to anybody who'd ridden across Mongolia on a motorcycle. And you know, it's the trip of a lifetime, so would putting an extra week on the schedule be the end of the world? And would it be worth missing all the cultural and spiritual aspects of this country – and I can see they have touched you – just for the sake of getting back on asphalt? Especially when we could recognise we made a mistake with the scheduling and we could decide we can only do fifty miles a day and regain the lost time in America.'

And as David was speaking, I thought back to the previous evening, when we'd eaten testicles in the ger and I'd gone outside afterwards to phone Eve. Walking away from the camp, I had stood in the rain, watching the sons of the wonderful nomad family, who had been so hospitable to us, bringing in the herd. There were about four hundred beasts – goats, sheep, cows and yaks. The sun had set about an hour earlier and it was getting dark. Watching these young lads work, silhouetted against the darkening sky, riding across a huge, open, twilit plain was the most beautiful sight. Shapes from centuries ago: men on horseback, herding animals in silence, their outlines softened by the rain. It was beautiful and it moved me.

'Ewan, in the end it's up to you.' It was David, still speaking on the phone. 'Obviously it rained last night and now the roads have gone from tough to being virtually impossible because the mud is so fucking heavy, and you don't know where the ditches are really in the grass, so it's not easy. Only you can decide, but I've seen that already you've been affected by this place. Hold on to that, Ewan. Even if you arrive in New York a week late, does it really matter?'

By the time David had finished speaking, I was completely turned around. He was right. I might never pass through Mongolia again and I would always regret pulling out when the going got tough. I told Charley and he took it well. 'Let's adjust our route,' he said.

'We've really got to change our plan,' I said. 'Just do as much as we can a day. We've said before that we'd stop chasing targets, but we never really meant it. We've still been rushing to get to UB by Saturday. But if we keep rushing for a deadline, then what happened to Russ in his car could happen to us on our bikes. And none of us needs that.'

Charley got out the map and we studied it. There was a thicker red line, which probably didn't mean anything, but it looked to be a more direct route to UB.

'Let's just do that,' Charley said. 'And it means we go through Moron.'

'I've always wanted to go through Moron,' I said. 'Let's get going.'

But Charley wanted to meet up with Russ and David. He wanted to see for himself that they were all right, whereas I thought we really should just push on. 'Look, this is their drama,' I said. 'We're having a tough enough time on our own. We don't need their problems as well.'

I was also worried that Charley was still not quite sure about camping and that, for him, it was just too easy to be with everyone else. It *was* easier, but because there would be so many of us, it would mean we would be less likely to meet other people. When it was just Charley, Claudio and me, anything could happen. We might end up spending the evening with some nomads in their ger. And in the morning we got away quicker than when we were in a big group. Despite everything that had happened to the support crew, I wanted to break away and be on our own.

While we had been deliberating, our Mongolian guardian angels had got Claudio's bike running and had disappeared behind their jeep. They reappeared with a little green plastic oil can. 'They want some gas,' I said. Then one of them said something in Mongolian that included the words 'vodka, vodka'. Unscrewing the lid of the canister, he offered it to Charley. It seemed that few transactions in Mongolia were complete without a vodka toast, and this was no exception. Out of all the Russian traditions the Soviets exported to their satellites, it was a shame that the most enduring legacy was a predilection for frequent vodka toasts that hadn't previously been part of their culture. The formalities completed, the Mongolians departed in their orange jeep and we continued our trek towards Baruunturuun.

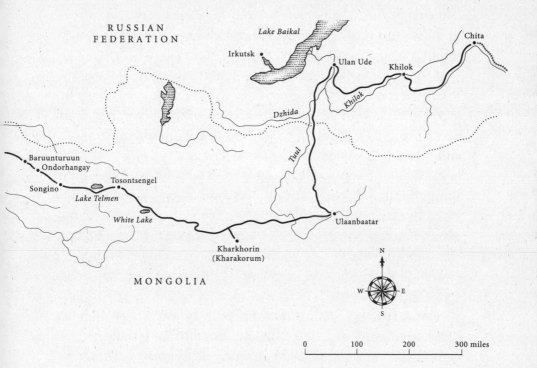

CHARLEY: Inevitably, we fell over again. And, equally inevitably, the Red Devil broke down again. I was getting really fed up and starting to regret buying the bike. If we'd stuck with the support team, Claudio could have continued in one of their cars. This time a different set of Mongolians came to our rescue. Two wore western clothes. The third, a ninety-seven-year-old in a purple silk tunic and trousers, with a pink scarf wrapped around his head, sat to the side, smoking a long wooden pipe with a metal bowl and watching the other two tinker with the clutch. Looking at all our Snap-On tools laid out on the grass, one of the Mongolians said something to the other two. They burst out laughing and I knew what they were saying. All the kit and no know-how. It didn't take them long to fix the bike. When it was finished, the old boy offered us all a snort of his snuff. In return, we gave him some Kendal Mint Cake and some of our whisky miniatures.

I'd got used to the idea of not heading for Russia. Riding along, I thought about it. It was only three or four months out of my life and now was the time to grow up and stop being homesick. There was something pathetic about sitting in the middle of Mongolia and thinking about leaving. Just suck it up and enjoy it, I told myself, don't pussy around. And while I was thinking about this, Baruunturuun appeared ahead. The town at last. But first, there was a river to be crossed. There was a wooden bridge nearby, but it was in a terrible state. The columns looked rickety. The deck was a loose collection of planks and railroad sleepers. Thinking it wouldn't take the weight of a bike, I stripped off my boots, socks and trousers.

'Our first river crossing,' I said nervously. We'd been dreading rivers ever since we'd left London. 'Better that I walk it. Then we'll know how fast and how deep it is.' Entering the water, I stepped cautiously across the riverbed.

'It's shallow here,' I shouted. 'We should be okay.'

'Hey! Look at that!' Ewan shouted. A Russian motorcycle was phut-phutting along the far riverbank. When it came to the bridge, it simply turned on to the deck and casually crossed over, while

I stood in the water below with no trousers on, looking a right idiot.

'I'm sorry, I think you should go over the bridge,' Ewan said as we both cracked up. 'I'm not riding through the river if I can go over the bridge. How deep is it, anyway?'

'Deep enough to get into fucking trouble,' I said.

The bridge rattled like hell as we crossed it one by one, but we made it to the other side. 'What are we going to do now?' I said.

'Get something to eat and move on,' Ewan said. 'Let's keep ahead of Russ and David.'

'Look, I think we should wait for them. They've had an accident and I just want to see for myself that they're all right.'

'Don't you like camping with us, Charley?' Ewan snapped.

'Yeah, I do. It's just . . .'

'I mean, have you got a problem with just the three of us camping?'

'No, no . . .'

'Because I don't want us to be stuck with them just because it's easier for you.'

'No. I just want to be with Russ,' I said. 'They've had a fucking accident and it's important after something like that for us all to be together. I just want to sit around with Russ and talk about it.'

I looked at Ewan. He looked really tired and very pissed off. I felt a deep need to be with Russ and Vasiliy. I just hoped he understood where I was coming from.

'It's okay,' Ewan said. 'You're probably right. I've lost the perspective on this. We should camp with Russ and Dave. No problem. Let's do it.' And that was that. The great thing about Ewan was that he could be so determined to do things his way, but when he realised that maybe it wasn't the best or the only way, he would immediately concede. And he didn't hold any grudges. The minute it was spoken about, it was done, it was dusted.

Baruunturuun was a sizable town, full of vibrant people. There were buildings with satellite dishes and a shop selling groceries, clothes and stationery, water, tobacco and vodka. We bought some coffee and chocolate. Ewan was so weary he could hardly stand up. Outside the shop, we were surrounded by locals, including dozens of kids, wanting to know how our bikes worked and offering directions and advice on hotels and places to camp. A middle-aged clean-cut Mongolian man in an expensively cut suit approached us. He spoke English, said he lived in Ulaanbaatar, and had worked on the Camel Trophy when it passed through Mongolia in 1997. We chatted for a long time and he went through the route with me. The bad news was that we had six hundred miles of the same kind of tracks ahead of us. It would get a little bit easier, he said, and the route was very scenic. The good news was that the last four hundred miles to UB were tarmac. It was more than we'd thought and something to focus on.

Then the support team turned up, the Animal at the front, trundling into town looking as if it had been through a crusher. I was gobsmacked. The windscreen was missing and David was wearing ski goggles to drive it. 'We didn't have a good day,' he said. They'd used a rope and pulley to drag the Animal upright, then a hydraulic jack to lift the dented roof so that they could shut the driver's door. The tailgate was wide open, pointing at the sky. It could no longer be closed.

We drove in convoy out of town for an hour or so until we came to the top of a hill. After everything we'd been through that day, it was the perfect place to camp. The sky was clear of clouds at last and the orange-red sun was setting. Most importantly, we were all together.

'Tick city,' said Russ and he told a story about how he had been running his hand through his hair after the accident when he discovered a lump on his skull. 'Just my bloody luck, I thought. First an accident, now a tick. But it turned out to be a bit of glass embedded in my head.'

'I'm just glad you're here,' I said. 'We had that conversation this morning after the testicle soup and then the next thing I hear you're in an upside-down car. I can tell you, there was some crying in my helmet, I was so worried about you.'

'Did you hear what was playing on the stereo when Russ turned the Animal over?' Ewan said. 'It was that Coldplay track with the video that has the guy walking backwards from the car accident. That's the song that was playing when he crashed the car.'

'Poor Vasiliy,' I said. 'He has a crash, he's trapped beneath Russ in the car and he has to put up with Russ's fucking loud music.'

While the others chatted and prepared something to eat, Ewan took me aside. 'I'm upset with myself because my reaction was to look at the map and get freaked out by how far we've got to go,' he said. 'I let it get me down and I'm annoyed because my reaction to it getting difficult was to bail out.'

I told him I felt the same way.

'Yeah, but I thought I was made of tougher stuff than that. I let us down.' Ewan was being very hard on himself.

'It's hard here, it's really hard,' I said. 'But it's also really beautiful and we just have to concentrate more on the beauty and less on the hardship, you know. No one said it would be easy.'

'I didn't think it was going to be easy,' Ewan said. 'But I also didn't think that my first reaction would be let's just short-cut, let's just bypass Mongolia. What kind of attitude was that? But it was a low moment, I guess.'

We decided to carry on along the new route and we vowed to take it easier. We needed to open our eyes to our surroundings. Any journey would be difficult when the field of vision was just 5 feet ahead of you.

'I think it's also because we set Mongolia up in our mind as this fantasy,' Ewan said. 'That it would be idyllic and smooth. That we'd start at nine and finish at three, camp by a river and do some fishing. But it just kicked our arse as soon as we got in here.'

The next day started well. We took a track up into the mountains and had the best morning's trail riding we'd ever experienced. It was like being in the Swiss Alps. With snowcaps in the distance, we passed gers and nomads riding with their camels, yaks, horses, sheep and goats. There were rivers running through pine forests and green lush pastures. Ewan was in a really good mood, on a high because the road was so good and the scenery so spectacular, but I couldn't shake off my fear that the easy conditions wouldn't last and that we'd get lost. And I was right: we descended into a valley, it had been raining and the ground just turned to bog. In less than an hour, the track had gone from bliss to the worst nightmare. And, most worrying of all, I couldn't see any tyre tracks anywhere. For some reason, this route was rarely used.

We rode on, coming to a river. There was a bridge, but part of it had collapsed. It was a difficult river crossing, but we got through it fine and soon stopped for lunch. While we were eating, two Mongolian couples, one of them with a young child squeezed between them, passed by on Red Devil motorbikes, just like Claudio's but customised with ornate Mongolian fabric over the seats. We had a chat with them and gave the boy a lollipop. I realised that they had followed the same track, and that encouraged me that we hadn't taken a wrong turning.

We pushed on, the tracks becoming much more boggy, and then we came to our first really wide river. We crossed it with little difficulty, kept going and then crossed it again as the track and the river wove around and across each other. On our third crossing there was a ger on the bank and a couple of herdsmen nearby. Ewan went first. He got as far as halfway, then stopped. He'd hit a rock. Watching Ewan trying to hold his bike up as it slipped away beneath him, I hoped he'd manage to hit the kill-switch as the bike dropped beneath the water, preventing the engine from sucking in water. I couldn't put my bike down because there was nowhere to put it safely on its stand, so Ewan was stuck in the middle of the river, trying to hold on to his bike on his own. I shouted at the herdsmen. They saw what was happening and steamed in to help. Eventually, I found somewhere to leave my bike and waded in to the river. We hauled the bike out of the water. It started on the first try: Ewan had hit the kill-switch just in time. Thanks to his quick reactions, the engine hadn't flooded.

Then it was my turn. I entered the river with my stomach in my mouth, but made it across. Claudio was last. And of course he just scooted through on the Red Devil without a care in the world.

'Funny how quickly a great morning can turn into a really crappy afternoon, isn't it?' Ewan said.

'Yeah,' I said. 'Let's move. Let's get on. We've got to get some miles under our belts.'

'On to the next river crossing,' Ewan said. 'Can't wait to discover that joy.'

We rode on for another two miles, until the road faded. Ewan was leading, but I decided we ought to turn back. It was clear to me that we'd taken a wrong turning, but it meant that we had to cross back over the river again. Ewan was understandably very nervous about it, so this time I decided to park up and walk behind Ewan's bike, holding the back of it as he rode through the water. But while I was finding somewhere safe to leave my bike, Ewan lost control of his, dropping it from the top of a bank of pebbles, so that it was lying almost upside down, smashing one of the fog lamps and scratching the petrol tank. It was all going wrong and, like the previous day, I had that sense of the world closing in on us, everything becoming too much and too difficult. Again, the herdsmen helped us get the bikes across the river and we set off on a different track. The conditions became increasingly boggy and we all fell a number of times. Ewan's bike got bogged down on several occasions, sinking into the mud up to its axle. 'At least I can now get my feet on the floor,' he despaired. The only way out in such circumstances was for the driver to gun the engine while the other two of us lifted and pushed the bike. Our stamina was flagging and the weather was closing in, but we had to press on. The boggier the conditions, the less distinct the track became. At times, there were hundreds of tracks running in parallel. Just choosing the right path was challenging enough on its own. Then it started to rain very hard and I got really worried. If we don't get a move on and it continues raining, I thought, we'll get stuck in this valley. We'll never get out.

And then it started to snow.

I was crawling along, not knowing where to go. I couldn't take it any more. I couldn't function. I didn't know what to do. At times we were like the Keystone Kops. Stuck in a bog, I caught my bike before it fell, but it was too heavy: I was unable to pull it upright on my own. Ewan ran over to help me lift it, then returned to his bike and moved off gingerly, entering a puddle and immediately falling over himself. Claudio then ran to Ewan's aid and in pushing him out of the bog was completely drenched in mud.

'Oh, Claudio, fucking hell. I'm sorry, mate,' Ewan said. 'Whatever happened to just a bit of tarmac, you know, just a little bit of asphalt? And what happened to third, fourth, fifth and sixth gears? Whatever happened to dry clothes? Whatever happened to being able to sit on a motorbike without falling off it? And why is it that you've hardly fallen off at all?'

It was too much. A huge storm was coming in and I'd lost the ability or the will to ride my bike. I didn't know how to do anything any more. Ewan was soaking wet after he'd fallen in the river and he'd fallen in the mud a couple of times as well. He was caked in dirt and really miserable. And I was so low. I was no longer riding my bike; I was waddling it through the bog. I had no idea what I was doing there and I just burst into tears in my helmet. I was blubbing like a baby, the inside of my helmet steaming up as the tears rolled down my cheeks. I was tired and frustrated. It had taken us two hours to ride six miles. It was slow and hard. The fully laden BMWs were so heavy and unwieldy in mud. It was a nightmare and all I could think was that we still had Siberia ahead of us. I stopped and thought about it. It was only four o'clock in the afternoon and we'd covered less than thirty-five miles that day, but, with even darker clouds approaching, I thought there was nothing for it but to head for a copse of trees in the near distance to camp.

We made it to the trees. As we climbed off our bikes, the rain stopped for a short while and a little patch of sunlight appeared between the clouds. Claudio, usually the last to suggest anything, spoke up. 'Let's get out of this valley,' he said. 'If it rains tonight we'll be stuck here for days. We're right at the bottom and it's all mud. It'll be completely impossible tomorrow.'

Claudio was right. I realised it was the correct thing to do. We had no choice but to press on. 'Let's get the fuck out of here,' I said.

'Just wait a second!' It was Ewan.

'C'mon, we've got to get going,' I said.

'You've got to give me more time . . .'

'What?'

'I don't process things as quickly as you do,' Ewan said. 'You've got to let me come up with my point and have my say, so that it's a joint decision. Our decision, instead of always your decision.'

'No,' I said. 'It was Claudio who said we should get over the mountain before it started to rain, not me. If we get going, we might make it to Ondorhangay and maybe there's a shitty little hotel or a ger we can stay in there.'

It seemed to me that Ewan just needed to have a nark. He was cold, tired and fed up and he needed someone to take it out on. I shrugged and we moved off. But it didn't become any easier. It became a lot worse. We climbed several passes and in every valley into which we descended the ground was softer. We crossed several rivers, the water getting muddier and muddier. The tracks became less and less distinct, merging into one big squirming mess, and the grass became more and more sodden and slippery. Eventually we spotted some telegraph poles and used them to navigate. The road became slightly better and we climbed a long hill. When we got to the top, everything changed. It was if someone had drawn a line across the landscape. Behind us, a mud bath. Ahead, rocky desert.

The track now dry, we rode another twenty miles to Ondorhangay. As we entered the town, I spotted a white car passing through very carefully, which I took to be a good sign. We followed it and as we were reaching the edge of the little town I raced over to the car, stopped it and asked the lady who was driving it how to get to Songino, our next destination. She said to follow her and took us to a track by the river that we'd crossed to get into the town. We rode through the river and then followed her directions on to the smoothest piece of road we'd yet seen in Mongolia. We glided along at 40mph. It was fantastic. Ewan was very wet and very cold, so we decided to continue for another forty-five minutes to let his clothes dry. Then we stopped and camped.

I was euphoric. At last we were back on good, smooth desert roads. I was elated that we'd survived the mud, rivers and bogs. We'd done it. It was a fantastic achievement, especially after our decision not to head for Russia.

'At least it's good practice for Siberia,' I said. 'Surely it can't be any worse than this.'

'Oh, great,' Ewan said. 'You know, we could've gone to Cannes instead of this, or to southern Spain, or . . . I don't know . . . Mexico or somewhere. But no, I wanted to go to Siberia to see the fucking gulags. And you know what? I can't remember why. I can't remember anything any more. I've completely lost my brains today.'

While Ewan dried his belongings and cooked the supper, Claudio and I climbed to the top of the hill on which we had pitched the tents. We could see the road that we'd just pulled off sweeping away to the south, but then coming back around our mountain and heading down the valley in the direction we wanted. It looked good and we knew we'd be on the right track the next day. At last there was the prospect of some easier riding, but as we camped that night and ate our supper, I spotted the dark cloud that had been following us ever since we had entered Mongolia. Every day we'd ridden away from it. Every evening it had caught up with us. It meant that every night, so far, we'd had rain. And so I went to sleep, wiped out and worried that it would pour again and that the misery would start all over again the next day.

The ride the next day from our camp near Ondorhangay via Songino to Nomrog, however, was fantastic. Running through the desert, the track was as smooth as glass. It was easy, it was good and it was simple. The sun was shining, it was windy, we didn't make too many mistakes and the scenery was just fantastic. Ewan dropped his bike, knocking off the end of the gear shifter, but it was a piffling setback by the previous days' standards. By early afternoon we'd put nearly one hundred miles under our wheels. We stopped to look at a temple near a ger village and knelt in front of the shrine. Still wobbly after the events and exertions of the previous few days, I felt a lump rise in my throat. For the first time in four days, we weren't being buffeted by the wind or drenched by rain. I'd forgotten what it felt like to be in a calm, quiet place.

We rode on for a short while until we reached Lake Telmen. The black cloud was approaching as we lay down on the ground, leaning against our bikes to shade ourselves from the howling wind. 'We'd better get the tent up quick,' Ewan said. 'I think it's going to rain.'

As we raced to erect the tent, an old man on a horse turned up. We said hello, shook hands and he immediately helped us bang in the pegs for the tents. The guy ropes had never looked so good. Another, younger, horseman came up, dismounted and crouched nearby, watching us silently while we went about our business, preparing our supper. It was the first time I'd been conscious of the equipment we were carrying. As he watched us unpack, set up the camp, light the stoves and bring out the camping food, I wondered what we must look like. We cooked some soup and noodles and shared it out in metal cups. They seemed to quite like it. After dinner, the older horseman's wife turned up. We showed her the pictures of our children that we'd stuck to our bikes and she invited us into their ger. Hoping we wouldn't be faced with another bubbling cauldron of nut soup, we followed the family back to their tent, chased by a dog with the longest legs I'd ever seen. The ger was beautiful inside and much bigger than the previous one. We sat down and drank Mongolian tea. Made with a lot of milk, a dash of tea and some salt, it tasted good and was very good for rehydration. On a fire in the middle of the ger, what looked like milk was bubbling away in a big pot shaped like a large wok. The older horseman spent a long time standing by the bowl and aerating the liquid, lifting a bucketful and slowly pouring it from a height back into the main pot in a slow, repetitive swinging motion. His wife called it '*so*' and asked us if we'd like some. It tasted like warm milk and sugar, with a nutty aftertaste from the yak's dung they burned to heat it up. It was delicious. They also gave us something that tasted like clotted cream on a cracker with sugar sprinkled on it. Again delicious.

After we'd eaten, the woman showed us her pictures, arranged in a large clip frame on the wall of the ger. We gave her one of our postcards and she slipped it into the frame, next to some photographs of her relatives. Somewhere in Mongolia, there is a ger with a black and white photograph of an old man – the woman's father – sitting in front of his Russian motorbike, looking very proud. And immediately above it there is a colour photograph of Ewan and me, standing in the courtyard at Bulwer Street, looking just as proud of the bikes and tool cabinets surrounding us. The woman showed us round the rest of her ger, explaining various bits and pieces of it to us in Mongolian. It was delightful to see such a loving, tightly knit little family. The woman and her husband were so obviously in love, holding hands as they chatted to us and constantly looking after each other. It was a really beautiful evening, but eventually it was time to head back to our tents. As we stepped outside, we could see the eldest son riding in the distance. He was holding a long stick and bringing in the animals. There were sheep, goats and cows. The father indicated to us not to move and as the animals approached he gestured to us to help him separate the younger animals and put them in pens. As the sun set, we were leaning over the animal pens, stroking the sheep and goats and letting them suckle our fingers. 'Thank you very much,' Ewan said to the son on horseback, who was silhouetted against the dimming red and purple sky. 'It's been a wonderful evening. We'll see you in the morning at breakfast.'

We had a very long journey the next day from Nomrog via Tosontsengel, where we had a fantastic lunch, to White Lake. We wouldn't have made it but for a truck driver who drew us the most fantastic map. All it had on it was a sketch of a river with a bridge, a road with some dots on it and a mountain with two little houses and two sets of trees. Sure enough, once we crossed the bridge we came to a road with some dotted markings on it. We followed it for more than twenty miles, when we came to a mountain. About halfway up, we passed two strips of trees. A little further we found two little houses. Directly behind the houses was a path leading to the right, which we would never have noticed without the map. It was a brand new man-made track, whereas the route that our maps indicated we should take was a mess. We skimmed along at about 40mph, whooping with delight at being on what was almost a proper dirt track. Along the way, we crossed several rickety bridges, stopped off at a tree draped in shaman ribbons, and passed the skeletons of dozens of horses and many vultures. Inevitably, Claudio's bike broke down several times, but we managed to fix it ourselves on each occasion.

In the late afternoon, we came screaming down a long pass towards a large bridge. There, standing beside the bridge, was the support team. It was great to see them. It meant we'd all got through the toughest part of the journey, a fantastic achievement. The support team decided to leave for Ulaanbaatar while we continued to White Lake, a long ride that took until after ten o'clock that night. After so many ups and downs, the days of misery in the bogs, the aborted plan to head to Russia, the tetchy arguments in the rain, the aching limbs and the exhaustion, I'd come to love Mongolia. It had been hell at times, but some part of me had actually relished the misery. I'd enjoyed meeting people along the road and I'd been blown away by the helpfulness of complete strangers. We couldn't have done it without them.

And it had rekindled memories from my childhood of being stuck in the middle of nowhere in County Wicklow with a broken-down bike and having to fix it to get home. I hadn't felt this happy for a long time: probably not since I'd been at home, in the arms of my family. It felt great to be over the worst of it.

EWAN: It was an immense relief to reach White Lake. I'd never done anything harder in my life than that ride there from the Russian border. Not in my wildest dreams could I have imagined how tough it would be. Once we got to White Lake I spent a whole day lying in a ger, too tired even to unpack, unable to think about the rest of the trip or even what was happening the next day. I couldn't face making a decision about anything.

I woke up very early to find a wee man lighting my stove. I watched him blow the fire into life, then he left and I made myself some coffee. I took my fishing rod down to the lake and walked for about an hour to find the right spot. I got my hook caught in some rocks, but it was a treat to be on my own. After two weeks on the go, I needed to be away from Charley, Claudio and everyone else. On the way to the fishing, I'd come across a little shrine. The Mongolians build little piles of stones, like cairns, and passers-by tie blue ribbons on them. I didn't know if it was appropriate to make a wish, but I did and I'd added a stone to thank the Big Man for the day and the beautiful landscape. On the way back to my ger, I added another stone, to thank him for not giving me a fish to catch. I didn't really want to catch a fish; I just wanted an excuse to stand in the landscape. That afternoon, I went out in a rowing boat with a couple of the locals from the little ger camp. They pulled their nets in and there were eight or nine large fish. As they landed them in the boat, I realised I didn't like it. Although I eat fish and meat, and I've worked on a trout farm clubbing hundreds of fish a day over the head to kill them, I don't really like to see animals die. Maybe I should be a vegetarian.

It was great to do very little for two days. The ride from the

border had been exhausting and I found my mood really [...]
when I was tired. And so, therefore, did poor old Charle[...]
I got a bit grumpy. Lying on the bed, I felt physically sic[...]
accumulated exhaustion of two weeks' riding in very diffi[...]
conditions. It was almost like having food poisoning, I felt so out
of sorts. I wondered how we had managed to make it that far. At
times, it seemed the only thing that had kept us going was the
Kendal Mint Cake. If it was good enough for Shackleton and
Edmund Hillary, then I suppose it was good enough for us.

Before we left London, I thought I was going to miss knowing
what was going on in the world, but I realised that day, as I
listened to the wind whistling round my ger, that being
completely out of touch was one of the glories of the trip. We'd
travelled a third of the way around the world on the back of three
bikes; people's faces had changed, their homes had changed, the
way they led their lives and what they believed in were different.
But with everything that was going on in the world at that time,
if we hadn't been so isolated we might very easily have travelled
through these countries without becoming aware that ultimately
we are all the same: we all love our kids, we all need somewhere
to sleep and some food. We all want the same things; the world
isn't that big a place. I lay in my ger thinking that if the likes of
President Bush, who might even struggle to find Mongolia on a
map, had spent some time finding out what was happening
outside their own countries, they would recognise what all people
of all nationalities and religions have in common, instead of
focusing on the differences, and maybe the world wouldn't be in
such a mess.

Although it was blissful to have a day off, I felt extraordinarily
homesick, or more pertinently, family-sick. I'd spoken to my wife
and children, and my wife had told me that for the first time in
weeks my youngest daughter had got really upset that I wasn't at
home. I'd spoken to wee Esther on the phone the night before, but
she became quite angry with me and wouldn't let me go. Eve had
to prise her off the phone and that set Clara crying. It was too

much for me, sitting in that ger, thousands of miles away from them. I was miserable and went in search of Claudio and Charley. Just talking to them about it, instead of sitting on my own, helped a lot.

The next morning I woke up to find a little Mongolian lady feeding the stove. Looking up to a little hole which formed the chimney at the top of the ger, I could see snowflakes falling. Oh no, not snow now, I thought. I jumped out of bed, and peered outside. All the mountains wore a dusting of snow and we were planning to cross several mountain passes. Christ, what will they throw at us next, I thought. We've had rain and bogs. Now it's snow.

It was very cold, so we put on all our thermal gear and set off. It was a beautiful ride up the hill behind the camp, past an extinct volcano and the roads were fantastic. It was bitterly cold, but we ended up riding more than one hundred miles in the morning, partly because we were desperate to pass over the highlands into the warmer lowlands. Because the roads were slightly better, we had more time to look around and everyone's spirits were soaring as we crossed some stupendous mountain passes and swept through some stunning gorges. We stopped for lunch at a little café in Tsetserleg run by two English people. It was bizarre, to say the least, to find what looked just like an English café, with English music, burgers, all-day breakfasts and even Sunday roasts, in the middle of the Mongolian desert. As we were leaving town, we passed a huge rock on the first bit of tarmac we'd seen in Mongolia. I saw Charley avoid it. Then there was a crunch. Claudio had collided with it.

'It's his fault, you know,' Claudio pointed at Charley.

'How can it be Charley's fault that you hit the stone?' I said.

'Because he should have made a big turn around the rock, which he didn't. He just skimmed by it, so that I couldn't see.'

'Claudio, it was like a small planet,' Charley said.

'Yeah, but you rode so close to it that I couldn't see it. And I know you did it on purpose, so what do you expect?' Claudio said. 'It was the first bit of proper tarmac in Mongolia and I was thinking everything is wonderful. I was looking left and right, enjoying the view and the countryside.'

'So whose fault was it then?' I asked.

'Charley's,' Claudio said without a hint of irony. 'Because he was driving in front of me, so I couldn't see the rock.'

Charley cracked up. 'As soon as I passed it I was looking in the mirror because I *knew* Claudio was going to hit it.'

'See! It's your fault!' Claudio insisted. 'Until now, I was always trusting you. Wherever you drive, I drive. And so I was following you nicely but you went close to this rock to make sure that I hit it.'

'Is that how you hit your pannier on the rock on the mountain top?' I said. 'By going right behind Charley too?'

'No, he went off and left me behind, so I couldn't keep up.'

Charley and I burst out laughing. 'Did you see Claudio just before lunch?' I said to Charley. 'When he was riding too close to you again and you stopped? He had to throw his bike on the floor to stop the fucking thing. And he got up and looked at you as if to say "That was your fault".'

'But ... but I pulled in there so slowly,' Claudio said indignantly. 'I was pointing at a fence. Where else was I going to go?'

It was a fair point. The Red Devil was a bitch to ride and Claudio had been a real trouper in persevering with it. I really didn't know how he had put up with it. But now the back brake was broken – the only brake that worked on that bike – and the exhaust pipe was bent. Fortunately it was made from such weak metal that we could straighten it with little difficulty. We rode on, Claudio's bike breaking down with monotonous regularity, until I had a spill. I was getting overconfident and cocky, jumping over ruts and flying over bumps, not really taking care. Two tracks were converging; Charley was on one and I was on the other, trying to beat him to the intersection. I dropped into a dip and although I could see that I couldn't make it out the other side, I stupidly thought I'd give it a go. I crashed and came tumbling off. Early on in the trip my pride would have been bruised, but as falling off had become a daily occurrence, this only made me laugh. I was okay. And the bike was hardly damaged. It had taken so many knocks from me and been fed low-grade 76 octane petrol for two weeks, yet it just ploughed on, a quite brilliant machine. The indicator was smashed and the pannier bracket was cracked after my fall, so I strapped it together using tyre levers and cable ties like Charley's botch on Claudio's bike.

About ten minutes later, Claudio came off, going very fast. He was riding through some ruts and tried to avoid a dip filled with water, but he got his tyre caught and the bike spat him off. He landed heavily on his ribs and was in quite a lot of pain, unable to kick-start the little Red Devil afterwards.

'How are your ribs, Claudio?' Charley asked. 'Not that I really care . . .'

'They're okay,' Claudio said, but we could tell from the way he was standing that he was in a lot of pain. Charley let Claudio drive his bike and rode the Red Devil the last few miles to the ger camp. A few hundred yards from the camp, the dirt track ran out and the tarmac began. That was it. No more ruts, mud and dust. Asphalt all the way to Ulaanbaatar and past the capital to the Russian border. For Charley, it was all too much. He hopped off the Red Devil and threw himself on the ground.

'Aaah,' he sighed. 'Such beautiful tarmac. Look how smooth it is. And it's warm and hard.'

'And it's Mongolia . . .,' I said.

'Mwah!' Charley was kissing the road. 'Oh, it's so nice.'

'Charley,' I said. 'C'mon. We're just about there, c'mon!'

'Where are we?'

'We're here. The camp's over there. Oh, fucking hurry up!'

'I might just chill out here for half an hour,' Charley said. 'Just enjoy the tarmac.'

'I'll see you over there,' I said, pointing at the ger camp.

'Oh, that's great,' Charley said sarcastically. 'We go together through the whole of Mongolia and he fucks off now. You know? That's it. Our relationship is over. It's *over*!'

But there was some truth behind Charley's joke. Charley was 'moving out', we liked to joke. After more than seven weeks constantly in each other's company, we'd had enough. We were going to ditch the tent we'd shared since Kazakhstan and get two one-man tents in Ulaanbaatar. We'd come to realise we couldn't be in each other's hair twenty-four hours a day. It was too much. We needed some privacy if we were going to maintain our sanity. We rode up to the ger camp, where we had our first showers for ten days, our limbs still shaking after riding nearly two hundred miles to Kharkhorin, the old capital from which Genghis Khan had ruled an empire that stretched from Vienna to Beijing.

Claudio looked dreadful the next morning. He hadn't slept all night because of pains in his chest. 'I couldn't lie down,' he said. 'I was hoping it was just bruised muscles, but the moment I tried to lie down there was a huge pain in my chest. I think I might have broken a rib. I hope not, because if I have, then that's the end of the trip for me.' Nevertheless, Claudio hauled himself on to the Red Devil to ride the final 250 miles to Ulaanbaatar. It was freezing cold, the wind banged our heads and I was very tired when we first started off. Just after lunch, we finally got a long stretch of straight tarmac and the sun was glaring. Starting to nod off, I had to scream and shout at myself to keep awake, but eventually we made it to Ulaanbaatar, riding up to our hotel to find Ted Simon waiting in the foyer. We couldn't have hoped for a better greeting.

Ted, who had taken four and a half years to ride round the world on a motorbike before writing up his experience in *Jupiter's Travels*, was one of the reasons I now found myself in Mongolia. He was a bit of a hero of mine, and his book had inspired me. 'If I need anyone to blame for going round the world,' I said, 'Ted, you're the man.' It was great to hang out with him and just compare experiences on the road. Ted had done it in a completely different way. He'd set off on his own and spent much of the trip alone, and he'd not put a time-limit on it. It was a completely different philosophy. Ted said it was the delays that made the journey, and he was right, but we couldn't entertain too many hold-ups, so Charley and I were both concerned that Ted might have a dim view of our venture. But he couldn't have been nicer. Now seventy-three, he'd recently returned from undertaking the same journey a second time. He'd followed the same route, but found much of the world had changed for the worse since his first circumnavigation. As Ted had set off in 1973 wearing a leather jacket with sheepskin trim and riding a standard Triumph Tiger, we thought he might regard all our equipment – the GPS navigators, the satellite phones and the high-tech bikes – with disdain. But not at all. 'You use whatever's the best at the time,' he said, 'and whatever you can get your hands on.'

While recuperating in Ulaanbaatar, we spent three days with Ted, who was never short of a jovial anecdote about his days on the road. Claudio's BMW was repaired, so Ted was given the little Red Devil, declaring it a 'death trap' but cheerfully claiming to love every minute he spent on it with us riding around the city and into the nearby countryside. He also came along to the centrepiece of our stopover in Ulaanbaatar, a Unicef-organised visit to find out about street children.

The city was a strange place, an ugly blot on Mongolia's stunning landscape with a filthy power station near its centre expelling dirty smoke into the atmosphere and pumping hot water along city streets through massive asbestos-clad pipes. Since Mongolia shook off its Soviet satellite status in the 1990s and embraced independence, the number of street children had mushroomed. Unemployment had soared, welfare services declined and the gap between rich and poor widened as the country embraced free market economics. While the relatively well-off wore cashmere and toted cellphones on their hips in the city centre's bars and stores, beneath the bustling streets a community of children lived in a rabbit's warren of chambers built around the hot-water pipes, seeking warm shelter from temperatures that can drop to minus thirty in winter. Some were as young as two.

One evening we were taken by Unicef to visit some street children. We met a group of about ten boys in a busy street in a commercial district and then climbed with them through a manhole into the dusty, stifling maintenance pit they called home. They loved the attention and proudly showed us around the dark, stinking cavern. It was distressing to see children as young as six living in such conditions. They were tough and cocky, but, despite all they had seen and experienced, they were still very much young children. The boys were very tactile with each other and with us. One of them had a tattoo, so I showed them mine and they all wanted to touch it, the youngest stroking my arm in a really sensitive way. He kept touching the skin and I could see he was desperate for human contact. He was still such a young kid and all I really wanted to do was to throw my arms around all of them.

The next day we went to a government centre that provided shelter and food for the street children. In a city of nearly a million people, it was the only government-funded support afforded them. There were about forty children at the centre, most of them very young, including a two-year-old girl who had been living on the streets with her four-year-old brother. The hard-working staff were clearly overstretched and many of the children were left to their own devices. The conditions in which these children lived, even in a proper centre, hit me like a sledgehammer. A four-year-old girl was lying on the floor with her head against the wall. Her legs were withered and weak and she was trembling. It broke my heart to see her in such distress, so in need of love and attention, but so alone. I spent quite a lot of time with her, stroking her hair, touching her face and playing peek-a-boo with her. And then we had to leave. I hugged as many of them as I could, said goodbye and got into a car.

Back at the hotel, I was haunted by what I'd seen. It was lunchtime, but I wanted to be alone. I couldn't really face talking to anyone about it. We were planning to move on to Ulan Ude the next day, but that wee girl would still be there, lying on the floor of a bedroom, so obviously ill yet not getting the care she so clearly needed. I couldn't understand why she wasn't in a hospital bed. Then I found out that the government centre couldn't afford the medical bills. It had disturbed me so much because there are few things worse than a child having no real start to their life. I couldn't forget what I'd seen and I couldn't get my head around the fact that children as young and as vulnerable as my wee daughter Esther had been abandoned and were forced to cope on their own. That unfortunate little girl deserved much better. She had made a deeper impression on me than anything or anyone I'd seen so far on the trip. Maybe she was the mysterious woman the fortune-teller in Prague had predicted would have a profound influence upon me. Worried that unless we took action that little girl would be left to die, we found out how much it would cost to get proper medical treatment for her and left the money with the centre. But it was still only a drop in the ocean. Even if this little girl received better care, there would be another child and then another to take her place. Unicef, I had learned, was not about handouts but about working to prevent children ending up on the streets in the first place; helping them to stay with their families and communities; encouraging them to stay in school and ensuring they received proper healthcare. So I vowed then and there to devote as much time and effort as I could to Unicef once I returned home. The journey would be over in another six weeks but I was determined to make working with Unicef something I'd do for the rest of my life.

We set off the next day for Ulan Ude, across the border in Russia, meeting the support crew at the frontier. Having abandoned Russ's damaged pick-up, they were all travelling in one vehicle, their equipment and luggage piled perilously high on a roof rack and towed behind them in a trailer. I had very mixed emotions as we slipped effortlessly through the border controls. Mongolia had put me through a physical and emotional wringer.

My thoughts were still very much with those street children in the government support centre. Riding across Mongolia had been incredibly demanding, but it had offered everything I'd been looking for on the trip, a pastoral paradise full of curious, open-hearted people who welcomed me into their homes because I was a passing traveller, not because I was Obi-Wan Kenobi on a bike. Those dreadful first few days – the hardest days I'd ever had on a bike – had taught us a valuable lesson: if we had bailed out then and headed for Russia, we would have missed the most beautiful part of Mongolia. It had been like riding through the pages of *National Geographic*. Every time we blinked there would be a jaw-dropping sight to look at or think about. A land in which most of the people still rode horses and wore traditional clothes, it was timeless without being stuck in the past. Much of the rural population still lived in gers, but they'd have solar panels and satellite dishes. All the guys we met just wanted to be herdsmen, happy to spend their lives on horses, rounding up sheep and goats, while the girls all had ambitions to head for Ulaanbaatar to go to university. And it had been wonderfully liberating to walk around markets unrecognised. Anonymous. It was what I had dared dream Kazakhstan would be like, but we were prevented by the police and media attention from experiencing Kazakhstan in the way I had hoped. Mongolia couldn't have been more removed from that experience or from western culture. It was completely unspoiled and untouched and I felt really privileged to have travelled through so much of it as well as proud that Charley, Claudio and I had got through the toughest parts on our own.

CHARLEY: Although it was a long distance away, we decided to push through from the border to Ulan Ude instead of camping along the route. We had lunch in a café, which to Ewan's delight and my great surprise sold cans of Irn-Bru made in Scotland, and set off, arriving in Ulan Ude late at night, desperate for bed but having to stay up to wait for the support crew to arrive. The next day we had a look around. After the tranquillity of Mongolia, it seemed a particularly busy city. Music and announcements were piped out of loudspeakers that lined dusty squares full of people sipping dark beer from plastic beakers sold out of the backs of carts. There were trams, trolley buses and stalls selling cheap sunglasses on the streets. It had the standard Soviet-era parade square at its centre, surrounded by ministerial buildings and with a statue that was claimed to be the largest bust of Lenin in Russia.

'We've got to think about the next section in little chunks,' Ewan said as we wandered around the streets. 'The thought of riding from here to Magadan is just too much to get my head around.'

We were faced with a choice. The road from Chita to Tynda, six hundred miles further north, was – depending on who we consulted – non-existent, an old gravel track, a recently refurbished high-quality gravel track, the base layer of a proper road and a pristine stretch of tarmac. On the map it was a dotted line, which meant it was under construction, but we didn't know if it was finished yet. We could either chance the road or, like every other round-the-world motorcyclist who had followed a similar route, take the train.

'I'm not sure whether putting the bikes on the train is the right thing to do,' Ewan said. 'Can we say we've ridden round the world if we take a train for six hundred miles?'

'It would be terrible if we were on the train and we looked down and there was a beautiful tarmac road running beside us,' I said. 'That would be a bit of a shame.'

'You know, there aren't any rules to this,' Ewan said. 'We can do what we like. But I don't want to look back for the rest of my life, regretting that we took the train. At the same time, I don't want to spend eight weeks trying to get from Chita to Tynda because there's no road.'

David was even more downbeat about the route ahead. 'You know, everybody we've spoken to here has told us that we're crazy to be going any further,' he said. 'They say the roads just disappear and the rivers are very high because the winter was so bad and that we'll never get through.'

David had more than enough problems of his own. He needed to buy a second car to replace Russ's trashed Animal. His Shogun had a snorkel that would allow it to drive through about three and a half feet of water, but the rivers were apparently running at six and a half feet.

While we were deliberating about the route ahead and David was searching for a new support vehicle, Claudio had all his hair shaved off – his extreme version of a haircut – and Ewan met a shamanist who offered to arrange a meeting with a shaman priestess who would bless the rest of the journey. The next day we left the support team in Ulan Ude and rode out to Lake Baikal, the oldest freshwater lake on the planet. More than twenty million years old, it held one-fifth of the world's fresh water, the largest amount in any one place. Passing through pretty villages of wooden houses and riding through large herds of cows milling around on the roads, returning to their owners at the end of the day, we had high expectations of what we had been told was one of the most spectacular lakes on earth.

It was a big disappointment. We were at the mouth of an estuary to the lake. It was flat, marshy and uninspiring, hardly the mountain-lined beauty spot we'd been promised. Then the shaman turned up with an interpreter, who identified himself as a news journalist from the local television station. Not quite what we wanted. The shaman was a short, stout, dark-haired, sour-faced woman for whom nothing was ever quite right. With the shaman scowling beside us, we built a little altar, a tower of sticks and a fire on the silted-up shore of Lake Baikal. Then the ceremony began. There was lots of drum-beating, chanting and burning of twigs, frequently interrupted so that the shaman could have a go at Ewan and me for no reason at all. In the end, I became so fed up I excused myself, saying I was cold and needed to get a sweater. If I'd stayed there another thirty seconds, I would have ripped her head off, shaman or not.

We slept that night in a derelict lake-shore hut, then pressed on to Chita. Stopping for lunch, we met a truck driver who advised us to take the train from Chita to Tynda. He said we could do the Road of Bones in six days.

A little later, at a petrol station, we met a couple who were driving from Vladivostock to Moscow. They told us that a very large section of the road from Chita to Tynda was in a dreadful state. We knew we could cope with gravel – we'd had much worse in Mongolia – but having given the bikes their last service before Magadan, we were concerned that six hundred miles or more on gravel or worse would not only take a long time, but would place unnecessary pressure on the bikes and rip the tyres to pieces.

'It's not quite the Trans-Siberian Railway,' Ewan said, 'but since we are in Siberia maybe a train ride is something we shouldn't miss. And it's the way all the motorcyclists we've read about have done it.'

'There must be a reason for it,' I said.

'There is a reason for it, and now that it seems we can't do it any other way I can't wait,' Ewan said. 'Nice one: feet up, a day on a train.'

Our minds were made up. If we could take the train, we would. Otherwise, we would reluctantly ride the long gravel road, something we had all the more reason to want to avoid after events later that afternoon. We had been riding for several hours in really hot weather, the three of us struggling to keep awake. Spotting a petrol station where I thought we could get some coffee and water, I slowed down. Just as I made the right turn, I heard an almighty crash behind me. I turned round to see Ewan struggling with his bike and Claudio lying on the road. Claudio's bike was on its side and Claudio was covered in tar that had melted off the road in the heat.

'What the *fuck*'s going on?' Ewan shouted. Like me, he had been struggling to stay awake. His eyesight had been going out of focus and he'd been screaming inside his helmet, trying to force his brain to stay awake.

'Are you okay? Is everything all right?' Ewan asked Claudio. 'What happened?'

'I was asleep,' Claudio said.

It was a valuable lesson. We were still reeling with exhaustion from our trek across Mongolia. Maybe a train ride would be a safer option than six hundred miles or more on a dusty gravel road. We rode on, stopping that evening in a beautiful field beside a peaceful river lined by pine trees. The tents erected, I stripped off and jumped in the river for a wash. 'It's about that cold,' I said, holding my fingers about two inches apart. 'As opposed to that other river in the Altai Mountains, which was about this cold,' I added, holding my fingers about half an inch apart.

By midday the next day, two hundred miles through pine forests were under our belts and we were standing in front of the impressive art nouveau frontage of Chita's main railway station. While Ewan and Claudio set off in search of tickets, I waited outside, sweating in the heat and surrounded by a crowd of winos and drug addicts, all asking questions in Russian.

'How many litres?'

'How fast does it go?'

'How many litres did you say?'

'How *fast* did you say it goes?'

'How big is the engine?'

'How many *litres*?'

'Does it really go that fast?'

'Where are you from?'

'Where are you going?'

'What are you doing here?'

Struggling to explain to the crowd that I didn't speak enough Russian to answer their questions, I spotted a young guy trying to get my attention. He was tall and young, with a trendy haircut and a pretty girlfriend. 'What are you doing here?' he said. 'I'm studying English in college.'

'Boy, am I pleased to meet you,' I said. 'Don't bother talking to me. Go into the ticket office and you'll see a guy with a shaved head, and another guy dressed in a T-shirt and trousers like mine, trying to buy a ticket. Can you give them a hand?'

And off he went, leaving me with the drunks for a very, very long time.

EWAN: Claudio and I were queuing in the main hall of the station, panicking about how to ask if we could put three motorbikes on a train to Tynda, when this young lad tapped me on the shoulder. 'Are you Ewan?' he said. 'Your friend said you needed a translator.'

The kid was brilliant. There's nothing worse than Russian bureaucracy and the railways seemed to be the nadir of obstinate Russian officialdom. As we were sent from passenger ticketing to goods ticketing to the cargo office to the station master and then back around the carousel again, the young lad patiently translated and explained what we needed to do next. At each office, we heard the same refrain: *Niet*. It was impossible, we were told. The bikes were too heavy; they had fuel in them; there were no trains to Tynda; there was a Tynda passenger train, but the bikes would have to go on a separate train via Skovorodino and be switched between trains there; and so on. No one wanted to help us.

By the end of the afternoon, we were giving up hope and resigning ourselves to riding the gravel road to Chita. We had just walked out of one of the offices when one of the goods yard employees came up to us. 'It's just talk, you know,' he said. 'It's possible to get to Tynda, but you'll have to travel with the bikes in a goods car. Come back tomorrow and I'll sort you out.'

After a good night's sleep, we turned up early the next morning at the station. At first, the deal was off, then it was back on, but only if we paid the goods handlers in advance and didn't let anyone see us putting the bikes on the train. It was becoming increasingly dodgy and I wondered whether we'd be better off riding the gravel road. Suddenly the mood changed and the goods handler we had met the previous day turned up. There was a lot of whispering. We heard the word *nichevo* – Russian for no problem – several times, then the translator said: 'It's going to be six thousand roubles.' By this stage, anything seemed a good deal. Around $320 for three bikes and the three of us for a twenty-four-hour journey was a bargain. 'Wait there and when we come to call you,' the goods handler said, 'get the bikes on really fast, with no one noticing it.'

We waited for hour after hour. The train wasn't leaving at 10.30 a.m. or 11.30 a.m. By mid-afternoon, we were beginning to abandon hope. Then the goods handler returned. 'Come with me,' he said. 'Keep really quiet, drive quietly and try not to attract too much attention.' It was a struggle for three big BMWs with three riders in Legoland outfits to pass down the main platform to the end of the train without anyone noticing it, but we managed it without being stopped to where six railway workers were waiting beside the goods wagon, the floor of which was about 6 feet above the platform. In the blink of an eye they put the bikes on a metal trolley, pushed it as close as possible to the wagon, then grabbed the bikes and hoisted them into the wagon.

'Right,' one of the workers shouted as we climbed up into the goods car, 'where's the money?' Ewan handed over a thick wodge of Russian roubles. The doors slammed shut. We were in pitch darkness.

11

Bad hair never looked so good

CHITA TO MAGADAN

CHARLEY: 'I can't believe we've pulled it off,' Ewan shouted in the darkness. 'It's fantastic.' The train lurched forward, then settled. It was getting ready to leave; we'd made it on board just in time.

'Where the fuck are we?' I asked. It was blisteringly hot in the wagon and I'd already broken out in a thick sweat. 'Are we on the right train? Did they know we want to go to Tynda and not fucking Vladivostock?'

There was a manic banging on the door. Shit, I thought, we've been rumbled. Or maybe we *are* on the wrong train and we need to get off quick. The door crashed open. It was Claudio. He'd been locked out. It was the first time I'd seen him looking even slightly flapped about being left behind. He leapt up into the wagon and the door slammed shut again on our steel sauna. Slowly our eyes became accustomed to the darkness. Our bikes were in a corner, there were a few crates and boxes, but otherwise the boxcar was empty. The only light came from a tiny crack in one corner, near the ceiling. I climbed up towards it and tugged open a flap, letting in enough light for us to get around the wagon

In the town of Tomtor.

At last, Magadan. It had taken us almost four weeks to cross Siberia, and we had travelled three thousand miles.

Relieved to have made it.
The statue behind us
commemorates the millions
of Russians who died while
constructing the Road of
Bones (which runs from
Yakutsk to Magadan) during
Stalin's reign of terror.

At Magadan airport with Claudio.

Panning for gold in Alaska. Well, we had to pay for the trip somehow . . .

Ewan limbers up for the final leg of the journey at the Forest Festival in Alaska.

Outside Calgary.

Ewan auditions for the job of his own stunt double in Canada . . .

. . . a much more serious crash. After we'd survived so much danger, it was a Canadian freeway that nearly spelled disaster.

A highlight of the trip: working with a horse whisperer in Montana.

Chilling out at the 'Taste of Lincoln' street fair in Chicago.

At the famous Orange County Choppers, New Jersey.

With Paul Snr., owner of Orange County Choppers.

Reunited with our families.

Arriving in New York.

Ewan raises his arms in triumph as we reach New York. There were tears in our eyes as we rode in.

After nearly four months, and over 20,000 miles – back where we started at Bulwer Street.

without bumping into things. The first thing we did was to strap our bikes to the sides of the wagon. While we were doing that, a railwayman came in, demanding payment.

'I thought we paid your friend,' I said, but he was having none of it. Then it dawned on us that the first payment was just to get us on the train. Now we needed to pay this railwayman – who we soon found out was the guard – to stay in his wagon. I asked him how many roubles he wanted. 'Four thousand?' I said. 'Two thousand is more like it!' The guard haggled over every last kopeck, settling eventually for a little more than three thousand roubles, then showed us around. There was a little cabin with two benches, where he ate and slept, and a filthy, stinking toilet that doubled as a kitchen. It was early afternoon and the sun had been beating down fiercely on the steel-walled wagon since dawn. Outside it was touching 90 degrees. Inside that boxcar it was well into the hundreds. As the train pulled off, the railwayman tugged the two side doors that led directly to his quarters. The doors opened into the wagon, leaving a little stoop, where we could sit, catching the breeze and smoking, hanging out and watching the world go by. It was fabulous.

Half an hour or so after we left Chita, four men appeared. They were Uzbeks. Like us, they were being smuggled on the train and they had hidden somewhere while we had been in the station. Clearly the wagon guard had a nice little earner going on. He was making money out of us and our new companions. The train, pulled by a hulking dark blue electric locomotive with a red star on its front, had fourteen goods wagons. Each pair of wagons had a guard and I was convinced that, just like ours, every guard on the train was on the make. Shortly before each stop at a major station, the guards would rush through the train, ushering us and our travelling companions into the main part of the boxcar so that we wouldn't be seen when the station staff walked through the wagon. Understanding the protocol after a while, we automatically came in from the doors before each station. Not only did we not want the guard to be busted, we couldn't face being thrown off the train.

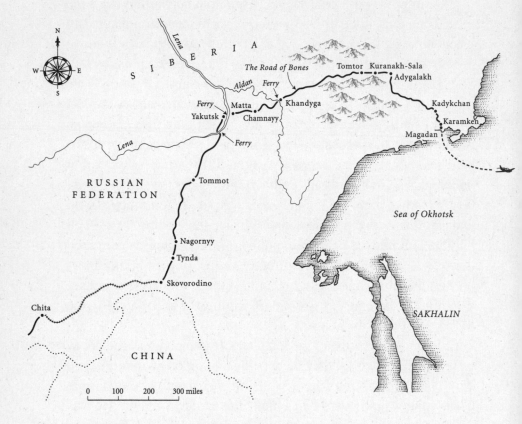

Cruising the valleys at a gentle 40 or 50mph, listening to my iPod and watching the pine forests and train yards slip by was just what I needed. I sat bare-chested on the stoop, my jeans oily and filthy from the train, just pondering things and letting my concerns about sticking to the schedule slip further away with each mile we clattered along the track. After crossing Mongolia and wangling our way on to the train, I'd come to realise that we'd solved every problem we'd encountered and we probably always would. Even when we were stranded in the middle of the

Mongolian desert, Claudio's Red Devil refusing to work, a local had turned up to help us fix it and there was no reason why that shouldn't continue to be the case.

Our Uzbek buddies were great company. We chatted with them as best we could and joined in their card games. In the evening, they cooked a fantastic borsch and invited us to eat with them. In return we shared out the last of our toffees, which they loved. At one of the stations, we poked our heads out of the boxcar to see one of the guards walking back along the train with a soft ice cream cone, wrapped up and with a lid on. Still absolutely roasting, we shouted at him to get us some. I gave him 50 roubles and he came back with more than twenty cornets. Our wagon companions and our guard didn't want any, so Ewan, Claudio and I ate our way through all of them. Just what we needed in the stifling heat.

We played poker long into the night, until the wagon cooled down enough to allow us to go to sleep beside our bikes. I dropped off immediately, but woke three times, convinced on each occasion that my bike was about to fall on to me. I'd tied it up as best I could with the few straps we had and had stuffed my bags under the pannier so that it would not crush me if it tipped over. Even so, I had a fitful night's sleep, constantly worried that the full third of a ton weight of my bike was about to kill me as I slept.

Twenty-three hours after we boarded the train, the door to the boxcar swung open and we found ourselves in Skovorodino. There was the same 5- to 6-foot drop as in Chita, only this time there was no one to help us down with our bikes. Our Uzbek companions would have been able to help us, but they couldn't show their faces in the station. The train stopped for about ten minutes, so we had to move fast. I grabbed a length of wood from the boxcar and carried it to the door, but it was too thin to take the weight of the bikes. Ewan jumped out of the wagon with Claudio and ran over to a pile of rubbish. They came back with a board, but that wasn't long enough. We were running out of time. Panicking, I thought we might have to drop the bikes off and take our chances. 'Fuck it,' I shouted. The board might not be long enough, but maybe it was sufficiently wide. 'Throw it up here!'

Ewan and Claudio propped the plank against the wagon. It sloped at more than 45 degrees but it would have to do. We didn't have much choice. With the help of the Uzbeks, I wheeled my BMW to the door and pushed the front wheel out of the wagon so that it was resting on its belly pan. While the Uzbeks lifted up the back of the bike, I grabbed the handles to skid it down the board. The hydraulic brakes barely worked without the engine ticking over. I teetered beside it, squeezing the brakes as hard as I could to get some grip on it, and tried to wheel it slowly down the hairy slope. It was a close thing, but I managed to get my bike down without losing control. I eased Claudio's bike down the ramp, then Ewan's. We'd done it. We had accomplished what we thought would be impossible. What a triumph to have made it from Chita to Skovorodino without damaging our bikes! A part of me felt slightly guilty that we hadn't ridden the road from Chita, but that regret was heavily outweighed by the thrill of our experience on the train. And to make the victory even sweeter, we were ahead of schedule for the first time, by four days.

Skovorodino was a dump. There was a railway junction, but little else. It was difficult to see how the locals managed to scrape any kind of living. We stocked up on water and food, and left almost immediately. Our diet had become quite rudimentary, just boil-in-the-bag survival meals and pot noodles, but I no longer cared. Living on my nerves and apprehensive about the Road of Bones, my appetite had diminished and I'd lost a lot of weight.

The road to Tynda was a succession of very long and extremely dusty straights. We'd become accomplished gravel-road riders by now, quite capable of cruising at 50 or 60mph and occasionally topping 90 or 100. But the problem with gravel roads was the dust, particularly as the stretch north from Skovorodino teemed with trucks – not that we could see many trucks through the thick dust that enveloped them. The first indication of a truck ahead was a huge cloud of dust in the distance – the truck would be invisible, but we'd know it was there. As we approached, the billowing cloud would thicken until we reached a point at which we had a choice: either commit to riding through the cloud or slow down to ease back out of it.

The sensible option would have been to cruise along slowly at a safe distance behind the trucks, which were moving at about 35 or 40mph. But, despite our best intentions, Ewan and I were still obsessed with pressing on and keeping to the schedule, so we'd have to accelerate into the dust cloud, not knowing quite how near we were getting. Six to 10 feet from the rear of the truck, the dust cloud would thin and we'd be able to see it in the fug. We then had to pick the right moment to move out into the thick cloud thrown up by the front wheels. Unable to see if any traffic was coming towards us on the opposite side of the road, we had no option but to go for it, riding blind. As we drew level with the back wheels, the dust would thin out and we'd get a glimpse of the road ahead. Often, a big blue 20-ton colossus would suddenly appear. An oncoming truck! Usually there would be time to slam on the brakes and slip behind the truck we'd just overtaken if a vehicle was approaching, but there was always the chance that, by the time we saw it, it would be too late. To slip back behind the truck we were overtaking, we'd have to cross from the tyre track of compacted gravel on the wrong side of the road, over the hump of deep, loose gravel at the centre of the road, and find the groove of compacted gravel in the tyre track on our side of the road, all without being able to see the road surface and without losing control of the front end of the bike. And then, as the two trucks passed each other, we'd be enveloped in another thick fog of dust. A total whiteout. Without doubt, it was the most dangerous thing we'd done so far on the journey. To make matters worse, the dust clouds made it impossible to spot patches of loose gravel that could twist the front end of the bike away in an instant. But after half a day of dicing with all this and boosted by adrenalin, I started to look forward to the next cloud. It was exciting.

We rolled past Tynda and decided to camp. It was late afternoon and we were hungry; the only meal we'd had in the last forty-eight hours had been the soup on the train. But there was nowhere to stop. Open-cast gravel mines lined both sides of the road. We continued riding, not spotting anywhere suitable for camping until it was almost dark, when we turned off the road and crossed a riverbed. Behind me I could see Ewan getting stuck in the deep sand. His back wheel was spinning madly, digging itself into the ground. Claudio and I got off our bikes and helped Ewan free his. Then we stood back and looked at his bike. His panniers were twisted and his back wheel appeared to have been knocked out of alignment.

'There's something different about my bike,' Ewan said tetchily. I could see he was really annoyed with himself for getting stuck in the sand and was sinking into one of his moods.

'Oh, fuck,' Ewan said. 'The luggage frame has snapped in the same place as Claudio's did.' Walking over to my bike to get some tyre irons and cable ties, I noticed it also looked wonky.

'I think mine's gone too,' I said. We examined our bikes. Mine had a crack on one side; Ewan's had a crack on the left and a breakage on the right.

'Oh, God.' It was Claudio. 'Ewan, look under your seat.' One of the two main bars that supported the entire back end of the bike had snapped. A disaster. The Beamer had a trellis frame, so it wasn't going to fall apart immediately, but without the big, fat main bars intact, Ewan would soon have nothing to sit on.

'We've been carrying far too much . . .,' I said.

'. . . yeah, and now the straw has broken the camel's back,' Ewan said.

'There's nothing for it,' I said. 'We'll have to go back to Tynda.'

'Hey, hang on,' Ewan said. 'I was just thinking that this would give us something to do in Yakutsk, and now you're saying we have to go back to Tynda.'

'If we turn back, we'll hit tarmac in about twenty miles. If we press ahead to the next town, it'll probably be gravel all the way and we don't know if the town will be big or small. We just don't know.'

We removed the panniers from Ewan's bike and patched over the breakages with tyre levers and cable ties. The next morning, we ferried his luggage piece by piece to the road, a fifteen-minute walk away. I couldn't believe how heavy it was. 'This is crazy,' Ewan shouted. 'We've got to get rid of all this weight.'

It *was* ludicrous. We were carrying several things we'd never used. We had two full tool kits, including all sizes of spanner and nuts, two water pumps, two foldable basins and two of just about everything. We'd chosen expensive titanium cutlery to save on weight, yet we were carrying a thermos flask we'd never used, a completely unnecessary soap dish and a toilet roll holder that was, frankly, laughable. We even had four saucepans. Ewan's obsession with gear had got the better of us. I'd wanted to get rid of a few items earlier on, but he liked the idea of having all his things around him. Now they were luxuries we couldn't afford.

With our top boxes and panniers in a line beside us, we sat by the side of the road hoping someone would stop and help us. A large dumper truck pulled in, but we couldn't get the driver to understand that we needed a lift. A red Lada approached, empty but for the driver. 'Perfect,' said Ewan, attempting to flag it down. It drove straight past us. 'Bastard!' he hurled after it. Eventually, an articulated dumper truck stopped and the check-shirted driver, fag in mouth, unshaven and grumpy, stepped out. We explained our predicament. He nodded and pointed to the back of the truck. We threw our luggage into the dumpster, got on our bikes and followed the truck into Tynda, where a bare-chested welder and his silent assistant worked on the bikes for three hours, joining the broken frame sections. The guy was a genius with a welding torch and did a beautiful job, adding carefully shaped braces to the weakest points of the bikes' frames. Afterwards, we found a hotel and stripped our luggage of all the unnecessary fripperies.

Weeded of all but the bare necessities, we were about 40 crucial kilograms lighter.

The best thing about Tynda was the bar next to the welder's workshop. Called Café Diesel, it was the coolest place I'd ever seen. Most surprising of all was the fact that it was hidden away in what looked like any other polluted, half-derelict eastern Russian town. With an old Russian motorbike and some car parts embedded in the wall, it was a petrolhead's heaven. It had bare stone and brick walls, aluminium doors and fire escape steps up to a black granite bar. And the music was fantastic. We spent the whole evening in there, drinking, talking, dancing and letting our hair down properly for the first time in ages. The next night, when the support crew had caught up with us, we took Jim and Sergey there. Again, it was a long night. Jim drank so much vodka with Sergey that he collapsed with alcohol poisoning and pulled the sink off his bathroom wall when he got back to his hotel.

We left the support team nursing their hangovers in Tynda and resumed the long grind northwards to Yakutsk. The support team had bought a Russian Furgon 4×4 van to replace the Animal. It was ugly and boxy, but there was nonetheless something very charming about its crude practicality and it was as sprightly as a mountain goat across rough ground. But the best thing about it, Ewan thought, was its number plate.

'Have you seen that?' he said. 'Look: the registration of the Furgon is 955 BO. And 955 is the number that Steve McQueen used to race with on his dirt bikes. A bit of a weird coincidence, seeing as we're dirt-biking around the world and he's one of my heroes.'

It took us three days to ride the eight hundred miles from Tynda to Yakutsk along dusty roads heavy with truck traffic. Day by day, our skins became darker. At first I thought I was picking up a good tan, but it was just layer upon layer of ingrained dirt. My hands were leathery black, my face was caked in half an inch of dust and the zips on our jackets jammed they were so full of muck. To avoid riding permanently in each other's dust clouds, we spread out along the road, up to half a mile between each of us. I was bringing up the rear, Ewan was leading and Claudio was in the middle when I got my first puncture of the trip. I pulled over, expecting Claudio and Ewan to turn back to help me. When their dust clouds had dispersed, I stared into the distance at the open, empty road. Claudio and Ewan had disappeared out of sight, so I waited. And waited. After ten minutes, I started to get pissed off. This was beyond a joke. After twenty minutes, I was getting upset. So much for looking out for each other. Forty-five minutes later, Ewan appeared in the distance.

'Fucking Claudio,' he said when he stopped. 'It wasn't until I stopped for some water, and Claudio pulled in, that we missed you. Claudio's dust cloud settled and there was no Charley.'

Ewan was really angry with Claudio, who should have been watching me in his wing mirrors. 'I asked him, "Where's Charley?",' Ewan said, 'and he said "I don't know". He hadn't looked in his fucking mirrors for forty minutes. I thought you might be having a pee round the corner, so we waited a bit longer. Then I thought I'd ride back a little way and check. I rode for almost half an hour, about twenty miles, until I found you here.' It was hard not to take it personally. If I'd had an accident, I would have been lying on the side of the road waiting for help for almost an hour.

Then Claudio turned up. He climbed off his bike very slowly, took his helmet off and started loosening the straps on his camera.

'Has anyone got any food?' he said.

'Claudio! You've got your head up your arse half the time, you know,' Ewan snapped. 'You've got to keep your eye on your mirrors, because we can't afford for this to happen again. If Charley had fallen off, it could've been the difference between life and death.'

Claudio didn't say anything.

'Did he really say that?' Ewan said to me. 'Did he ask about food?'

'It's all he cares about,' I said. 'We're riding around the world and all Claudio wants to know is when he's getting his next meal.'

'Like the porridge today,' Claudio said. 'It was disgusting. Like soap powder. Terrible. Crap.'

'You know, I do my best,' I said. 'Middle of fucking nowhere and he's provided with food. He's actually putting on weight and all he can say is: "Can we eat now? I must eat now." I make soup for dinner every night and then he complains. It's quite hurtful, Claudio.'

Claudio looked as if he didn't quite know whether I was teasing or my complaint was serious. 'Last night, while I was cooking,' I said, 'Claudio came up to me and said "Can I take me some water?". So he went off and shaved in the cooking pot and left all his bits of hair in it. How awful is that? They never feed me, he says, and he shaves in the cooking pot. Yuck.'

Claudio had become the scapegoat for all our frustrations. He was really getting it in the neck. 'I had a real moan about you when I got back and found Charley with his wheel off,' Ewan said. 'I'm coming clean now . . . I laid all the blame on you.'

'I'm getting used to it,' Claudio said and went in search of a chocolate bar.

The long journey to Yakutsk gave us plenty of opportunities to quiz truck drivers about the Road of Bones from Yakutsk to Magadan. Along the way, we accumulated so much conflicting information that we could read it any way we wanted: either the whole road was impassable or it would all be a breeze, depending on which advice we chose to believe.

'Why do we keep asking everyone all the time about the Road of Bones?' Ewan said. 'Every time we ask someone we get different information. And we'll just have to do it anyway, so it doesn't matter what they say. Ultimately, very few people have ever done it on a motorbike. That's why nobody really knows.'

However, it did become clear that there was one section that would be particularly tricky and it was likely to be worse now than at almost any other time of the year. Those few truck drivers who had driven the whole route had done so in the winter, when the rivers were frozen. We'd be trying it when the rivers were in full spate, swollen with meltwater running off the mountains.

Just before the last stretch into Yakutsk, we had to take a ferry. We followed directions down a dodgy road to a sandy riverbank where a column of trucks and two cars were waiting. A barge carrying three diesel tankers, pushed by a small tugboat, appeared around a bend in the river, wobbled in our direction and slammed into the riverbank. The trucks drove off and the ferry captain jumped ashore. He was immediately surrounded by truck drivers screaming, shouting and waving their arms in an effort to outbid each other for a place on the ferry. Some of them had been waiting two or three days to cross the river. Meanwhile, the three of us could just slip into the spare space between the trucks on the ferry.

After a short crossing, we rode into Yakutsk, an ugly, industrial, grey city full of dangerous and drunk drivers, one of whom nearly knocked Ewan off his bike. Yakutsk spent about half the year gripped by snow and ice, the average temperature in January was minus 43 degrees Celsius and the houses had to be built on stilts because of the permafrost, so it was hardly surprising that it looked so rundown and the locals drank beer and vodka like water.

We didn't do much in Yakutsk except rest and prepare our bikes and worry about the journey ahead. We desperately needed to catch up on sleep, but I spent most nights tossing and turning, unable to sleep for worry about the Road of Bones. When I did fall asleep, I was plagued by nightmares about crossing rivers and getting to Magadan. On the last morning, we discussed our plans over breakfast. If necessary, we'd hire a truck to carry the support vehicles through the rivers, but Ewan, Claudio and I would try to ride the entire Road of Bones on our bikes. 'This is the beginning of the end of the journey,' Ewan said as we swung our legs over our bikes that morning. 'Or maybe it's the end of the beginning.'

We rode for about twenty miles to a shanty village, where we caught a ferry across the Lena River. Meandering by inlets, the river was several miles wide at this point and as flat and still as a mirror. 'It's taking us round the wetlands,' Russ said on the boat. 'But we'll have to ride through them later on.'

'Wetlands?' Ewan said. 'Nobody mentioned anything to me in the prep about wetlands. You know how I hate water.' We'd crossed some small ponds on the way down to the ferry, but they were mere puddles compared with what we knew we were likely to face on the Road of Bones.

'Don't worry, Ewan,' I said. 'It'll get easier.'

'I fucking hope so. The gravel's got easier, the sand's got easier, maybe the water will get easier too, but something about riding a bike through water still freaks me out.'

The ferry dumped us in the middle of nowhere. With no ferry terminal or quay to aim for, our landing point was any old sandbank that took the captain's fancy. We disembarked and rode for a few hours, making slow progress across the tundra until we found a dirt road, which we followed through small towns of log cabins, until we camped in the early evening.

The next day and a half was spent riding through the wetlands, via Matta and Chamnayy, to the next ferry. The riding was much easier than it had been in Mongolia, mainly because the bikes were so much lighter after we had dumped so much of our equipment in Yakutsk. We made quick and easy progress, eventually arriving at an empty ferry whose captain wanted $2500 to take us on a twelve-hour trip up the river.

'You know the truck drivers pay really good money,' he said.

'Yeah, but there aren't any truck drivers here,' I replied.

By the time we'd got off the phone to his boss, the fare had gone down to $900 and we were on the long, narrow barge, just wide enough to take two articulated trucks. We boiled up some camping rations and ate them as the boat drifted through the twilight. After dinner, I sat on the edge of the landing ramp, one leg dangling over the side while I spoke to my wife on the satellite phone and watched the river slip past. The water was as flat as glass, the air completely still and again I had that feeling of not being at all concerned if things didn't go to plan. Since the train journey, I'd realised that if we wanted to get somewhere we'd do so eventually and that there was little point in worrying about how or when. If only I could remain so positive when things were going against us.

We left the boat the next morning and immediately came upon the deepest gravel we'd ever experienced. The stones were about three inches across, several feet deep and a nightmare to ride on. The road had a life of its own, shifting beneath the wheels as we rode across it. It was terrifying. 'If it's going to be like this for the rest of the way, we're fucked,' I said to Ewan, not for the first time in the course of the trip. This was the type of road surface that could really inflict serious damage, particularly as we had no desire to take it easy. It continued for mile after mile, graduating to smaller stones a few miles past Khandyga and then disappearing altogether to be replaced by hard-packed road the next day. Once we hit those hard-packed roads we screamed along at 60mph. It was a perfect surface: a well-travelled and well-kept track on which the mud had become quite polished and there was no dust. We pushed on, getting as many miles as possible under our belts while the going was good, riding through stunning countryside in monochrome: black mountains with white snowcaps, grey dirt beneath the wheels and dark rocks lining the road. We climbed several mountain passes on a tricky single-lane road with a huge drop on either side and passed an ominous signpost: Magadan 1430km. Parts of the road had been washed away by rivers and we crossed dozens of shallow stretches of water, often having to ride along the riverbed, against the current, as much as across it. And then we came to the first big river. The water was about 6 metres deep, with a ferocious current. There was a bridge nearby, but it looked like the broken spine of a dinosaur skeleton. Made of wood, the deck was buckled and twisted and the uprights jutted at strange angles, all higgledy-piggledy in the river. Two-thirds of the way across, it had collapsed. A wooden ladder spanned the 30-foot gap between the two sections, so it was possible to cross on foot, but a bike crossing was out of the question. We were stuck.

We had no choice but to set up camp and wait until the river fell or a truck on which we could hitch a ride came along. I crossed the river in search of help. The town on the other side was a shithole. Looking like a bombsite, it was in fact one of the former gulag concentration camps that had housed the political prisoners Stalin's regime had forced to build the Road of Bones from Magadan to the gold and diamond mines that dotted the area. I went from hut to hut through the eerily silent camp, hoping to find some inhabitants. Just about every building was derelict. The streets were full of rubbish, scrap metal and rusting, broken-down vehicles. I knocked on the door of a hut beside a petrol station. An emaciated, pale young man and his toothless father opened the door and eyed me with suspicion.

'Hello. *Strasvitye*,' I said. 'Uh, good to see you.'

They regarded me blankly, then the toothless older man shouted something in Russian.

'We have three *mototsikl* on the other side of the river and we need a truck to . . .'

More Russian. I wished I'd paid attention in the Russian classes back in Bulwer Street. This was embarrassing.

'Yeah, a *mototsikl*, and we need a truck to get across the river. Can you help?'

Nothing.

'I thought this looked like a *benzin* station – let's hope there's petrol here – anyway, nice to see you. I'm English . . . er . . . *Inglesky*.'

They perked up. Maybe they were starting to understand.

'Er, English? I'm English.'

The young lad gabbled something in Russian.

'Yeah, yeah . . .,' I said. 'On the other side of the river. Three *mototsikl* and we want to get across.'

More Russian, this time from the toothless one.

'Yeah, just here . . . it's too big for us . . . no bridge . . . no . . . do you know if there's a *benzin* here?'

They pointed at what I had guessed might be the petrol station.

'Okay, thank you.'

They nodded and smiled.

'Do you know if there's like a truck or something that can get across?'

They looked at me blankly again.

'Nothing here?'

The young lad said something in Russian.

'Over there maybe?' I said, ever the optimist.

More Russian.

'Maybe? Er, okay.'

Just as I was about to walk away, the young lad beckoned me into his toothless father's car, a back-firing old Lada that was fit only for the scrapheap, and drove me around the camp to someone who fixed passing trucks. He couldn't help, so I returned to our camp on the other side of the river, hatching a plan along the way to build a ramp out of some planks, span the two bridge sections and wheel the bikes down it if the level of the river did not drop the next day. When I got back to the tents, Ewan had built a large fire to ward off bears and was nursing the wounds of our first serious encounter with Siberian mosquitoes, the dreaded east Russian summer plague that we'd been warned about.

'Look at this,' he said, dropping his trousers and baring his arse. I counted the bites. There were five in a vertical row, all on the same cheek.

'He really helped himself, that one, didn't he,' I said.

'The greedy bastard,' Ewan replied. 'And that was in just one squat, one sitting.'

We made some supper and ate it in the pouring rain, then Claudio, whose tent had been stolen, crossed the river to sleep in one of the abandoned huts.

All through the night we listened for approaching trucks but none came. It rained until dawn, causing the river to rise even higher. At about nine o'clock I heard the sound of a vehicle in the distance. I leapt out of my sleeping bag, pulled my clothes on and crawled out of my tent. There, on the ridge of the road, was the young lad I'd met the day before, driving a Russian jeep. Beside him, in the passenger seat, was a fat old lady who I assumed was his mother. I waved at them as they passed by, irritated that the vehicle I'd heard hadn't been a truck, and watched them disappear from sight. Seconds later, the horn started to sound and it didn't stop. I hurried in the direction of the blaring horn, over the top of the ridge and down the other side to where the jeep was lying on its side. The windscreen had been smashed and was hanging loose, still half attached to the jeep, and I could hear screams coming from inside the vehicle. I pulled the windscreen completely off it to find the fat old lady lying on top of her son, who was struggling under her considerable weight. I pulled the old woman out and then dragged the lad out of the cab on to the mud, where they stood in the pouring rain looking shocked. I looked down. The old lady didn't have any shoes on, so I climbed into the jeep, found her shoes and helped her put them back on. The lad was clearly very distressed. As far as I could make out, he'd just borrowed the jeep and immediately crashed it. Ewan, Claudio and I helped him pull it upright and then spent half an hour trying to start it, getting thoroughly soaked in the process.

'We can't do the bikes down the plank business in the rain,' Ewan said after we'd returned to our tents for some breakfast. 'It's much too dangerous. We'll have to fall back on the truck idea – hope that a truck passes by that can take us across.'

We decided that I would wait on the road in case a truck arrived, while Claudio and Ewan would climb over the bridge to the camp to dry our rain-sodden clothes and damp sleeping bags inside one of the derelict huts in which Claudio had found a heater. I waited for hours, pacing up and down, often thinking I could hear a truck in the distance but then, when nothing came, realising it was just my mind playing tricks on me. It was now early afternoon, and I'd just finished pacing a length of the road and was about to turn around when I felt something behind me.

I turned and there was David in the Warrior. The one time a car did come along, and I hadn't heard it.

'Boy, am I pleased to see you,' I said, leaning into the Warrior to explain to David our problems with the bridge. I explained our dilemma, then stepped back, turned around and got the fright of my life. Just 30 feet away, two huge trucks had stopped. Again, I hadn't heard them. One was a Kamaz with an open top; the other was a Ural with a large passenger cabin, like a bus, on its back. They were just what we needed. Both were formidable heavy-duty trucks, with six-wheel drive and powerful engines. Trucks made by Kamaz – company motto: No Roads? No Problem! – had been developed by the Soviet Union in the 1970s specifically to deal with the most impenetrable fringes of the country and became the vehicle of choice in the Arctic, across deserts, in the tropics and on mountains.

A burly driver climbed down and introduced himself as Vladimir. He was a big man, a human version of his muscular truck, with a wide smile and curious eyes.

'We have motorcycle,' I said. 'To go across the river in this truck is okay?'

Vladimir nodded.

'My friends on other side of river,' I said. 'They come soon. Bring bag.'

Vladimir nodded again.

I ran down to the bridge, where I met Ewan and Claudio. 'I've got some trucks,' I said. 'And they're going to take us across the river. It's all sorted.'

'Fantastic,' Ewan said.

'Come and see them,' I said. I was so excited. 'I've been waiting this whole trip to go on a truck like one of these. I get a little semi just thinking about them.'

Vladimir backed up his truck against the raised bank of the road and we rode our bikes on to it, strapped them fast and stood on its deck as it moved off. The Kamaz had incredibly low gear ratios which enabled it to climb extreme slopes. With its engine roaring, it inched its way down the riverbank, through the river, the water washing over its wheels, and up the other side, Ewan and I whooping as it deposited us safely on the far side. Vladimir then crawled back across the river to carry across the support vehicles one by one.

We'd been led to believe that there would be only two really big rivers on the Road of Bones, the one we'd just crossed and the last one before Magadan. In between, there would be lots of smaller rivers, but we'd be able to get through them all on our bikes, so we waved goodbye to Vladimir and the support crew and set off on our own. We rode through a succession of ghost towns, most of them remains of the old gulag camps, some with children's shoes still arranged neatly in rows in the rooms, looking as if the occupants had departed suddenly and were due back at any moment.

Walking around the old camps was a haunting experience. As many as two million prisoners were said to have died in the Kolyma region, many of their bodies used as landfill in the road we were travelling on. Hence the name the Road of Bones. It was built to service the gold mines, where, in temperatures down to minus sixty Fahrenheit, prisoners were lowered by steel buckets into the pits to mine gold on their knees for fourteen hours a day. It is estimated that for every kilogram of gold extracted from the mines one prisoner died. Many didn't last more than a month after their arrival from Magadan, where prison ships unloaded their human cargo and for which we were now headed. And those who had made it to the camps had endured a journey of unimaginable brutality. Across the Soviet Union by rail to Vladivostok, crammed so tightly into cattle wagons that many suffocated. Temperatures in the holds of the ships that then carried the prisoners from Vladivostok to Magadan often dropped below zero and entire shiploads of prisoners would arrive entombed in ice. Once at Magadan, the prisoners were marched to the camps, which could be many hundreds of miles away. No wonder Alexander Solzhenitsyn, himself a survivor of the gulags, called

Kolyma 'the pole of cold and cruelty'. We'd heard tales of prisoners being tied naked to trees in the middle of summer and left to the mosquitoes until they passed out or died. There was an overwhelming feeling of sadness about the buildings and, in the face of such extreme human suffering, our minor hardships on the Road of Bones paled into insignificance. It was humbling.

We rode on from the camp and came to another big river. I waded in to gauge the depth and the strength of the current. The water washed above my knees and nearly knocked me off my feet. 'It looks like the water's higher than the piston heads, so we could be in trouble,' I said. 'But even if it's lower, the bikes will catch more of the current than I did and I think they'll get swept away.'

While we were waiting for the Kamaz and Ural trucks to catch up with us, three Urals crossed the river from the far bank to the side on which we were waiting. They told us there were at least five high rivers before we would reach Tomtor, the halfway point on the Road of Bones, and that two Urals had recently been swept away on one of the river crossings. 'Four hundred kilometres snow and no bridges,' one of the drivers said. 'It was hard to drive here.'

We crossed the river on top of the Kamaz, unloaded and rode off on our own again. An hour or so later, in the middle of a pine forest, we came to another river, which had swept away a 30-foot length of road. Although the gap was narrow, the river ran deep and very fast. Vladimir refused to cross it. It would be safer in the morning, he said. We might have to wait three days, but eventually the river level would drop. I'd been watching Vladimir as he negotiated the rivers and come to trust him. He was a brilliant driver, who had been plying the same route for twenty-five years, ten of them in the Kamaz, which he owned. Nothing fazed him. He was very calm and steady and refused to be swayed by others. It was clear he would do things at his own speed and in his own time. If he said the river was too deep to cross, I believed him.

On the opposite bank stood three lumber trucks, their drivers arguing about whether or not to cross the river. We watched them shouting and waving their arms at each other. Then one of them jumped into an articulated truck used for carrying lengths of timber. He gunned the engine and the 30-ton truck lurched into the water. The cab twisted in the water, looking as if it was going to be swept away. Only the rear section, which was anchored on the bank, was preventing it from being washed downstream. Just when we thought the driver was about to lose control, one of the other truck drivers on the far side dragged the logging truck out of the river using a length of steel cable linking the two trucks. That lumber truck was stronger and heavier then either of ours, yet it had been tossed around in the river like a feather in the wind. The implication was clear.

EWAN: The lumber drivers partied all night. We saw them break open a case of vodka as we crawled into our tents and were woken at about six-thirty the next morning by drunken shouting and the sound of the trucks being revved up. Bolstered by Dutch courage, they were having another go. The same driver who had tried the night before powered the articulated logging lorry into the river, but again he couldn't make it across. The river level had dropped by about 3 feet overnight, so our bank was now too high to breach from the river. We set to work with spades and pickaxes, chipping away at the Road of Bones to construct a gentler slope. I loved being caught in a situation where there was no option but to solve the problem. It pulled everyone together really tight. We all did our bit. There were no arguments or fights or disagreements; it was all done efficiently. And as we made our way slowly eastwards, I felt proud that Charley and I had brought everyone together.

'Look at everyone,' I said to Charley. Ahead of us, Russ, David, Jimmy, Sergey and Vasiliy were cutting away at the riverbank. It was hard work and it was raining. We should have been miserable, but everyone was having a great time.

'If we hadn't decided to do this thing, none of these people would be here now,' I said. 'And Vladimir and the other truck driver wouldn't be here with a job to do and we would never have met most of these people.' It felt wonderful, magical.

An hour or so later, we had finished our ramp and the lumber truck drivers had another go. This time they made it. The driver steamed on to our side of the river, but then couldn't get the truck up from the surrounding marshland on to the raised road. With the engine bellowing black smoke, he careened along the road, one wheel up on it, the other in the mud, flattening bushes and small trees as he fought to gain a sufficient grip to haul all 50 feet of the logging truck on to the Road of Bones. Eventually he made it. The driver then tugged the other trucks through the river with a steel cable. Once they'd all made it across, more vodka was opened and the party resumed.

Then it was our turn. Vladimir engaged the lowest gear and the Kamaz dipped into the river, crawled through the water and climbed the far riverbank like a tortoise slowly but surely hauling itself up a rock. The Warrior was pulled through on a cable, David shouting with alarm as the back end slipped away and the current threatened to sweep the car downstream. Vasiliy refused to drive the Furgon through the water. He thought it was too dangerous and not something a doctor should be expected to do, so David volunteered.

'Don't do this if you think you might get hurt. It's not worth it,' I said. 'I couldn't forgive myself if anything went wrong. This trip's not important enough for somebody to die trying to cross a river. There's no way I could justify that.'

David eased the Furgon into the water, while I stood on the riverbank. I could hardly watch, I was so scared that something might go wrong. Foot by foot, he edged the van forward, his knuckles white, he was gripping the steering wheel so hard. And then he climbed the far bank. He had made it. I screamed with delighted relief.

We'd asked the lumber truck drivers about the state of the

roads ahead. They told us there would be hundreds of rivers to cross before we reached Tomtor. I looked quizzically at Vladimir, but he just tapped the side of his neck with his fingers: the Russian sign for vodka. In some circumstances, it would signal the offer of a drink. But on this occasion, its meaning was quite different: the lumber truck drivers were blind drunk and not to be trusted. Sure enough, Vladimir was right and we sailed through to Tomtor, easily crossing a few shallow rivers on our bikes.

Along the way, Vladimir spotted a baby brown bear and shot it, not because it was a threat but because its fur was worth $600. He skinned it quickly and tossed the fur into the back of his truck, leaving the bear's carcass to rot in the forest. I was appalled. Here we were in the middle of a wilderness, having to bow to Mother Nature several times a day, yet being so cavalier about our relationship with our environment. The loggers we had just encountered were illegally felling trees simply because they would get $100 for each tree trunk. Vladimir had shot the bear simply because its fur was valuable. I understood that their lives were not easy and that they might need the money, but it still didn't make it right. The bear had been a wild animal living in its natural habitat and nobody had any right to shoot it with a gun. I thought it was disgusting. Charley was also bitterly disappointed the bear had been shot, not because of the mindless waste of an animal's life but because he'd not seen Vladimir do it. 'You should have let me shoot it,' he wailed. Again, I was appalled and the arguments on the rights and wrongs of shooting wild animals kept us busy for days afterwards.

By that evening, we were tucked up in a stuffy, overheated hunting lodge where the windows couldn't be opened because of the mosquitoes. In the quiet of the hotel, I had time to think about home. It had been my wife's birthday the day before and I would have done anything to have been with her. I'd spent more than a year daydreaming about this trip. And now that I was on the journey, here I was fantasising about home – taking the kids to school, giving them a bath, or going to the park. My daydreams were now about everyday things.

I felt as if I had been drifting since we'd left Ulaanbaatar. Mongolia had had a profound effect on me: I hadn't expected to be so deeply touched by what I had seen and experienced. I had a real sense of where we were there and where we were headed, but since we'd arrived in Siberia, I'd lost my sense of place. All that mattered now was getting to Magadan. It had been a hell of a trip so far. Trucks, bikes, mud, camping and bears – it was everything I had hoped for. And when we were all working as a team to get across a river by building a ramp or moving a tree off the road, the sense of achievement was enormous. A tiny part of me regretted that Charley and I couldn't do the entire Road of Bones on our bikes without help from Vladimir and his trucks, but I had to face the fact that it was impossible. We couldn't do it without assistance. A motorcycle couldn't plough through a river that was 6 feet deep. The engine would flood and we would lose it in the current. That would be it. Trip over. And we only had one objective: to get to New York. The end justified the means.

Over the next three days, we crossed dozens of rivers, felled trees to fill in ditches and slowly ground our way towards Magadan. We rode for sixteen hours on the first day out of Tomtor, the most exciting sixteen hours of motorcycling I'd ever experienced. The roads deteriorated as we wound our way through mud, gravel, puddles, potholes, rivers and bogs. Just about everything was thrown at us all at once. But all I could think was how much easier it was than I had expected. Had we not ridden through Kazakhstan and Mongolia, I would have found the Road of Bones impossible. But I was now an old hand. I could feel the difference the off-road experience had made. I wasn't freaked out about mud. I was quite happy on it. And I'd conquered my fear of water by doing the thing that had frightened me the most: sucking water into my engine. During one river crossing I had dropped the bike on its right-hand side, just where the air intake was located. Instead of panicking, I had calmly removed the plugs, pumped the water out of the piston heads and cranked the engine. I'd put the plugs back in and turned over the engine. Water shot out of the exhaust and the engine fired up. I'd fixed it. I'd got the bike going again, at a vital moment.

But then things started to go badly wrong and we reached a point where we couldn't ride any further for two reasons. First, Charley injured his back. His bike slipped as he was taking it down from the centre stand and, thinking he was going to trap his leg between his falling bike and Claudio's, he tried to wrench his bike upwards, in the process pulling the muscles behind his shoulder blade. He was in agony and couldn't ride. Second, we'd reached rivers that were too deep to cross. I'd sucked water into my engine for the second time, Charley for the first. We had been crossing rivers in which we were waist-deep in water, the river flowing over the bike seats. The only way we could get across them was to take each bike over individually. Charley would push the handlebars, I'd push from behind and Claudio would inch the front wheel forward on a count of one-two-three. Afterwards, we'd have to strip each bike down to dry everything and ensure the engine was free of water. Eventually we'd had enough. With heavy hearts we had to concede that the rivers had beaten us. They were simply too high to cross in June. We'd survived eight days on the Road of Bones. Another month later, maybe, and we would have been okay, but we didn't have a month to play with. We loaded the bikes on the Kamaz and hitched a lift in the support vehicles, Charley dosed to the eyeballs on Vasiliy's painkillers. Within fifteen minutes I knew we'd made the right decision as we bumped through potholes the size of lakes, as wide as the road and deeper than the bikes. Even so, we still had a major challenge ahead of us: the river that all the other truck drivers told us even the Kamaz and Ural struggle to cross.

Over the next two days, we cut through dozens of rivers. Charley and I had become part of the support crew by now, hacking away at riverbanks to help the trucks drop down into the water, guiding the vehicles through rivers and watching open-mouthed as the Warrior took most of the Road of Bones in its stride. Out of all the vehicles, it was the most impressive. The Kamaz, Ural and Furgon were built for these kinds of conditions, but the Warrior was an off-the-peg Mitsubishi Shogun. At home, it would be a glorified shopping trolley. In Siberia, it was a *bona fide* off-road expedition vehicle. Amazing.

Nevertheless, there were plenty of hairy moments. The Warrior almost toppled over the edge of a section of road that had been swept away by a river and was saved only by the quick thinking of Vasiliy, who snapped on a rope and towed it to safety with the Furgon. On one river crossing, the Furgon started to float down the river, but Vasiliy bravely kept his focus on the riverbank and his foot on the accelerator and made it to safety.

On 25 June, we reached the *big river*, the one we had been warned about. The mother of all river crossings. Vladimir had been speaking about our Siberian nemesis for days. When he saw it, he just shook his head and said: 'We wait until tomorrow.' His decision was final. The river was about 300 metres wide and fast flowing, with whole trees floating past. We camped on the riverbank, near the rusting hulk of a bus that had turned over in the water. Charley and Vladimir stayed up late, drinking vodka into the night. Charley had grown very fond of the Russian, calling him his surrogate father, and I woke at four o'clock in the morning to hear them singing drunkenly.

The next morning, Charley looked dreadful. With Nat King Cole singing that we'd find life was still worthwhile if we just smiled from the Warrior's stereo, the rest of us began chipping away at the riverbank, while Charley, now nursing a stinking hangover as well as his injured shoulder, looked on. After a couple of hours' digging, the ramp was ready. The Kamaz inched its way into the water and we jumped on to its back. Trembling in the current, it carried us to the far riverbank, where we climbed over the cab and jumped on to the shore to begin working away at that section of the road. Another hour or so later we'd smoothed the lip of the drop sufficiently to enable the Kamaz to climb up on to dry ground.

'Yeaaaaaahhhhhh!' It was Charley, his arms outstretched, high in the air in defiance of his injured shoulder. 'We've fucking done it!' Tears were rolling down his face. We all threw our arms around each other. The unconquerable had been breached. Three and a half weeks after we'd left Ulaanbaatar we'd crossed Siberia. The last big river on the feared and fabled Road of Bones was behind us.

We unloaded the bikes from the Kamaz. Vladimir gave Charley and me the thumbs up, waved us up the road as if to say be gone with you and turned around to return across the river to pick up the support vehicles. I was changing my oil after getting water in the engine when I heard a car approaching, its horn parping. Kostya and Tanya, our Mongolian fixers, jumped out and came screaming towards us.

'You told us three days!' they shouted as they embraced us.

'We meant three days,' I said.

'But we've been waiting seven days for you to arrive. Seven days in that car.'

We apologised. In the face of Mother Nature, schedules had fallen by the wayside. Handing over little tubs of ready-made noodles, Katya outlined our options. 'We can spend the night here with all the mosquitoes,' she said, 'or up the hill where there is still water and there are fewer mosquitoes.'

'It's up the hill then. Let's go there,' I said. Later on they told us they were surprised to find us on our own, filthy, smelly and covered in oil, with our tools strewn around us by the side of the road, changing the oil on my bike. They'd expected us to have Winnebago trailers and a regiment of assistants, the full Hollywood entourage.

We rode on and then camped on the hill, the support crew and the truck drivers arriving a little later. For Vladimir, the job was done. He cracked open a bottle of vodka and in a very short space of time became very drunk. It was time to celebrate. And my God, he got plastered. I'd not seen anyone that rubbered for a very long time.

Charley broke down in tears again the next morning when he had to say goodbye to Vladimir. After a round of hugs, we rode nearly four hundred miles on dirt tracks to Karamken and camped that night surrounded by mosquitoes that circled us like a halo and got everywhere. In the time it took to boil a pot of water, ten or fifteen mosquitoes would land in it and bob around as if it were a jacuzzi. Every second mouthful of dinner that night had one of the little critters in it.

We woke early the next morning to find hoar frost on our tents and our breath condensing in the cold air. It was mid-summer yet well below freezing. It was 28 June and we were about to ride the last few miles to Magadan, one day ahead of schedule. We ate breakfast quickly, packed up and set off by seven o'clock. On the way, we passed a truck that had crashed into the ditch by the side of the road. We climbed up on to it to take a picture before realising the driver was inside the cab.

'*Harosho*? Okay?' I shouted in at the slumped heap, lying under a blanket with a woolly hat on.

'*Normalya!*' came the reply, with a wave that said get lost.

About five miles from Magadan, I stood up on my pegs, punched the air and screamed my lungs raw. We'd done it! From London right across Europe and Asia to the Pacific. I felt like Valentino Rossi winning a Moto GP. Elated. And then, as we came around a hill, Magadan suddenly revealed itself in the valley below. I stopped my bike at the Mask of Sorrow, a memorial to the victims of Stalin's prison camps, and climbed off. I felt numb. Charley and I walked over to the edge of a ledge that overlooked Magadan and sat down. Resting our chins on the handrail and with our legs dangling over the side, we stared in silence at the city below and the sea beyond. The last time we'd seen open sea, it had been the English Channel and we'd slipped underneath it in a train. Now here was the Pacific ahead of us. In a few days, we would take a flight across that ocean to America and the hardest part of the journey would be behind us. It didn't seem real. The map opened up in front of my eyes and I thought back over the previous eleven weeks. I couldn't believe it. We'd crossed two continents on a motorbike. It was too big to make sense of right then and I thought it probably wouldn't sink in until long after I'd got home to my wife and family.

Charley and I sat there for almost an hour, just letting our memories of the journey wash over us. We'd survived and relished every experience and not fallen out seriously once. Then we got on our bikes for the last time in Asia and rode into Magadan. As we pulled up outside our hotel, I turned to Charley and pointed at the watch on my wrist.

'You know what time it is?' I said.

'What?' Charley answered.

Since 14 April, the day we had left London, we'd had ambitions of setting off early in the morning, riding until mid-afternoon, and then pitching our tents early enough to give us time to look around, do a bit of fishing or go for a walk. In seventy-six days, we'd not managed it once.

'It's three o'clock,' I said. *'Three o'clock.* On the very last day, we left early and we finished at three o'clock. Can you believe it?'

12
Tears in my helmet

ANCHORAGE TO NEW YORK

EWAN: Arriving in Alaska was a complete shock. I'd half expected Anchorage to be a romantic, rustic frontier town, with a row of wooden buildings along one main street and a spit and sawdust port. Instead it was just like any other American city, with shopping malls, big buildings on a grid of streets and traffic lights at every corner. We'd been in untamed lands for such a long time, where people had nothing but were filled with hospitality and warmth, that it felt strange to be back in a place where *everything* was on offer. Having spent two and a half months revelling in the liberation from the most excessive aspects of western consumerism, one of the first things we did on arrival in Anchorage was to succumb immediately to the attractions of an American breakfast. Charley had stuffed French toast and I had Eggs Benedict, with side orders of crispy bacon, lots of orange juice and strong coffee. 'I'm not even hungry,' Charley said, tucking into his breakfast with relish.

It took some time to get used to the land of plenty. After breakfast, I went in search of toiletries. Bumbling through a supermarket, I picked up some toothpaste, a trimmer for my beard and something for my hair. I turned around and there on the shelves were a rifle, a Magnum handgun, ammunition, knives and crossbows. After spending so long in countries where sometimes we were lucky if we came across somewhere to eat in two days, being able to pick up a handgun with your groceries was genuinely disconcerting.

We spent four days recuperating in Anchorage, going on trips to see bears and killer whales in the wild, watching television and really appreciating the big, comfortable beds in the hotels. It was great just to have the opportunity to kick back and let our minds tune out. On one rainy afternoon, while doing my washing in a launderette, I fantasised about the perfect day's recuperation after more than two months on the road. It would be to wake up in my hotel bedroom, watch a couple of episodes of the original *Bewitched* series while eating breakfast in bed. Then straight into Michael Caine in *Blame It on Rio*. Fantastic. Soon as that finished, straight into Dudley Moore in *10* with Bo Derek. Go out for a nice lunch. Come back, get into bed again. A big pot of coffee, big plate of chocolate biscuits and then *The Cruel Sea* with Jack Hawkins and all the boys from the best British classics. Fabulous. Then out for an early dinner, get really full and straight back into bed for Mickey Rourke in *Angel Heart* followed by Nick Cage in *Wild at Heart*. And then to sleep.

But amid all this fantasising I found it difficult to shake off a hankering for being in the middle of nowhere. I missed the Road of Bones. I wanted to be back on those roads, stopping at the end of a day and really being out there, feeling that I was one of only a handful of people on the one dirt track that was going through a land mass that was bigger than the British Isles. I'd never been anywhere else that felt that remote and it had made me feel very comfortable. I yearned for the quiet and the easy camaraderie we had in Siberia, a sense of being able to do exactly what I wanted to do. If I didn't want to stand around and bullshit all day, I didn't have to. But if I did want to bullshit, I could. I'd gone in search of adventure and an alien culture. I'd found both and now I wanted more.

One of the real treats in Alaska was taking our bikes into The Motorcycle Shop in Anchorage for a full service. The shop was run by genuine bikers, lovely guys who sold all different kinds of machines and did a fantastic job with ours. In Anchorage, long-distance bikers were ten a penny; it took a lot to impress them. Every week, they'd see a few bikes arrive in town having finished the Pan-American Highway, a ribbon of more than sixteen thousand miles of continuous road from the tip of South America up to Alaska. We told them we'd come across the water from Siberia.

'We don't see too many who've come from the west,' said the bike shop owner, taking a bit more interest. Then he saw the BMW jacket that Charley had worn from London to Magadan. For seventy-nine days it had been splattered with mud, dust and dirt. It had been washed in streams, showers and hotel baths. When we had started out, it had been bright red with dark and light grey panels. The red had now faded to a pale washed-out orange. The dark grey panels were now light grey. And the previously light grey panels were a sludgy brown – the dirt would no longer wash out.

'Now *that* is impressive,' the bike shop owner said.

On 5 July we set off for New York, riding up towards Fairbanks, where forest fires were encroaching on the city limits and the local population was facing evacuation. On the way, we pulled into a petrol station. Charley and Claudio went inside to get a coffee, while I waited outside. When they didn't appear after a few minutes, I went after them. I found them wandering around inside, staring open-mouthed at the choice of food and drink on sale. For months we'd been used to petrol stations that sold petrol and nothing else. Occasionally we'd be able to buy some water or coffee, but that was the rare exception. This petrol station was nothing special by American standards, but it had row upon row of drinks, snacks and other goodies. For us, it was like being in Aladdin's cave.

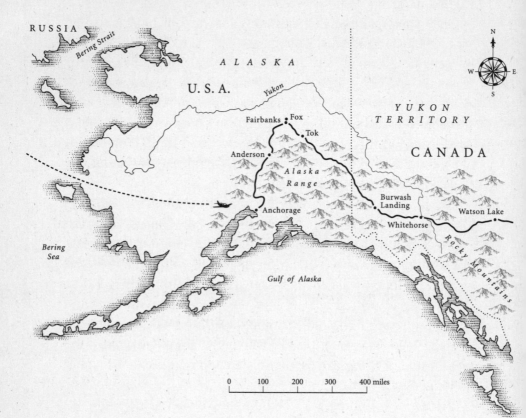

Long before we reached Fairbanks, we could smell the fires in the air. Once we got near, we spoke to some of the firefighters who were slowly bringing more than 1.8 million burning acres under control. There was a huge camp, with tents everywhere and helicopters flying in and out, carrying water to the fires, and it was really exciting to see it.

The next day we entered the Rocky Mountains and spotted a moose casually grazing beside a pond. A little later, I had to disappear into the forest to answer a call of nature. I was in there, doing my business, when I heard Charley and Claudio shouting

'Fucking hell!' I thought nothing of it until I came back out of the woods to see Charley and Claudio looking quite concerned. While I'd been squatting out of sight, a bear had emerged from the forest, very near to where I'd disappeared, and walked right past them.

The roads were wonderful, especially as we'd replaced the knobblies that had carried us across Europe and Asia with soft road tyres. They made the ride much more comfortable and enjoyable on twisty, high-speed roads. After a steady diet of gravel and potholes, it was a revelation to rediscover the pleasures of riding a good bike on good roads. It was also a treat to meet a lot of other bikers who had ridden for long distances. We met a couple in the early stages of a round-the-world trip that was much longer than ours. And we met an old guy called Harold on a 1978 BMW touring bike, who had ridden 875 miles the previous day. By the time he thought about stopping, it was three o'clock in the morning, so he felt he might as well carry on. Harold put us to shame. We'd been moaning after three hundred miles in a day and Harold had done almost three times that distance. The only downside to the excellent roads was the traffic. Compared with Siberia, the roads were teeming with vehicles: hundreds of camper vans, or RVs, and just as many heavy trucks.

And as we rode into more familiar surroundings, the outside world that I'd kept at bay for two and a half months increasingly encroached. For the first time since Slovakia we were easily contactable on the road. Mobile phones worked just about everywhere and consequently the pressures of work started to creep back in. I'd already started reading scripts that had been sent to me when we were in Kazakhstan and Mongolia, but back then I'd found it very difficult to make them mean much to me. There had been a time, when we were riding through the Ukraine and Kazakhstan, when I couldn't even imagine being back at work. Being in my trailer, waiting for the knock on the door and 'Five minutes, Mr McGregor' seemed like another world. Now I was taking calls from directors and agents and the idea of working again had become quite exciting, provided it was something good and interesting. After what we'd seen at the Unicef centres in Kiev, Almaty and particularly in Ulaanbaatar, the world of multi-million-dollar movies still seemed quite bizarre, but I knew then that it would all fall back into place by the time we reached New York. I could feel that, as we approached the end of our journey, the reality of nearly being home would coincide with looking forward to returning to work. I'd cleared my mind and I felt ready to go back to filming.

A week out of Anchorage it became clear to me that the journey would always feel like two separate trips. I wanted to marry up the London to Magadan leg with the Anchorage to New York section to make the journey feel like a single entity, but the two legs were completely different in almost every way. There was no longer any sense of the unknown or of a possibly unachievable target. It was much more manageable, everyone spoke English, the roads were excellent, and, with good motels everywhere, we didn't need to camp.

Charley was also missing the wilderness. 'I just feel a bit down about the fact that we are back in civilisation and staying in motels,' he said. 'I miss the adventure we had in Kazakhstan, Mongolia and Siberia.'

Maybe it was the absence of a challenge that made it feel so different. We'd been told that mountaineers who conquered Everest always warned that the accidents happened on the way down, when the toughest part of the journey was done and they'd dropped their guard. Jamie Lowther-Pinkerton had warned us that America was the most dangerous country on our itinerary, but, provided we didn't make any mistakes, there was no reason to assume we wouldn't arrive in New York bang on time and in good shape.

On 13 July, having stopped at Dawson Creek in British Columbia, we went in search of pizza. We found a restaurant with a bar and I was outside, smoking a cigarette, when a young guy approached me. He was slightly drunk, a little bit camp and his shirt was unbuttoned to his navel.

'Ewan McGregor,' he said.

'Uh, yeah . . . yeah,' I said, slightly taken aback because I'd got used to not being recognised behind my long beard.

He asked what we were doing so I told him about our journey. He talked about the Calgary stampede and all the cow girls there.

'I'm married, you know,' I said.

'Oh yeah, shit, yeah right,' he said, smirking. 'You've been away on a motorbike trip for three and a half months and you're married and you mean to tell me that's stopped you . . .?'

I was really offended. I was all for someone having a friendly chat, but this guy was being rude. We chatted a bit more, but it wasn't the same. He told me he owned a buffalo farm, but frankly I didn't really care much for his company any more. Pissed off, I went back inside the restaurant and sat down to an enormous pizza with Charley.

A little later, the buffalo farmer came up again and started chatting with Charley. They hit it off and I came to realise he was actually a really sweet guy. His name was Jason, he was great company, very genuine and quite a colourful character. If it hadn't been for Charley, I probably wouldn't have spoken to Jason again, but listening to him I realised that in many ways Jason was just like Charley: very gregarious with a take-me-as-I-am attitude that could be a bit disarming at first.

The next morning, we rode over to Jason's farm. It was a beautiful huge ranch, with great big red barns. He had reared three buffalo from calves, bottle-feeding them because their mothers had died. These buffalo were now mature, but they had become pets. I'd never been up close to one, but he let us sit on one called Lucy, who took quite a shine to Claudio, nudging him in the groin as he tried to film us riding on her back.

Having arranged to meet Jason a few days later in Calgary, we headed off south again. We were averaging three hundred miles a day and the accumulated exhaustion of fourteen weeks in the saddle was starting to take its toll. Several times each day I would find myself falling asleep at the handlebars, unable to keep my eyes open on the bike. My eyes would go out of focus and my eyelids would drop. The only remedy was to stop and lie down on the side of the road for a few minutes. Napping for just a quarter of an hour would give me enough energy for the next hour or two. I was dying to get to New York to see my wife. More than anything I just wanted to put my arms round her, but I was also desperate for a rest.

Two days later, we were approaching Calgary. It was early afternoon and we had a good lunch in our bellies, Charley was riding at the front with Claudio and I was at the back. We'd stopped wearing protective clothing. It was too hot. Wearing jeans, T-shirts and leather or canvas jackets, we were riding up towards the brow of a hill when the traffic ahead of us slowed suddenly. Charley put his hazard lights on. Riding at about 60mph, I reached forward to put my hazard lights on too. There was a screech of tyres and then the bike went completely out of control. It happened so fast, I don't know which came first. Charley said afterwards that he saw it all in his wing mirrors.

'Out of nowhere, a red car just whammed into the back of you,' he said afterwards. 'Your front wheel went straight up in the air, almost vertical, then slammed down on the road. You were all over the place, your handlebars weaving from right to left to right to left. Somehow, you managed to stay on and come to a stop.'

All I could remember was a bang, suddenly being out of control, seeing a big grass ditch about 6 feet deep to my left and thinking I was going to topple into it.

I'm not going on the grass, I'm not going on the grass, I repeated to myself and managed to pull the bike round. The next thing I noticed was that my bike was still running after being smashed in the tail end, that I was still on it and that it was riding straight and true.

I pulled off to the side of the highway, put my bike on its side stand and got off unharmed, unscathed. I didn't even have a stiff neck. Nothing. Fuck, this bike is amazing, I thought. I've just been hit from behind and I managed to ride in a straight line. It could have been very nasty, but I came away without a scratch.

'I was hit!' I said to Charley as I walked past him towards the car that had tail-ended me.

'I know,' he said.

A kid, about seventeen years old, dressed in big baggy pants with a chain wallet, got out of a red Honda Civic. The poor kid was in a bit of a state and his car was wrecked. The bonnet was crumpled. The front grill and the mudguard were lying on the ground.

I wasn't angry, but I felt as if I should be. 'What were you doing with your eyes?' I asked.

'I didn't see you, man,' he replied.

Charley was furious. 'What the fuck are you doing?' he screamed at the kid. 'You almost killed my friend!'

Charley looked ready to beat up the kid, but I really didn't care too much that he had hit me. I was just pleased to be alive.

'It's fine. It was just an accident and accidents happen,' I said. 'Are you all right?'

'Yeah, yeah. I'm all right, man,' he said.

Then he turned around. 'Oh, my fucking car's fucked, man. My fucking car's fucking fucked.' All I could think was that I was lucky to be alive and he was worrying about his car!

Meanwhile, I was as high as a kite. The adrenalin was pumping and I felt elated. We looked at the back of my bike. My pannier boxes had crumpled and the pannier frame was broken in two places. Protruding about 4 inches behind the back tyre, the panniers had saved my life, absorbing the impact that otherwise would've been straight on to my back wheel. There was no question that I would have hit the deck and slipped under the car if he had hit my rear wheel. It would have stopped it dead and I would have been run over, probably crushed under the bike beneath the car. In all likelihood, it would have killed me. We'd come through some of the most difficult road conditions in the world and our first accident was someone tail-ending me on a Canadian highway . . .

I felt so sorry for the wee guy. When the police turned up, he didn't even know which document was his insurance policy. Nevertheless, it was difficult to understand how he hadn't managed to see me. I was on a huge BMW right in the middle of the highway. We looked at the skid marks. The marks began where he had started to brake. Then there was a skid mark from my back tyre where he hit me. And then there was another skid mark where my front wheel hit the ground and twisted from side to side. The Honda's skid marks went on for about 30 yards after he hit me, so I would most probably have gone underneath the car if I hadn't stayed up. When the police asked him, the wee hip hopper tried to make out I'd been changing lanes, but soon abandoned the pretence when I showed the policeman the skid marks and made it clear that we'd both been travelling in a straight line.

I got back on my bike and rode off. Charley was behind me and I felt a real bond with him there. I could feel him looking out for me. He knew that after an accident I'd be a bit shaky for a wee while and he was watching over me. As we approached Calgary the adrenalin wore off and depression set in. Thoughts raced through my mind of what might've been, how it would have impacted on my family and what a silly waste of everything that would've been. We got to the hotel and I had a bath. As I lay in the tub, I felt my spirits rise again. It was as if I'd been given a second chance. I felt extraordinarily alive. I felt great.

We went out for dinner that night. Arriving at the restaurant, I felt on top of the world, really buzzing, chatting away to the waitress. It was so unlike me, but I was still as high as a kite. We had a fantastic steak dinner, everything sparkled and everybody was great company. Charley got a bit drunk and started making speeches about how much he loved everybody at the table. He went on at length about how much Claudio meant to him and how we couldn't have done the trip without him. I could see the red wine in his eyes and, of course, when someone mentioned it the next day, he tried to brush it off.

'Yeah, it was nothing,' he said with a grin. 'I was just a bit pissed.' Then he looked a bit more serious than usual. 'No, actually I meant every word of it.'

CHARLEY: Ewan phoned the guy who had hit him the next day and checked he was okay. In the meantime, we got his bike and panniers repaired at the biggest bike shop any of us had ever seen. They did a fabulous job. By the time they'd repaired the panniers, they were in better shape than they'd been when we'd set out three months earlier. By chance, there was a stunt rider at the garage. He did some stunts for us outside, a couple of tyre burns, some stand-up wheelies, sitting on the tank wheelies and some stoppies. It was the beginning of the season and he was a bit rusty and the stretch of road was a bit short, but he was still fantastic. Afterwards, we jumped on our bikes and somebody shouted: 'Go on then, do a wheelie.' With most of the bike shop employees watching, I was very nervous, but I still popped a beauty, a nice long wheelie along the road.

That evening, we met Jason, the buffalo farmer from Dawson Creek, in a bar and had a few drinks. 'It's the best fun you'll have with your boots on,' he said as we headed off to the stampede, where I promptly lost Ewan and had to borrow money from Jason all evening. My wallet had been stolen a week earlier, when we had stopped off for a dip in some natural hot springs. Other than some little changing rooms and some decking, it was just hot water coming out of the ground. I stupidly left my wallet in the pocket of my jeans, which I'd hung up on a peg. When we got back from the spring, it was gone. I'd just put $500 and about €400 in it that I had previously been carrying in my pannier. I also lost all my credit cards. Claudio had had a bag stolen in Russia, but Ewan and I had travelled all the way through some of the poorest countries in Europe and Asia without having anything stolen. It was my fault for not taking more care and putting my wallet in one of the lockers, but I'd lowered my guard once we'd arrived in North

America, thinking that I was less likely to have something stolen. Strangely, the gypsy in Prague had said that I would lose some money before the end of the trip, but, then again, it was a fair guess that, out of a group of six men travelling around the world for three and a half months, one of us was likely to lose some cash.

We rode on to the American frontier, our last border crossing. Having crossed frontiers into France, Belgium, Germany, the Czech Republic, Slovakia, the Ukraine, Russia several times, Kazakhstan, Mongolia and Canada, we thought we had borders sussed. We passed through the Canadian section without a hitch and carried on to the American boundary. About 20 yards short of the huts, Ewan and I stopped to take off our helmets while we waited for David and Jimmy in the support vehicle. Immediately, a female American border guard came running out and screamed at us.

'You cannot stop there!' she shouted. 'You *cannot* stop there! Proceed through the checks! You cannot stop *there*!'

'Uh, we're just waiting for our . . . we're just waiting for our friends,' I said.

'You have to go back. You have to wait back there. You cannot stop,' she said. She was ridiculously aggressive. The idea that two guys on motorbikes were a major security threat was daft, but, more than anything, we were embarrassed for her. She was making such an arse of herself, screaming and shouting. It freaked me out, so I jumped back on my bike, turned round and rode back as she had told us.

'That's a one-way road!' she shouted. 'You cannot go back there!'

Behind me, Ewan was facing her down. 'Calm down,' he said. 'He's going back because you just said we had to go back.'

'No, you have to clear the American border and then if you want to go back . . .'

'Listen, he's going back because you just told us to go back.'

'I did not tell you!'

Claudio and Ewan gave up. They rode up to the checkpoint, where the border guard treated them like dirt until she asked why they had a carnet. As soon as they explained that they had filming equipment in the support car, her behaviour changed. She became a little kitten, putty in our hands. It was equally embarrassing to see her behave in such an obsequious manner. We got through the checks, hugged each other because it was our last border crossing, and set off into Montana.

As we rode into America, I realised I was fulfilling a dream I'd had since I was a teenager: to ride across America on a motorbike. I'd been so focused on our final target of New York, that it had taken two weeks on the smooth roads of North America before it dawned on me that one of my longest-held dreams was coming true.

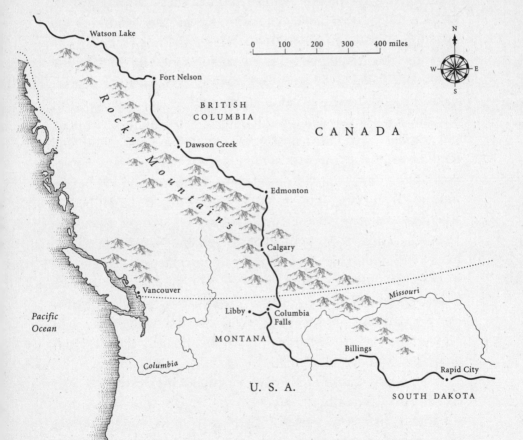

But mixed with my joy was disappointment that the journey was approaching its end. We were now in the last country on our itinerary and much as I couldn't wait to see Olly, Doone and Kinvara in New York, I also knew I would desperately miss this journey that had changed my life. We'd had difficult times, but we'd come through them stronger than before. My biggest worry had been that the stresses of the journey would drive Ewan and me apart. In many ways we were chalk and cheese, but we'd come to respect the differences and love what we had in common. I felt very lucky to have emerged from the trip having gained so much.

Montana was fabulous, with beautiful scenery. We stopped off for one day at the ranch belonging to the guy who was the inspiration for the film *The Horse Whisperer*. His ranch was an extremely luxurious place, with fantastic food and an amazing attention to detail in the pretty log cabins that Ewan and I slept in. After a big supper, we had a great night's sleep and the next morning we were invited to see the horse whisperer train a horse. It was great to see this man at work. He was so light and in tune with the animals. Afterwards, we helped round up some horses and lasso a cow, then we sat down to a delicious lunch before setting off for the long ride west. Passing through Native American country, it was difficult not to draw comparisons with Mongolia. Like the Mongolian herdsmen, the Native Americans of the Great Plains had been nomadic, living in tepees and moving on to follow the buffalo herds and find their animals fresh pasture to graze. The difference was that the nomadic lifestyle was still fully operational in Mongolia, whereas the white man had stopped the Native Americans from living the way that they and thousands of other people had lived for a very long time.

'Why was it possible in Mongolia, but not in America?' Ewan asked. He was really angered by the unjust way the Native Americans had been treated. 'There are Native Americans all around us, but they're driving pick-up trucks and working in petrol stations instead of living the way they want on what has always been their land. It's a wide open country and it's just not right.'

We rode on via Rapid City, a charming place like a town from a Frank Capra movie, to Waseca in Minnesota. It was a long ride under the big skies of South Dakota, interrupted only by stop-offs at Mount Rushmore and the Little Big Horn, the scene of Custer's last stand. By the time we reached Waseca we had ridden 542 miles. Fuelled by Mountain Dew Amp, a high-energy drink, it set the one-day record for the trip. In Waseca, we stayed with Chantelle, the sister of Kyle, the American embassy employee we'd met while he was surveying military radio installations in Mongolia. Kyle had given me a little medallion for his sister. Having carried it halfway around the world from Mongolia, I was determined to get it to her. Chantelle and her husband were lovely. They put us up, gave us breakfast, the first home-cooked meal we'd had since we had been in a ger in Mongolia, and the next day showed us around their large arable farm, letting us climb over their massive John Deere tractors like little boys.

From Waseca, we rode via Madison to Chicago, stopping off at the Harley-Davidson factory along the way. Arriving at the factory on three dusty, slightly damaged BMWs that had been around the world was great. We lined up beside the rows of gleaming Harleys, mostly belonging to employees, and felt very proud. They showed us around the plant, where we watched an engine being built, travelling along the factory production line, being customised to the purchaser's requirement. There were engine blocks and boxes of pistons and cylinders everywhere. For Ewan and me it was like letting children loose in a sweetshop. At the end of the line, a lovely lady plugged in the engine and fired it up. Bam! It started up straightaway and we'd just witnessed the woman giving birth to the engine. It made us feel like getting out the cigars and celebrating.

Afterwards, they let us ride a couple of Harleys. I'd never been a great fan, thinking Harleys weren't really suited to the British climate, but I could absolutely see the point of them in the States, where they were ideal for cruising in a long, straight line in T-shirt and shades.

EWAN: The next day we followed Jimmy's dad on his Kawasaki cruiser from our hotel in Chicago back to his house in the suburbs of the city for lunch with Jimmy's family. Living in a comfortable all-American neighbourhood, where most of the houses had a veranda and an American flag flying outside, they'd laid on a fantastic spread, which we ate out on the balcony while Claudio played ragtime on the piano. That evening, David and I went to see *Frankie and Johnny in the Clair de Lune* at the Steppenwolf Theatre Company, where John Malkovich had started out. I'd been gagging to see some theatre and it was just gorgeous, a great production. I was so excited to be sitting back in a theatre. When the lights went down, I knew it was time to get back to work. The ride across America had become a decompression chamber from the isolation of Mongolia and Siberia and I felt as if I was at last ready to come up for air. It was really good for me to go and see a great play, particularly as it was completely by chance. All I'd known was that I wanted to see a Steppenwolf production. We went along, picked up the tickets and it just happened to be a phenomenal play with a great cast. We had dinner afterwards and then went to two busy bars where some great blues was being played. I went to bed very satisfied with my evening and hungry to get back to work, my creative energies recharged by seeing the world and immersing myself in the cultures of different people.

The next day, my wife and Charley's family arrived in New York. Eve was now only seven hundred miles and one time zone away, the closest we'd been for three months. The only time I'd seen her was on a video that I'd watched in Anchorage and at the time I couldn't get my head around seeing her on the screen, moving and talking and breathing. I was very excited about finishing the journey and seeing her again, but also strangely nervous. Although we'd spoken almost daily, we'd lived separate lives for a quarter of a year and we'd got used to existing day to day on our own. I'd become acclimatised to moving on every day, always being on the road and sleeping in a different bed each night. Every day, as I rode my beautiful bike further east, I'd have little flashes of the people we'd met and the places we'd seen along the way. And those flashes would be intercut with fantasies about being at home, taking the children to school, or the park, or just eating a meal all together.

Before we were reunited with our families in New York, we each had one last treat planned. Charley wanted to visit an amusement park that was home to some of the world's highest and longest rollercoasters – not my idea of fun – and I wanted to visit Orange County Choppers.

Just before we left Chicago, Charley got a note from David. 'I know the time in New York might fly by without a chance to say that this has been a thing of incredible beauty to me on every level,' it said. 'Thank you for letting me be a part of it, I'm crying and I don't know why and I don't want to stop. Dave.'

One of the reasons it would be so difficult to end the trip in a few days' time in New York was that it would mean we'd all go our separate ways. Without David and Russ's complete devotion, the trip wouldn't have turned out such a great success. Every day, they'd faced some kind of difficulty or challenge, and with the help of Jimmy, Claudio and all the office staff in Shepherd's Bush, they'd conquered them all. Charley and I were both really touched by what David, an honest, hard-working, loving person, and Russ had done for us. Starting out just as business associates, we'd come to respect each other and in the course of the journey we'd become the closest of friends, forming a relationship we'd treasure and cherish for the rest of our lives. We'd started out as colleagues and ended up a band of brothers.

But it wasn't just David, Russ, Jimmy, Claudio and Charley who felt special to me. I had also fallen in love with my bike. The next day I was standing outside a motel, smoking a cigarette, and I looked at my BMW. I felt really sad. It looked so fantastic and yet I'd soon have to say goodbye to it. I couldn't get over its beauty. I stood beside it for ages, smoking one cigarette after another, just staring at it like some infatuated lover. I was so proud of it. It looked awesome and it looked like it had gone round the world for the simple reason that it really had.

For the next couple of days just about everything we did – the last full tank of petrol, the last night Charley, Claudio and I spent on our own, the last long day's ride – was tinged with a mixture of sadness and excitement. On the evening of 27 July, we passed a signpost that read 'New York 166 Miles'. We tapped 'hotel' into the GPS and were led to The Chestnut Inn on Oquaga Lake in upper New York State. It was a beautiful place, just the right setting for Charley, Claudio and I to have our last meal together. The next evening we were scheduled to meet up with David and Jimmy, and the night after that we'd be with our families in New York. As we sat down for dinner, I realised I had no regrets over the trip. Sure, there'd been hard times, but they had always led to good times. And the hard times were the ones that I was likely to remember most fondly.

The next day, we rode about eighty miles to Orange County Choppers in Montgomery. Eighteen months earlier, when I'd been busy with work, I'd whiled away the downtime in my trailer, waiting to get on to a film set, by watching the first series of Orange County Choppers on DVD. It became an obsession and after a while I'd be itching to finish a take so that I could get back to my trailer and watch some more of the show. 'Okay, are we done?' I'd say. 'Right, can I . . .?' and I'd horse back to the trailer. And by all accounts, I was not the only person hooked on the show about a father–son team – Paul Teutul Senior and Paul Junior – building custom bikes with a third guy, Vinnie, in their workshop and arguing like hell. The show had three million viewers in the States and fifty thousand people turned up to see the Teutuls when they appeared at a bike show. The two Pauls were incredibly friendly and showed us around the workshop. I got our world map out and showed them where we'd been. They were very interested and then they said what I'd been really hoping for: 'Let's go for a ride.'

They gave me a chopper about 12 feet long and on which my backside was lower than the top of the rear wheel. It was ridiculous, but it felt so good. I wheeled it back – you needed to pick your spot if you wanted to do a U-turn – and, not realising it had a big mudguard at the back, I dinged it into the wall. Paul Junior was standing next to me. 'Woah, woah, woah!' he said.

I was mortified. Fortunately, I'd not chipped the beautiful paint job. Charley was such a sports bike rider that I hadn't expected him to be particularly excited by the experience, but when I looked over at him on another chopper I could see he was absolutely thrilled. Sitting on two enormously long bikes, we fired them up and were blown away by the roar of the engines. Their primary belt drives were winging around on the left of the bike, terrifying us with the thought we'd get our trouser legs caught in the 3-inch-wide rubber belt. The exhaust pipes on Charley's chopper swept along the side of the bike and then tilted upwards. Whenever he blasted the throttle, my hair would be blown back by the exhaust from his pipes. Paul Senior was riding a Santa Claus bike with Christmas lights and reindeer antlers and his son was on a prisoner-of-war bike, a huge big thing.

We knocked the choppers into first and pulled up a hill that led on to the road. The two Pauls led the way and stopped at the top. Oh, for fuck's sake, don't stop there, I thought. The bikes were worth around $70,000 and I was terrified I was going to drop mine. Charley was in front of me. I was playing with my handlebars a bit and I saw Charley looking down. I was tapping his leg with my front wheel; I hadn't realised it was so far ahead of me.

And then we got out on the road. My chopper felt just fantastic. With 103-cubic-inch V-twin engines, they were much more industrial than our BMWs or a sports bike, and we really had to thwack through the gears, but they just had so much grunty torque. In a straight line, they rode like a dream. You could hear the electric guitars twanging. I looked over at Charley. We didn't have helmets on and Charley was in his T-shirt and jeans. His long hair was blowing in the wind and he had a smile on his face as big as the Cheshire Cat's, and he suited it. Charley really did. I imagined us by the ocean, cruising through California on those choppers, and I thought that if I ever ended up living in Los Angeles I would definitely get a couple just so that when Charley visited we could go riding along the coastal highway. It looked perfect.

After visiting Orange County Choppers, we rode for about an hour to a beautiful hotel. David had said he wanted us to spend the last night in a special place. We were sitting in a little pagoda, having a drink and chatting about the trip, waiting for our rooms to be ready. Charley had already wondered if Eve, Olly, Doone and Kinvara were already at the hotel, and I suddenly had the strangest feeling that he might be right.

'They're not here, are they, David?' I said. My heart was racing, I had butterflies in my stomach and, all of a sudden, I felt really anxious about seeing Eve again.

David looked really surprised. 'What?' he said.

'The girls; they're not here, are they?' I said.

'No, they're in Manhattan,' David said. 'Why, did you think they might be?'

'No, no . . . I didn't . . . it's just . . . Charley and I . . . it's just I wanted to know if they're here so I can stop my heart beating like this,' I said.

'No.'

'They're in New York,' I said. 'Aren't they. We'll see them tomorrow.'

'That's what you said you wanted.'

'No, that's right . . .'

'You spoke to them in New York, remember?'

'Yeah, yeah. It's just . . . That's good.'

'What do you think it's going to be like when you see your wife for the first time?' David asked.

'Insane. No, it won't be insane. It'll be . . .,' I said, trying to find the right words, but I was interrupted by a scream.

'Daddy! Daddy! Daddy!' Doone was running across the grass towards us. Kinvara was frozen to the spot, so excited she was unable to move.

'Oh my God,' Charley said.

'Oh my God,' I said.

They were there. I jumped over the railing of the little pagoda thing, ran up to Eve and took her in my arms. It was just the most incredible feeling. A weird, heady, out-of-body feeling of actually seeing Eve in the flesh. I tried to kiss her, but I hadn't trimmed my moustache and beard, so every time I tried to make contact with her lips, I was kissing my own facial hair. It was getting irritating, so I lifted it up to give her a proper kiss. I'd missed it so much.

'I knew you were here,' I said.

'Why?' Eve said, her voice trembling.

'I could just feel your presence. I knew it.'

Eve was obsessed with my beard. She didn't like me with it. 'I want to see it off you!' she said. 'Oh God, it's so bizarre.' I hadn't realised until that moment quite how long and bushy my beard had become. 'It's not really you because you've got this *thing*. I know it's you, but it doesn't quite feel like you.'

Charley was hugging and kissing his wife and daughters, going through much the same experience as me, only without the beard in the way. He had a little goatee, but his wife said she quite liked it.

'Oh, I've dreamt about this for so long,' I heard Charley say.

David was watching us all, the look on his face a mixture of sheer joy and slight embarrassment that by now he ought to be somewhere else. 'Ten fingers, ten toes, a little more hair, but otherwise just the same. Now it's over to you, ma'am,' he said to Eve. 'He's back to you and I'm outta here.'

My daughters were with their grandparents in France, so Eve and I walked alone into the hotel. I couldn't take my eyes off her. I couldn't stop staring at her and touching her. But by the time we got into the elevator to go up to the room, it felt completely natural to be with Eve, because we do belong together. All the apprehension and anxiety had disappeared. The moment we saw each other again, it just felt right.

That night we all had dinner together and told our families about our adventures. Then we went upstairs. Olly had a terrible headache, so Eve and I went downstairs to a gift shop to get her some aspirin. As we were walking back to the lifts we passed a big ballroom where there was some line dancing going on. I looked in the door. There, in the middle of the dance floor was Olly with Charley, Doone and Kinvara dancing in a big ring, holding hands. I watched them for a wee while. It looked fantastic. Charley was completely at home again with his family and I could see the excitement on his daughters' faces.

The hotel was a big old building. It reminded me of the Crieff Hydro, a hotel near where I'd grown up, which was full of creaky floorboards and a lot of elderly guests. It had the air of a place to which families went for their summer holiday year after year. But as Eve and I returned to our room, none of it meant anything to me. As far as I was concerned, there were only two guests in the hotel: Eve and me. I climbed into bed with my wife again. It felt so right.

By the next morning, however, I was focused again on the journey. Eating breakfast with Eve, I felt my bike beckoning. I was terribly anxious to go and get it sorted for the very last time. It felt like Christmas Day or some other big event. From the moment I'd woken up, there had been a sense of something quite special about the day. As we sat eating breakfast, I turned to Eve. 'Look,' I said. 'I'm just going to have to go and pack my bike.'

'All right, go and be with your bike instead of me,' Eve joked. And having not seen my wife for nearly four months, I left her sitting at the breakfast table on her own, so that I could head upstairs and sort my bags out. My bike had temporarily become a third party in my marriage and I needed to honour an appointment with her.

A short while later I was sitting in the sun in front of the hotel, my bike packed beside me, thinking back over the trip. Mongolia had been the undisputed highlight. It had been so hard and so good and so amazing and magical. All sorts of things popped into my mind, some of them significant, some of them trivial, like a restaurant in which we ate lunch or somewhere we had to stop for a pee at the side of the road. And the randomness was what was nice about it, I thought, hoping that for the rest of my life the memories would just keep coming back.

What I'd miss most of all was the sense of having a lot of time on our hands. Even on days when we put four or five hundred miles under our wheels, once we'd stopped, parked up and pitched our tents, the rest of the day was ours. And I'd also come to enjoy all the hold-ups and stops, whether it was a rest stop for something to drink or an enforced stop because the Red Devil had broken down. Most times, we'd have a laugh and kick around. It was like kicking stones around in the streets when I was a child, something I'd not had time to do for years. Charley and I had already joked about how we would get home and the first weekend one of us would phone the other to arrange a meet at the petrol station on the King's Road, where we'd stand for half an hour kicking stones around. I knew I'd also miss the time for reflection I'd had on the bike. That time when we were chasing the daily mileages had been really special and important, an incredibly enriching opportunity to let things go through my mind.

David and Jimmy turned up a short while later. Pretending to be upset because I'd left her at the breakfast table alone, Eve got into a car with Olly, Doone and Kinvara. Charley and I got on the bikes for the last time and immediately became like kids showing off to the girls we fancied at school. We pulled wheelies and other stunts to impress our wives, dying for them to tell us to stop in case we hurt ourselves. David pulled us aside and told us we had to do an interview with someone from BMW on the way to Orange County Choppers, where we were going to meet up with Paul Senior and Paul Junior. An interview was the last thing

Charley or I wanted to do, mainly because we were dying to get back to the choppers, which I wanted to show Eve. David said we couldn't get out of it and that he had arranged for us to meet the BMW executive at a coffee shop about ten minutes away. We pulled up as arranged outside the coffee shop in the little town and waited for him. A short while later, we spotted Russ and the executive approaching, both riding BMW bikes. Having not seen Russ for a while, I was really pleased to see him and went up to him as he took his helmet off.

'Great to see you,' I said. 'We really missed you on the last leg.'

'Yeah, me too,' Russ said. 'Let me just introduce Laurence from BMW.'

I turned around. Laurence had his back to me and was taking his helmet off. As he removed it, I suddenly thought, hey, it's Ted Simon, simply because it felt a bit odd to be introduced to someone who had their back to me. The mystery man turned around and for a split second I was speechless, then it just burst out of me: 'Daaaaaaaaaddd!'

I hadn't had the slightest idea my father was going to be there. No inkling at all. It was a brilliant surprise and I was so proud that my dad could join us for the final push. We hugged and kissed, each of us as excited as the other, then set off for Orange County Choppers, where we picked up a few more riders, including Paul Senior, Paul Junior, Vinnie, and some of the mechanics and bike builders, most of them on Harleys rather than their very precious choppers.

With a mixture of heavy hearts and extreme excitement, we moved off for the very last time. Destination: Manhattan. As we rode towards New York beneath a clear blue sky, the emotions of finishing started to snowball in my mind. For a few moments I thought it was all wrong, that it should be just Charley, Claudio and me. I thought that maybe we'd made a mistake riding with about forty other bikers who hadn't seen what we'd seen or done what we'd done, but when I turned around and saw a phalanx of bikes stretching back along the road as far as the eye could see,

I realised it was exactly the right thing to be doing. All I really wanted was Charley up next to me, so that the two of us could be side by side, and by the time we got to the George Washington Bridge, Charley had caught up, I had my dad in my rear-view mirror and I was overjoyed that we were surrounded by bikes. Waiting for everyone to pay their toll, I was shaking my head. I couldn't make sense of it all. I wanted to gather my thoughts, but they just wouldn't come. It was awesome having all the bikes around us. It added to the sense of achievement, which I really felt warranted a procession of noise into the city.

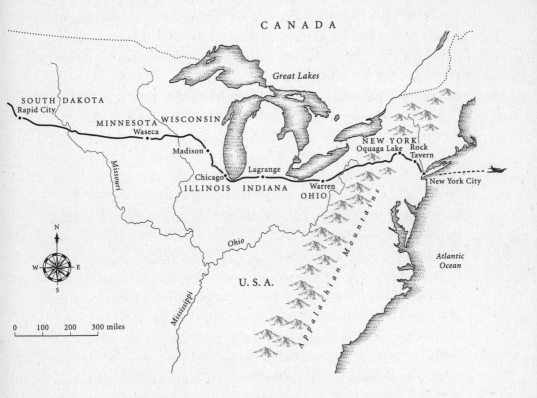

And then we set off. Riding down the ramp on to the bridge, Charley and I stood up on our pegs and the glorious Manhattan skyline suddenly appeared on our right, stretching down the Hudson River. A helicopter was flying level with us over the water, a cameraman hanging out of its door, and I was gone. I burst into tears, crying like a baby, the tears rolling down my face as I blubbed into my helmet and pulled a V for victory sign to the helicopter swooping nearby. All the way across the bridge and halfway down the West Side Highway, the tears kept flowing. I was overwhelmed, looking at the buildings through my tears and thinking we've done it, we've done it, we've done it. I'd been excited about finishing and I was looking forward to the adulation, to people saying 'Well done, you're the business', but I really hadn't expected to feel this way. The noise of all the bikes was deafening. Some of the Orange County bikers were doing burn-outs, great clouds of blue tyre smoke rising into the warm air. At traffic lights, all forty of us would rev our engines to the red line and beep our horns, then race away from the lights when they turned green.

'We did it,' I shouted across to Charley. 'We fucking did it. We wanted to do it. We said we'd do it. We fucking did it.'

At the next traffic lights, Charley leaned over to me. 'I can't really take all this in,' he shouted over the deafening din of the bikes. 'It hasn't really hit me yet that it's nearly all over, but I just want to say it's the best fucking thing I've ever done and I want to thank you for that.'

As we rode away from the lights, I was still in bits and I could feel Charley's love supporting me as we rode through the concrete canyons of New York. Two blocks away from our finishing line at Battery Park, I suddenly thought, shit, I'm going to burn my clutch out a block away from the finish, but I made it into the park. There, standing in front of me, were loads of friends. I saw Ciara, my publicist, and hugged Lindy, my agent. But more than anything I wanted Eve. I needed to see my wife, but I couldn't find her. I scanned the crowds and then I spotted her on the other side of the fence. I ran over and grabbed her. Again I was gone, weeping into Eve's hair and neck. I was just completely blown away by it. We'd done it, we were there.

Then I had to find Charley. Again I scanned the crowd. There he was. I ran over, threw my arms around him, hugged him tight and buried my head in his shoulder.

'We've done it,' I sobbed into his shoulder. 'We've done it and I love you.' I couldn't get much else out between the sobs.

'Thanks, mate,' Charley said. 'It's been great.' We'd spent fourteen weeks in each other's company and not really fallen out once. 'It could have gone either way,' Charley said. 'We could have ended the journey never wanting to see each other again. But it didn't happen that way. You've become the brother I never had.'

Pulling the corks on two magnums of champagne, we sprayed them all over each other and the onlookers; we were hot and sweaty, our hair was matted and my beard was all over the place. Charley just looked like he'd crawled out of the river.

'You'll never look better in your life,' Ciara shouted over at us, 'because you look exactly like you've done what you've just done.'

We gave a series of interviews and posed for photographs, feeling on top of the world and loving every minute of it. Then Charley, Claudio, my father, Russ and I got back on our bikes and rode up through the streets of Manhattan. It was baking hot and I looked over at my dad. 'Never in my wildest dreams did I think I'd be riding on a motorcycle around Manhattan with you,' I shouted to him. It couldn't have been better.

My father was usually the most law-abiding of bikers, never breaking the speed limit, but he was following us over pavements and cutting across the corners of sidewalks to get round traffic lights. He was really enjoying it, keeping up with everybody. We returned the bikes my father and Russ had been riding to BMW, and then Charley and I took our two beloved bikes around to the Maritime Hotel where the Black Rebel Motorcycle Club were going to play at our homecoming party that evening.

There was a lot still to come. That night we'd go to the party, where I'd have a very strange reaction to seeing our riding suits, helmets and boots displayed in Perspex cabinets as if they were museum pieces – I'd just want to put them back on, get on my bike and head off west to do the whole journey in reverse – and where I'd be blown away by the huge enlarged photographs taken on the trip. It was strange to see the wee faces of the guys at a petrol station in Mongolia and to think that we had been there not very long ago. A few days later, Charley and I would watch our two BMWs being loaded on to a flight from JFK to London. After that, we'd pick them up from Heathrow and ride them the twelve miles from the airport back to Bulwer Street, where we'd finally cross the line we hadn't seen since that warm April morning we'd ridden away from our families and friends. It was important for Charley and me to return to the point at which we'd started, but, that formality aside, the journey was over. We'd made it from London to New York, 18,478 miles according to my odometer, plus several hundred miles by train and a few thousand miles by air.

Outside the Maritime Hotel I unstrapped my luggage and unloaded the panniers from my motorbike, threw them in the back of a yellow New York taxi and stepped inside. It was strangely mundane to be sitting in a taxi on my own after nearly four months with Charley always at my side, but as the taxi bumped along the avenues of New York, somehow it just felt right. Five minutes later, the taxi was standing outside the hotel where I was staying with my wife. I gave the driver a good tip, walked in, took the lift up to our room, ran a bath and lay back in the suds with a contented sigh. At long last, it was done.

Appendix A

ROUTE

	Destination	Country	Mileage between destinations	Cumulative mileage
WEEK 1				
April 14	Brussels	Belgium	244	244
April 15	Nürburg	Germany	170	414
April 16	Prague	Czech Rep.	428	842
April 17	Prague			842
April 18	Jedovnice		145	987
April 19	Bojnice	Slovakia	128	1115
April 20	Turna Nad Bodvou		146	1261
WEEK 2				
April 21	Uzhhorod	Ukraine	80	1341
April 22	Lviv		153	1494
April 23	Kiev		329	1823
April 24	Kiev			1823
April 25	Kharkiv		295	2118
April 26	Krasnyy Luch		188	2306
April 27	Belaya Kalitva	Russia	125	2431
WEEK 3				
April 28	Volgograd		208	2639
April 29	Volgograd			2639
April 30	Astrakhan		249	2888
May 1	Atyrau	Kazakhstan	223	3111
May 2	Atyrau			3111
May 3	20 miles south of Qandyaghash		305	3416
May 4	50 miles south of Qarabutaq		268	3684
WEEK 4				
May 5	Aral Sea		160	3844
May 6	Qyzylorda		298	4142
May 7	Shymkent (Cimkent)		271	4413
May 8	Almaty		419	4832
May 9	Almaty			4832
May 10	Almaty			4832
May 11	Almaty			4832
WEEK 5				
May 12	Charyn Canyon		113	4945

	Destination	Country	Mileage between destinations	Cumulative mileage
May 13	15 miles west of Kalinino		158	5103
May 14	Ayaköz		379	5482
May 15	Semey (Semipalatinsk)		221	5703
May 16	Bamaul	Russia	274	5977
May 17	Gorno-Altaysk		159	6136
May 18	Tashanta		314	6450
WEEK 6				
May 19	Tsagannuur	Mongolia	33	6483
May 20	5 miles south of Hotgor		110	6593
May 21	Ulaangom		64	6657
May 22	Uvs Lake		36	6693
May 23	Baruunturuun		67	6760
May 24	Ondorhangay		39	6799
May 25	Lake Telmen		94	6893
May 26	White Lake		169	7062
WEEK 7				
May 27	White Lake			7062
May 28	Kharkhorin (Kharakorum)		168	7230
May 29	Ulaanbaatar		240	7470
May 30	Ulaanbaatar			7470
May 31	Ulaanbaatar			7470
June 1	Ulaanbaatar			7470
WEEK 8				
June 2	Ulan Ude	Russia	340	7810
June 3	Ulan Ude			7810
June 4	Ulan Ude			7810
June 5	Ulan Ude			7810
June 6	Khilok		210	8020
June 7	Chita		203	8223
June 8	on train (from Chita via Skovorodino)		580	8803
WEEK 9				
June 9	15 miles north of Tynda		132	8935
June 10	Tynda		15	8950
June 11	Tynda			8950
June 12	Nagornyy		60	9010
June 13	10 miles north of Tommot		286	9296
June 14	Yakutsk		270	9566
June 15	Yakutsk			9566
WEEK 10				
June 16	Yakutsk			9566
June 17	Matta		48	9614
June 18	Chamnayy		151	9765
June 19	on ferry heading for Khandyga		56	9821
June 20	20 miles east of Khandyga		36	9857
June 21	30 miles west of Tomtor		236	10,093
June 22	Tomtor		30	10,123

	Destination	Country	Mileage between destinations	Cumulative mileage
WEEK 11				
June 23	Tomtor			10,123
June 24	20 miles east of Kuranakh-Sala		69	10,192
June 25	20 miles west of Adygalakh		35	10,227
June 26	Kadykchan		58	10,285
June 27	Karamken		390	10,675
June 28	Magadan		61	10,736
June 29	Magadan			10,736
WEEK 12				
June 30	Magadan			10,736
July 1 (i)	In flight Magadan–Anchorage (crossing IDL)			
July 1 (ii)	Anchorage, AK	USA	2505	13,241
July 2	Anchorage			13,241
July 3	Anchorage			13,241
July 4	Anchorage			13,241
July 5	Anderson, AK		292	13,533
WEEK 13				
July 6	Fox, AK		89	13,622
July 7	Tok, AK		214	13,836
July 8	Burwash Landing, YT	Canada	212	14,048
July 9	Whitehorse, YT		174	14,222
July 10	Whitehorse			14,222
July 11	Watson Lake, YT		274	14,496
July 12	Fort Nelson, BC		326	14,822
WEEK 14				
July 13	Dawson Creek, BC		284	15,106
July 14	Edmonton, AB		360	15,466
July 15	Calgary, AB		189	15,655
July 16	Calgary			15,655
July 17	Libby, MT	USA	383	16,038
July 18	Columbia Falls, MT		104	16,142
July 19	Billings, MT		483	16,625
WEEK 15				
July 20	Rapid City, SD		374	16,999
July 21	Waseca, MN		542	17,541
July 22	Madison, WI		267	17,808
July 23	Chicago, IL		148	17,956
July 24	Chicago, IL			17,956
July 25	Lagrange, IN		143	18,099
July 26	Warren, OH		259	18,358
WEEK 16				
July 27	Oquaga Lake, Deposit, NY		353	18,711
July 28	Rock Tavern, NY		102	18,813
July 29	New York City		74	18,887
	to London		3458	22,345

Appendix B

EQUIPMENT

Modifications and additions to Ewan's and Charley's
BMW GS 1150 Adventures

All by Touratech: Zega pannier system, Remus exhaust system, steering stop, headlight cover, sump guard, wide foot pegs, rally mudguard, additional fog headlight pair, oil-cooler guard, ROK all-purpose flat straps, cigarette lighter sockets, accessory sockets, power data lead, lockable GPS brackets, windscreen spoiler, handguard spoiler, 2l holder and canister for panniers, pannier inner bags, Arno stretch bands, tool kits, tyre puncture repair kit, Ortlieb dry bags, Cascade compression bags.

AirHawk seat cushions.

Camping equipment

One of the following: Northface three-man tent, Northface one-man tent, Coleman Viper one-man tent. CamelBak, tent lamp, torch, toilet roll holder.

Two of the following: Touratech tent bags, large packsacks, Pack-it All Aboard II, Poly Survival Bags, bivvy bags, Mountain Equipment Snowline sleeping bags, sleeping-bag inners, Thermarest chair kits, Thermarest mats, collapsible aluminium stools, mosquito head nets, fishing bags, tackle boxes, Giant Soft Fibre Trek towels, drysacks and assorted stuff sacks.

Cooking

Optimus stoves, firesteels, MSR fuel and water bottles, Ortlieb folding bowl, polythene drinks bottles 0.5l, polythene drinks bottles 1l, Aladdin flasks 0.5l, titanium cutlery sets, titanium mugs, Miniworks water filter and maintenance kit, tea towels, heavy duty wiresaws, survival tins, ten disposable lighters, MSR Alpine Classic Cook set, MSR Mini Cook set, can opener, salt and pepper, curry and herbs, cooking oil, OXO cubes (mixed), Tabasco sauce, skimmed milk powder, Bovril, Marmite, cordial.

Food

Camping meals, rice, couscous, pasta, Supa noodles, cereal bars, dried fruit, Oatso

Simple (assorted flavours), packet soups, sweets, chocolate, Kendall Mint Cake.

Personal items

Mosquito repellent jacket, mosquito repellent trousers, Belstaff jackets, Gortex jackets, Gortex trousers, fleece jackets, lightweight trousers, canvas shorts, sweatshirts, short-sleeve shirts, T-shirts, silk long johns, underwear, hiking socks, walking boots, hat, snoods, sunglasses, wristwatches, eye masks, travel soap, dry wash, toothbrush, toothpaste, razors and blades, shaving gel, moisturiser, lip salve, sun protection – factor 30, baby wipes, hand sanitiser, soap, soap dish, shower gel, shampoo, 100 per cent deet, Berocca, antacid tablets, multivitamins, cod liver oil tablets, aspirin, Ibuprofen, allergy tablets, nail clippers, tweezers, scissors, clear plasters, brush and comb, magnifying shaving mirror, whistles, penknives, passport and money cases, compass, head torches, earplugs, tin foil, cling film, Ziploc bags, rubbish bags, toilet rolls, travel washing powder, clothes lines, guidebooks, reading books, two Russian phrase books, binoculars, pens, string, strong cord, rubber bands, strong glue, black binliners, postcards, stickers, cigarette battery charger plus rechargeable batteries, Dictaphones, iPods and chargers.

Communications and navigation

Two of: Iridium phone, cellphone, phone chargers, Garmin GPS unit.

Video and photography equipment

Two of: on-bike camera, Panasonic NV-GS70 camcorder (plus allied car battery charger, stereo zoom microphone, filter kit, lens protector), digital stills camera (plus additional battery, charger and memory cards), 35mm stills camera. Tripod and mini-tripod. Mini DV tapes.

Bike spares on support vehicle

Eighteen Continental tyres (three sets for three bikes), replacement bulbs covering headlight main and dip beam, side lights, indicators and brake light, three sets of rear brake pads, pad retaining pins and anti-rattle clips, six sets of front brake pads, pad retaining pins and anti-rattle clips, spare front and rear ABS wheel sensors, eight front wheel spokes with mounting nipples and securing grub screws, eight rear wheel spokes with mounting nipples and securing grub screws, two sets of replacement front wheel bearings, two replacement saddles, low height option, three fuel octane coding relays (for poor fuel quality), three oil filters, six air filters, four replacement rocker cover gaskets, six spare spark plugs, two front brake levers, two clutch levers, three oil-pressure switches, three auxiliary power sockets.

Also on support vehicle

Full bike tool set, Charley's personal box, Ewan's personal box, extra clothes, extra helmets, extra motorbike boots, extra videotape, extra film, extra food.

Ending with a sense of hope

When Unicef invited us to see its work helping and protecting some of the world's most vulnerable children, neither of us had anticipated it would have such an impact. The three visits to Unicef projects in Mongolia, Ukraine and Kazakhstan stand out as some of the highlights of our journey.

We were able to catch a rare glimpse of the kind of bravery that some children need to survive, growing up alone, in poverty, at serious risk of exploitation and largely forgotten by the rest of the world. From the boys we met that sleep in the filthy manholes of Ulaanbaatar and the young people living with the fatal legacy of Chernobyl, to those uprooted and displaced by poverty in Almaty, their unfortunate stories were powerful and shocking. It is hard to believe that life can be so bleak at such a young age.

But what will remain in our memories is a sense of hope, because in each country we saw that something was being done to help. Unicef was taking action. Their staff – real heroes to the cause – work with a tireless passion and purpose to make a lasting, positive change for children. They have been an inspiration to us. Unicef is successfully giving children and young people all over the world opportunities and hope. Just like the ones we met. Unicef is protecting them from exploitation and is giving them the chances that we all take for granted.

As fathers, we know what a force for life children can be. They represent all of our futures. This trip has offered us the opportunity to help Unicef and to see first hand some of the life-changing work they're doing in the world.

We support Unicef; we hope you will do the same.

Charley Boorman and *Ewan McGregor*

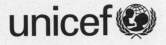

UNICEF, the United Nations Children's Fund, is the world's largest organization working specifically for children, protecting and promoting their rights. It works in 157 countries of the world to help every child reach their full potential through long term and emergency work on child health and nutrition, quality basic education for all boys and girls, and the protection of children from violence, exploitation and AIDS.

By working in partnership with others, from governments and teachers to youth groups and mothers, UNICEF is a driving force for people throughout the world working to ensure a better future for children.

UNICEF receives no funding from the UN, and relies entirely on voluntary donations to fund its work. UNICEF needs people like you to help protect children from exploitation and to build a world fit for children. You can make a difference. You can donate, or purchase UNICEF cards and gifts, or become a volunteer or campaigner.

To make a donation or to learn more about UNICEF's work, you can call 1-800-4UNICEF or visit www.unicefusa.org.

Checks and money orders should be made payable to the U.S. Fund for UNICEF and sent to:

U.S. Fund for UNICEF
P.O. Box 98006
Washington, D.C. 20090-8006

To find out more about Ewan and Charley's UNICEF visits, please go to www.unicef.org.uk/longwayround

Acknowledgements

Very special thanks to:

Olivia, Doone, Kinvara and the whole Boorman clan
Eve, Clara, Esther and our family

David Alexanian and Russ Malkin, our partners.

Alexis Alexanian, Luke Boyle, Julian Broad, Totty Douglas, Ailsa Fereday, Manus Fraser, Julia Frater, Sergey Grabovets, Kash Javaid, Lindy King, Robert Kirby, Asia Mackay, Jo Melling, Andrew Mer, Rachel Newnham, Vasiliy Nisichenko, Ciara Parkes, Claudio von Planta, Jake Roberts, James Simak, Lucy Trujillo, Robert Uhlig and Scott Waxman.

Tamsin Barrack, Nann du Sautoy, Antonia Hodgson, Marie Hrynczak, David Kent, Alison Lindsay and Diane Spivey at Time Warner Book Group UK, and Tracy Behar, Brigid Brown and Judith Curr at Atria Books.

BMW Motorrad GB: Steve Bellars, Howard Godolphin, Tony Jakeman
British Airways: Murray Lambell, Clare Sweeney
Chiron: Rob Budge
Mitsubishi: Gabi Whitfield
Sonic Communications: David Bryan, Darren Roper, Liam Thornton
Unicef: Sarah Epstein, Alison Tilbe, Wendy Zych

Maps and guidebooks donated by Stanfords in Covent Garden – the world's largest map and travel bookshop.

Photographs in the picture sections were taken with Pentax cameras.